GIRL POWER
BRAIN BOOSTERS

BY SARAH PARVIS

downtown bookworks

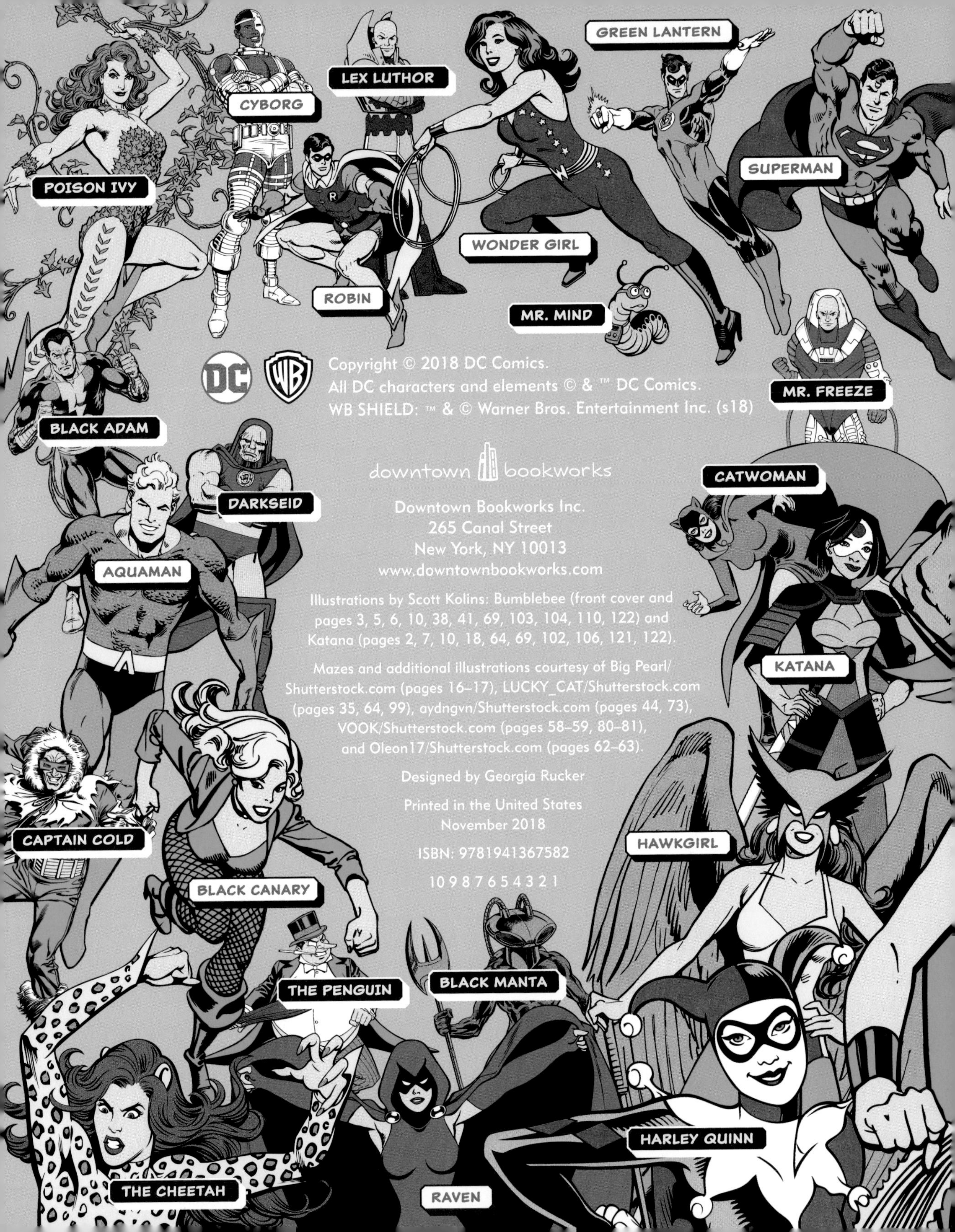
GREEN LANTERN
LEX LUTHOR
CYBORG
POISON IVY
SUPERMAN
WONDER GIRL
ROBIN
MR. MIND
MR. FREEZE
BLACK ADAM
CATWOMAN
DARKSEID
AQUAMAN
KATANA
HAWKGIRL
CAPTAIN COLD
BLACK CANARY
THE PENGUIN
BLACK MANTA
HARLEY QUINN
THE CHEETAH
RAVEN

downtown bookworks

Downtown Bookworks Inc.
265 Canal Street
New York, NY 10013
www.downtownbookworks.com

Illustrations by Scott Kolins: Bumblebee (front cover and pages 3, 5, 6, 10, 38, 41, 69, 103, 104, 110, 122) and Katana (pages 2, 7, 10, 18, 64, 69, 102, 106, 121, 122).

Mazes and additional illustrations courtesy of Big Pearl/Shutterstock.com (pages 16–17), LUCKY_CAT/Shutterstock.com (pages 35, 64, 99), aydngvn/Shutterstock.com (pages 44, 73), VOOK/Shutterstock.com (pages 58–59, 80–81), and Oleon17/Shutterstock.com (pages 62–63).

Designed by Georgia Rucker

Printed in the United States
November 2018

ISBN: 9781941367582

10 9 8 7 6 5 4 3 2 1

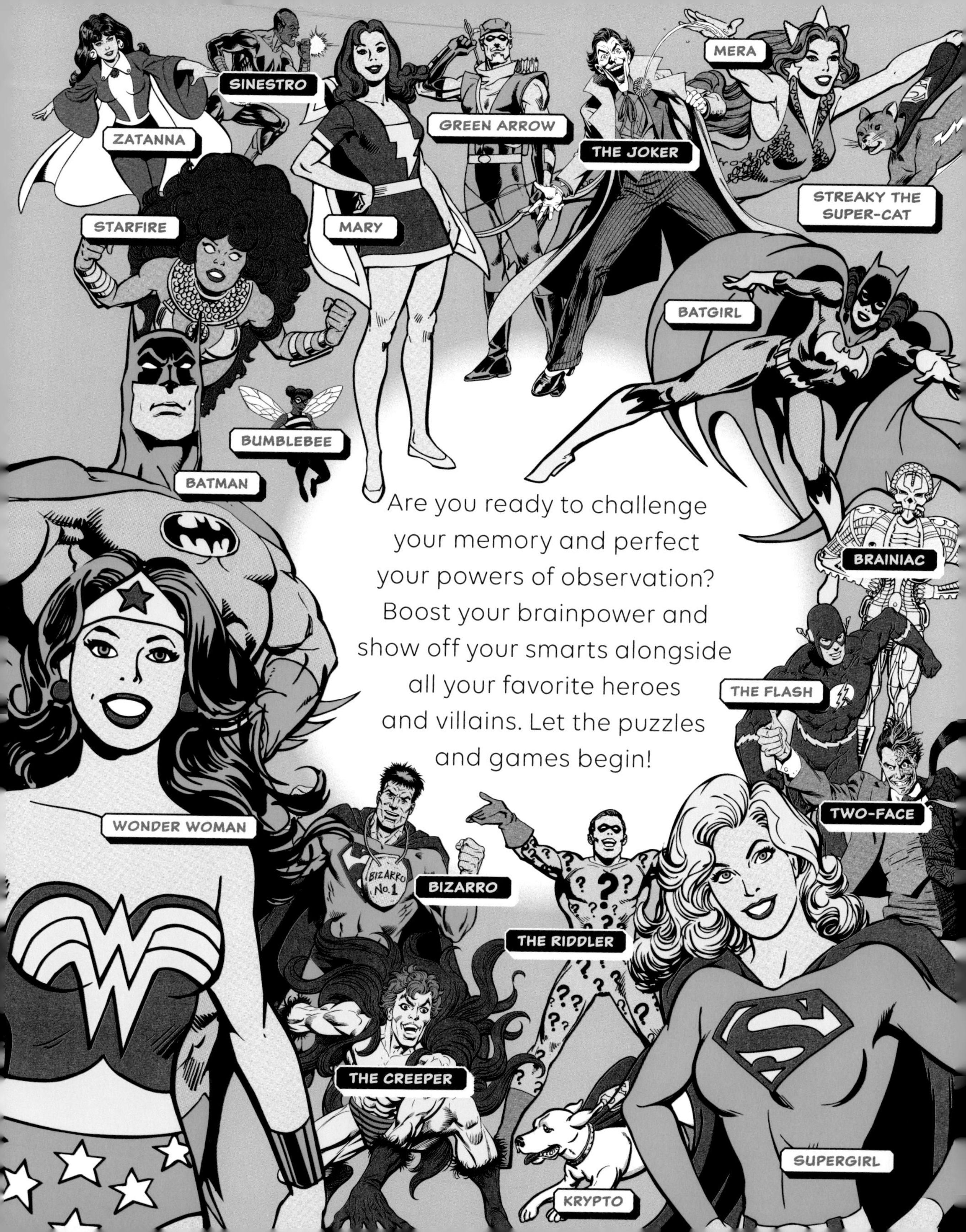
ZATANNA
SINESTRO
MARY
GREEN ARROW
THE JOKER
MERA
STREAKY THE SUPER-CAT
STARFIRE
BATGIRL
BUMBLEBEE
BATMAN
BRAINIAC
THE FLASH
TWO-FACE
WONDER WOMAN
BIZARRO
BIZARRO No. 1
THE RIDDLER
THE CREEPER
SUPERGIRL
KRYPTO

Are you ready to challenge your memory and perfect your powers of observation? Boost your brainpower and show off your smarts alongside all your favorite heroes and villains. Let the puzzles and games begin!

Which Wonder Woman?

One of these super heroes is not like the rest. Can you spot the imposter?

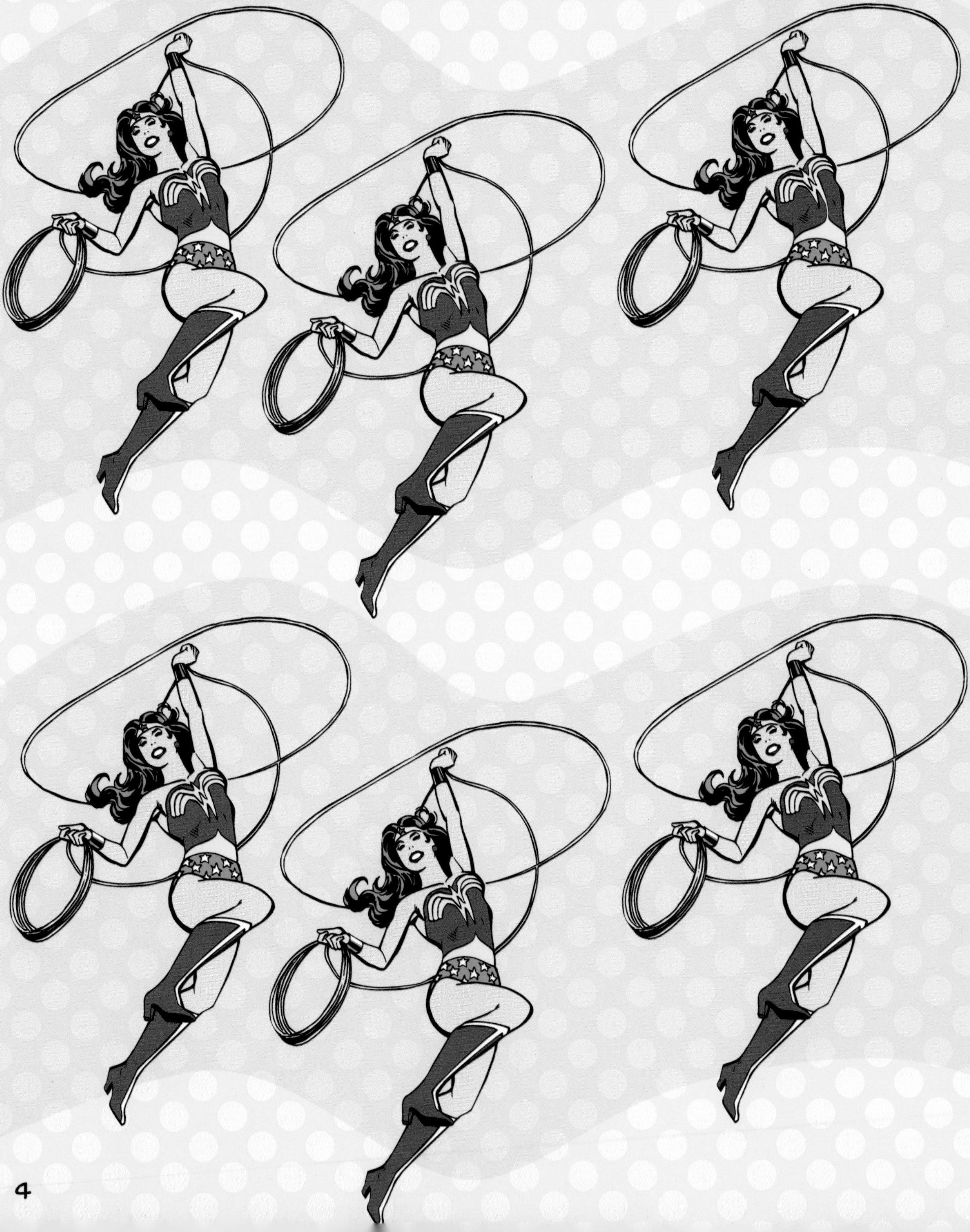

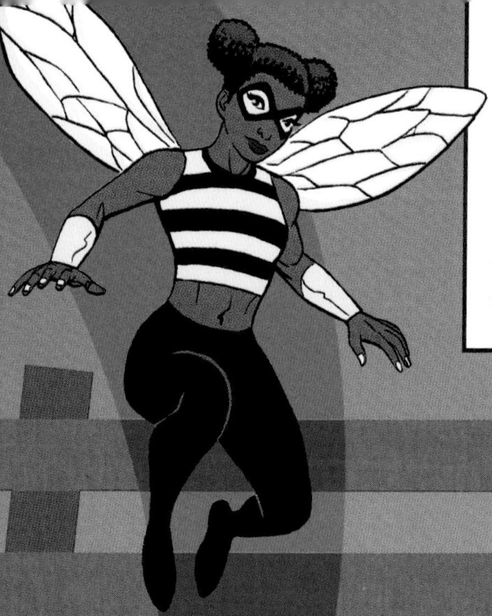

Bumblebe
Word Lad

Bumblebee is a wh
and she's got a chc
Change one letter in each line to get from the top word to the bottom word.

Buzzy insects	B	E	E	S
Uses her eyes				
At the park, kids love to play on the swing ______.				
What you use to scoop up fish				
Almonds, cashews, pistachios, and pecans				
In baseball, each team has three ______ per inning.				
Many cereals are made from ______.				
Green Lantern recites an ______.				
Where you might soak in hot water				
Winged creatures of the night				

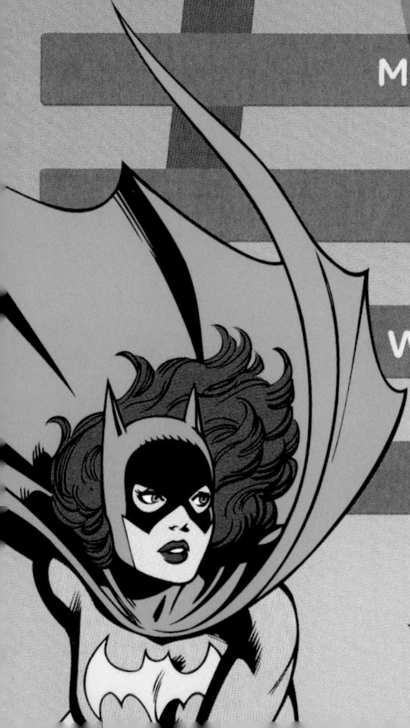

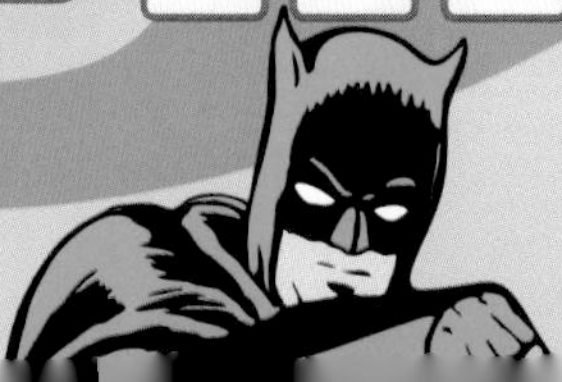

Master the Pattern

Follow the pattern on the right to help these incredible super heroes foil a plot by scheming villains. You can go right, left, up, or down—but not diagonally. Watch out for Harley Quinn!

THE PATTERN

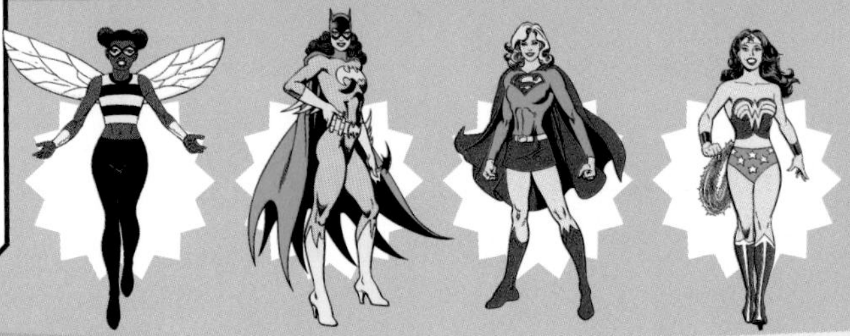

START

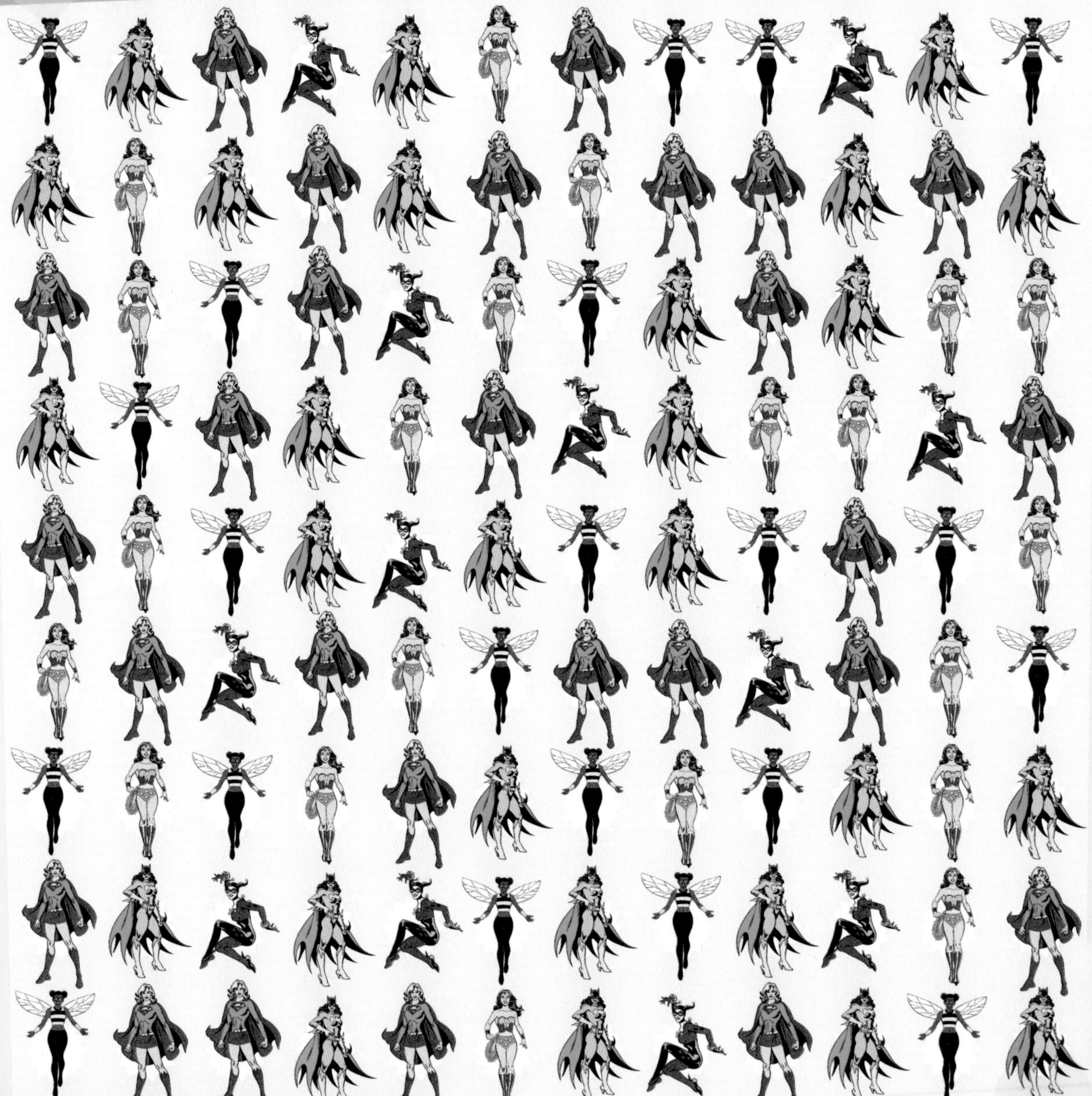

END

Time to Rhyme

Super heroes in training need to be ready at a moment's notice to solve riddles and decode messages. Make sure your skills are sharp by figuring out the missing words in each sentence. They all rhyme with **"hook."**

1 Batgirl loves to read. She ends each day with a __ __ __ __.

2 Supergirl used her X-ray vision to __ __ __ __ through the wall and see what Lex Luthor was up to.

3 Giganta is so huge that when she ran, the ground __ __ __ __ __.

4 Bumblebee saw a thief run from the jewelry store, so she flew after the __ __ __ __ __.

5 To track down a villain who was a posing as a student, Batgirl flipped through the

__ __ __ __ __ __ __ __ __

to see pictures of everyone in the school.

6 Knives are useful in the kitchen. But Katana uses her blade to fight, not to __ __ __ __ __.

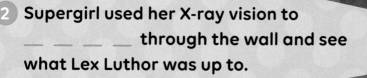

Upon Further Reflection...

Wonder Woman's mirror images might look just like her, but these pictures aren't identical. Find and circle 8 things that have changed in the scene on the right.

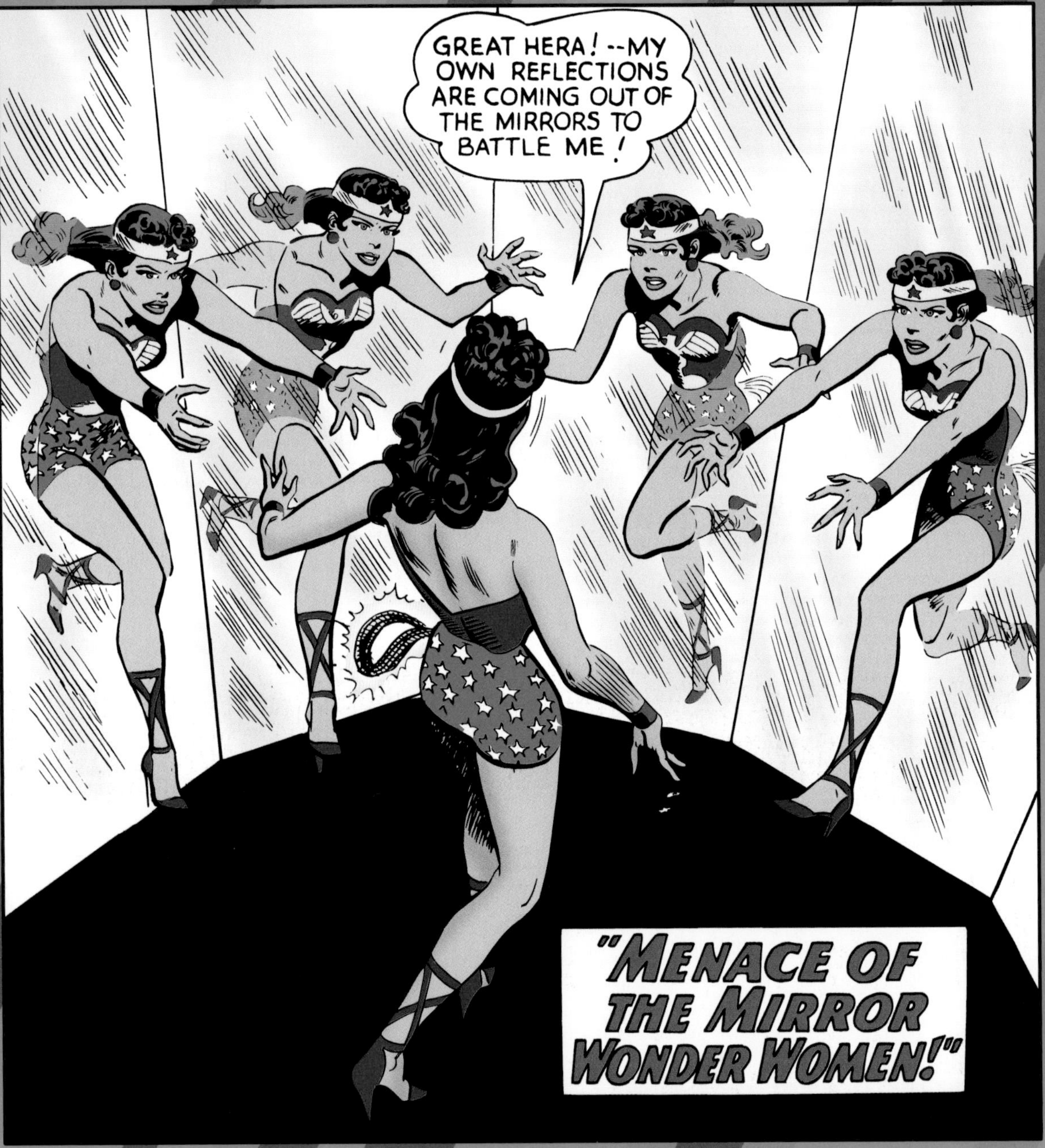
GREAT HERA! --MY OWN REFLECTIONS ARE COMING OUT OF THE MIRRORS TO BATTLE ME!
"MENACE OF THE MIRROR WONDER WOMEN!"

Perplexing Paths!

Draw a line that connects each pair of awesome characters. You can draw lines horizontally and vertically, but not diagonally. Make sure no lines cross. When you are done, every box in the grid will have either a line or a picture in it.

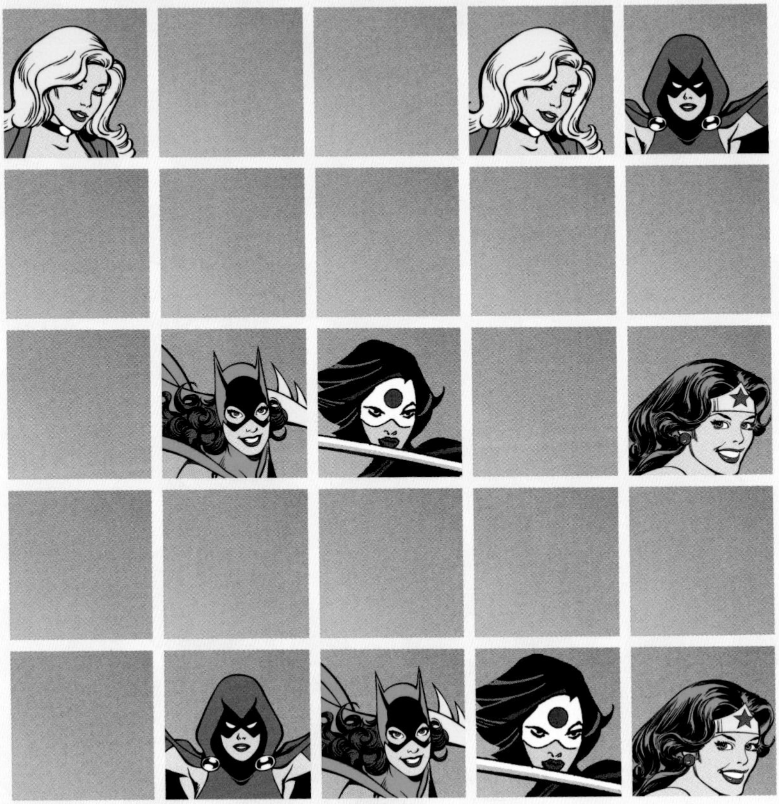

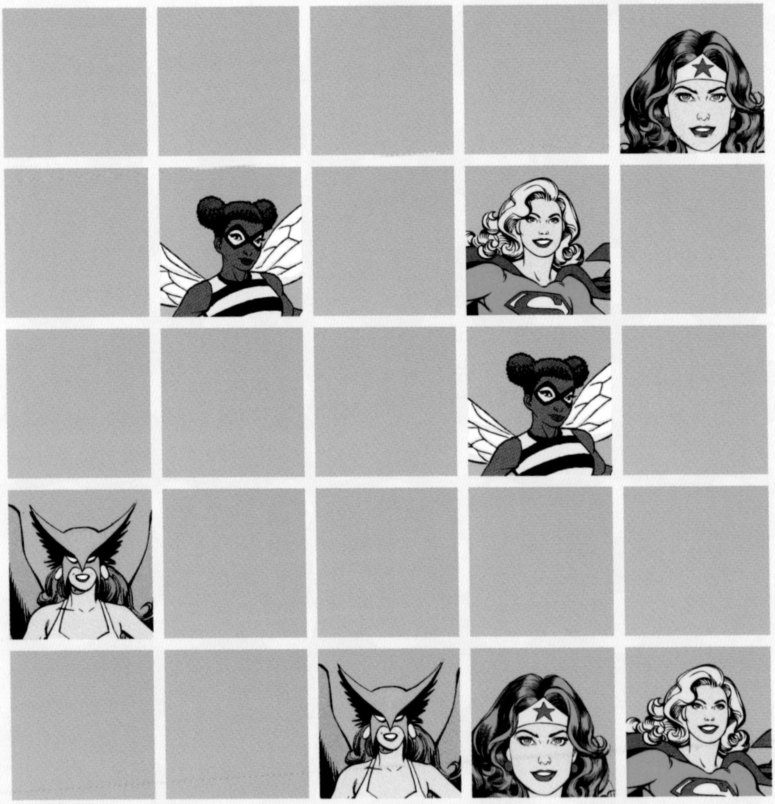

Mighty Drawing Challenge

Can you recreate this picture of Batgirl? Let the grid be your guide! Start with the black lines. When you are done, add color.

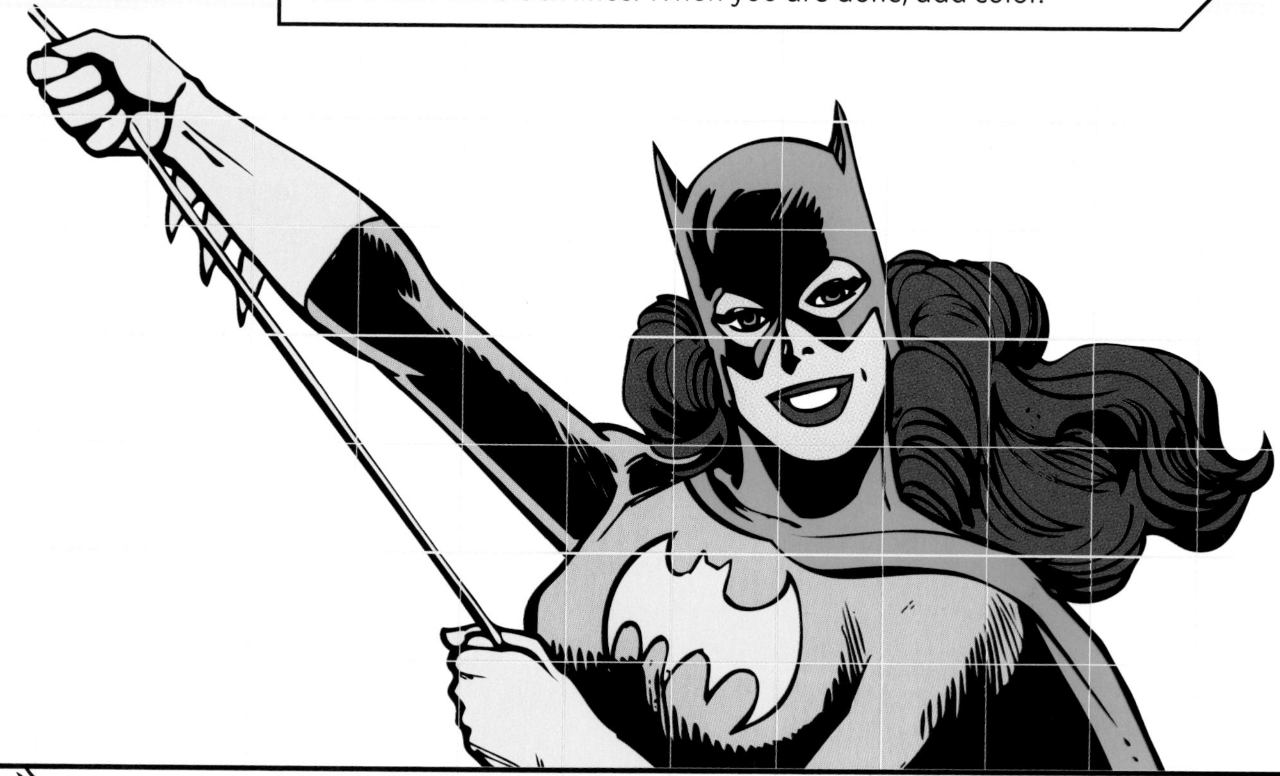

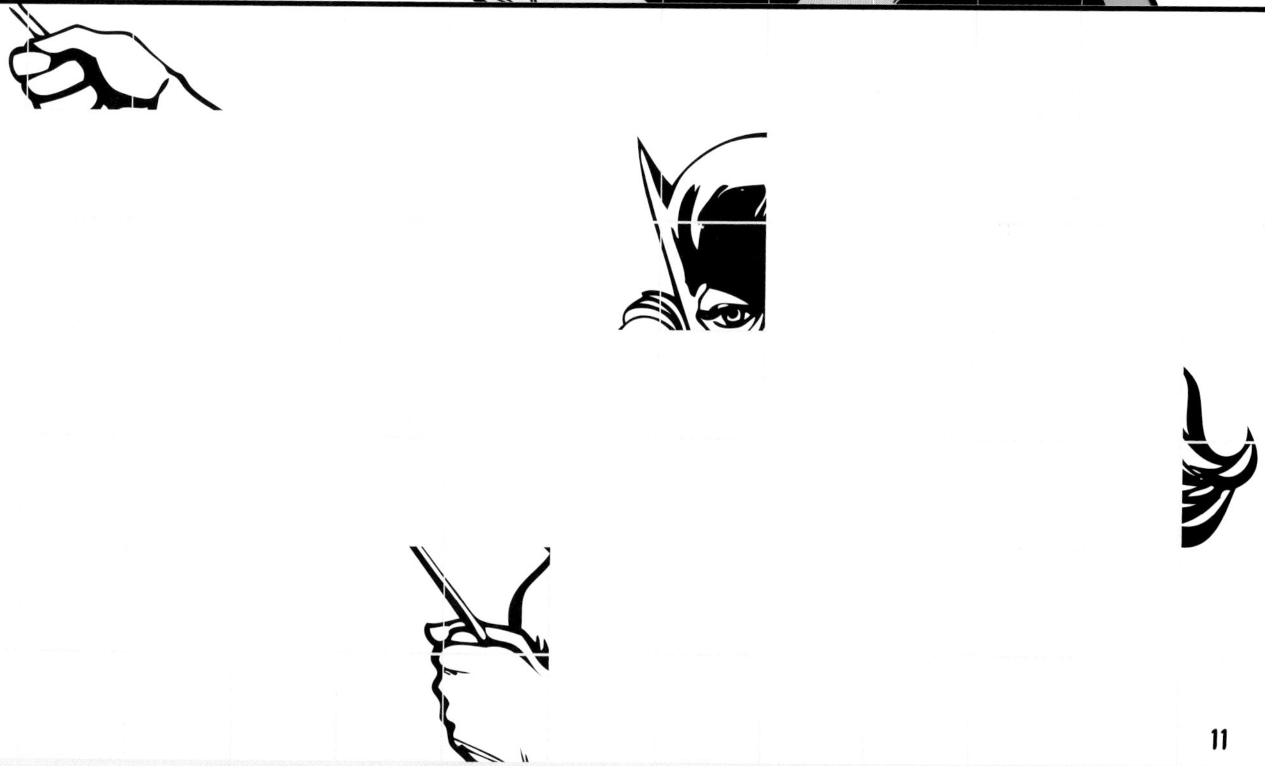

X-Ray Visionary

Supergirl has lots of incredible powers. With her X-ray vision, she can look through walls and even see what's happening inside this robot. Draw what she sees.

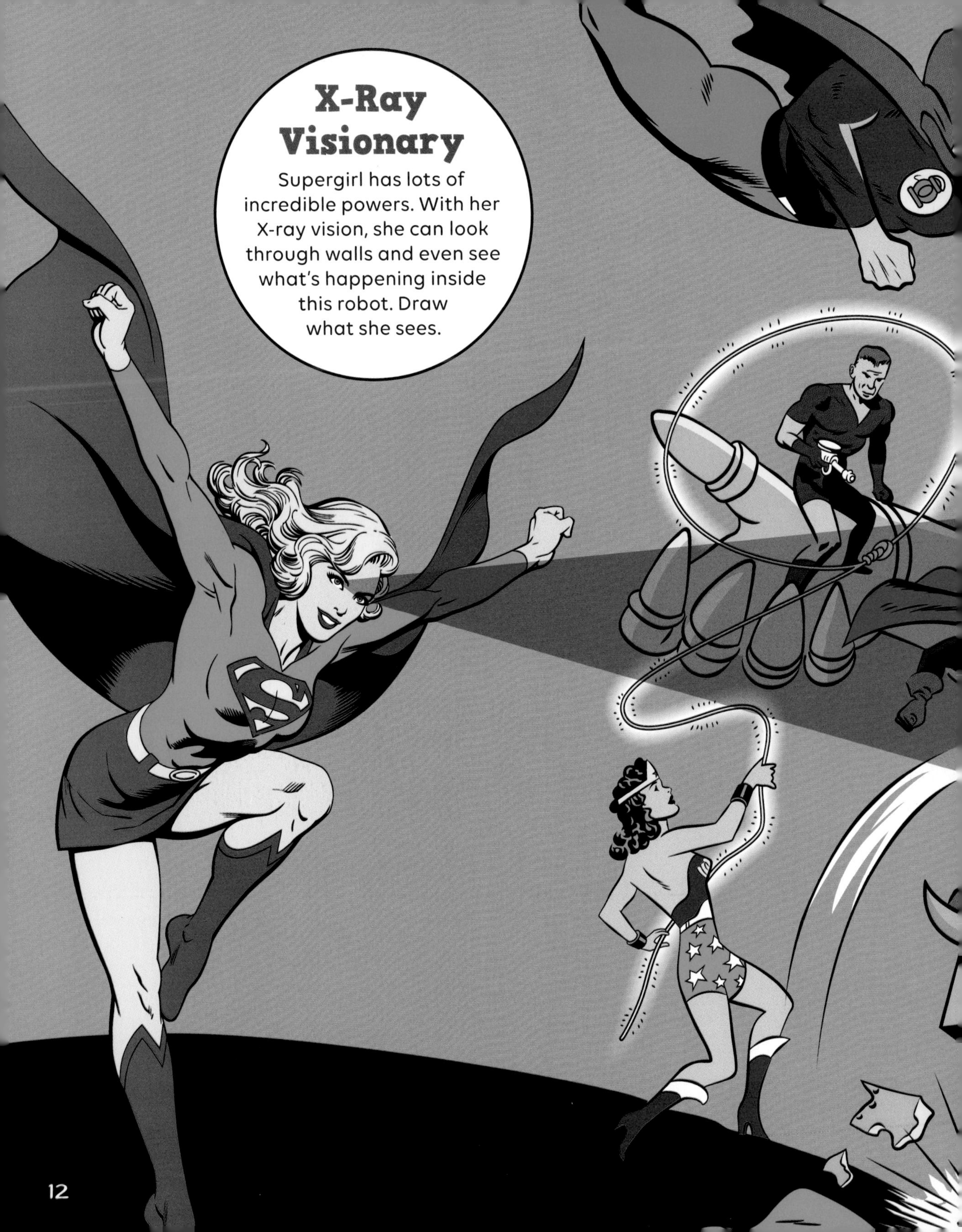

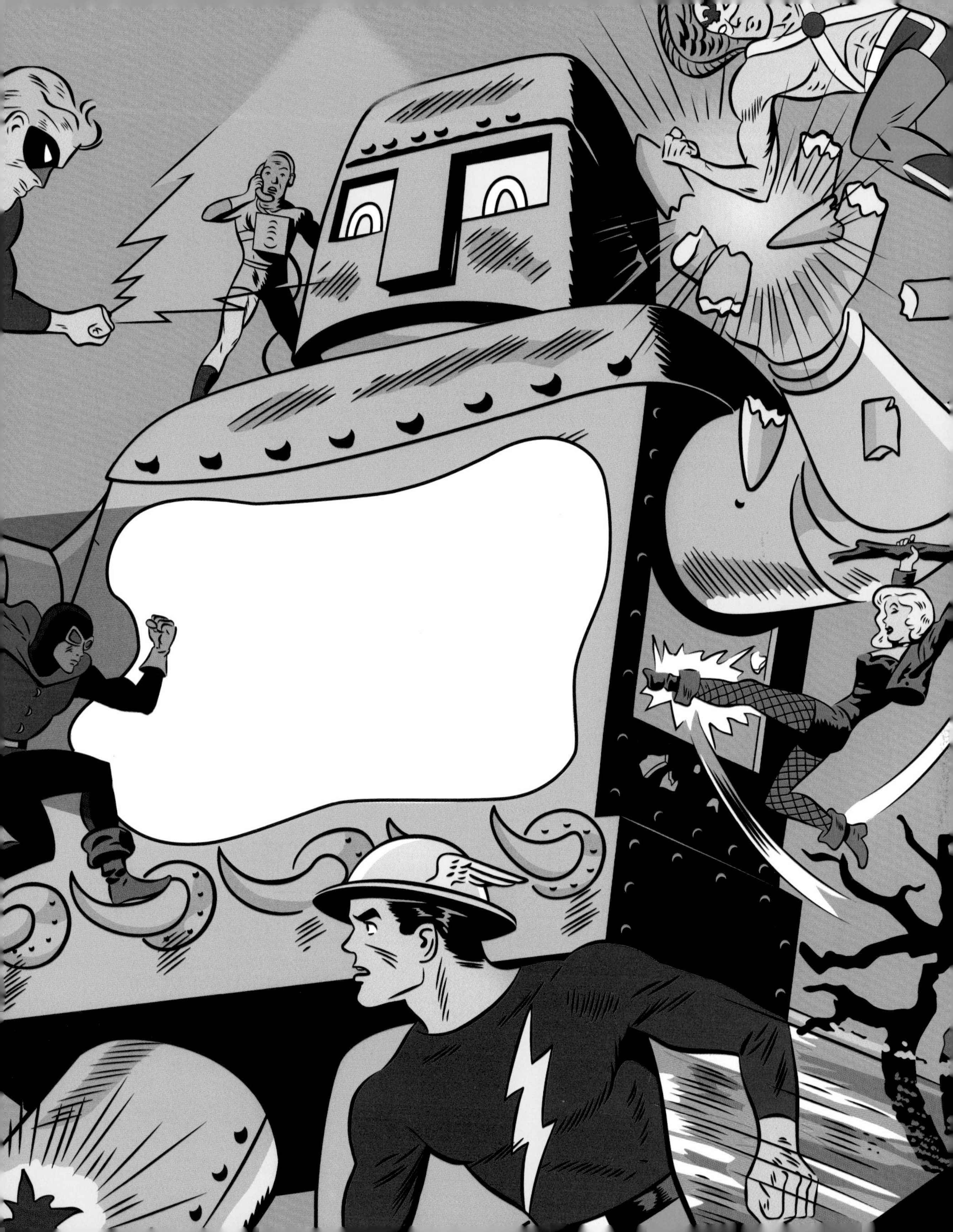

How Do You Say "Word Search" in Tamaranean?

Starfire has an amazing ability to learn new languages by touching people who speak them. In fact, she learned English from Robin. Can you find all the languages listed below? They appear forward, backward, up, down, or diagonally.

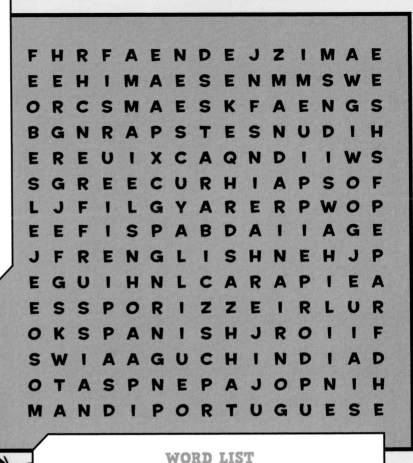

```
F H R F A E N D E J Z I M A E
E E H I M A E S E N M M S W E
O R C S M A E S K F A E N G S
B G N R A P S T E S N U D I H
E R E U I X C A Q N D I I W S
S G R E E C U R H I A P S O F
L J F I L G Y A R E R P W O P
E E F I S P A B D A I I A G E
J F R E N G L I S H N E H J P
E G U I H N L C A R A P I E A
E S S P O R I Z Z E I R L U R
O K S P A N I S H J R O I I F
S W I A A G U C H I N D I A D
O T A S P N E P A J O P N I H
M A N D I P O R T U G U E S E
```

WORD LIST

Arabic	German	Portuguese
English	Hindi	Russian
Finnish	Japanese	Spanish
French	Mandarin	Swahili

Out-of-this-World Word Generator

Are you a word whiz? Prove it!

There are 8 letters in the word Starfire. How many other words can you make from the letters in S-T-A-R-F-I-R-E?

IT

EAT

FAR

Starfire is Tamaranean, from the planet Tamaran. How many words can you make from the letters in T-A-M-A-R-A-N-E-A-N?

Starfire has superhuman strength, endurance, and agility. She can fly, create energy blasts, shoot eye beams, and survive in space. She has bulletproof skin and is an incredible warrior. But, like many Tamaraneans, she is allergic to metallic chromium. Do you have any allergies? Do your classmates?

After Him!

Mary, Raven, and Hawkgirl have Black Adam on the run. They take off after him. Which super hero catches up with the villain?

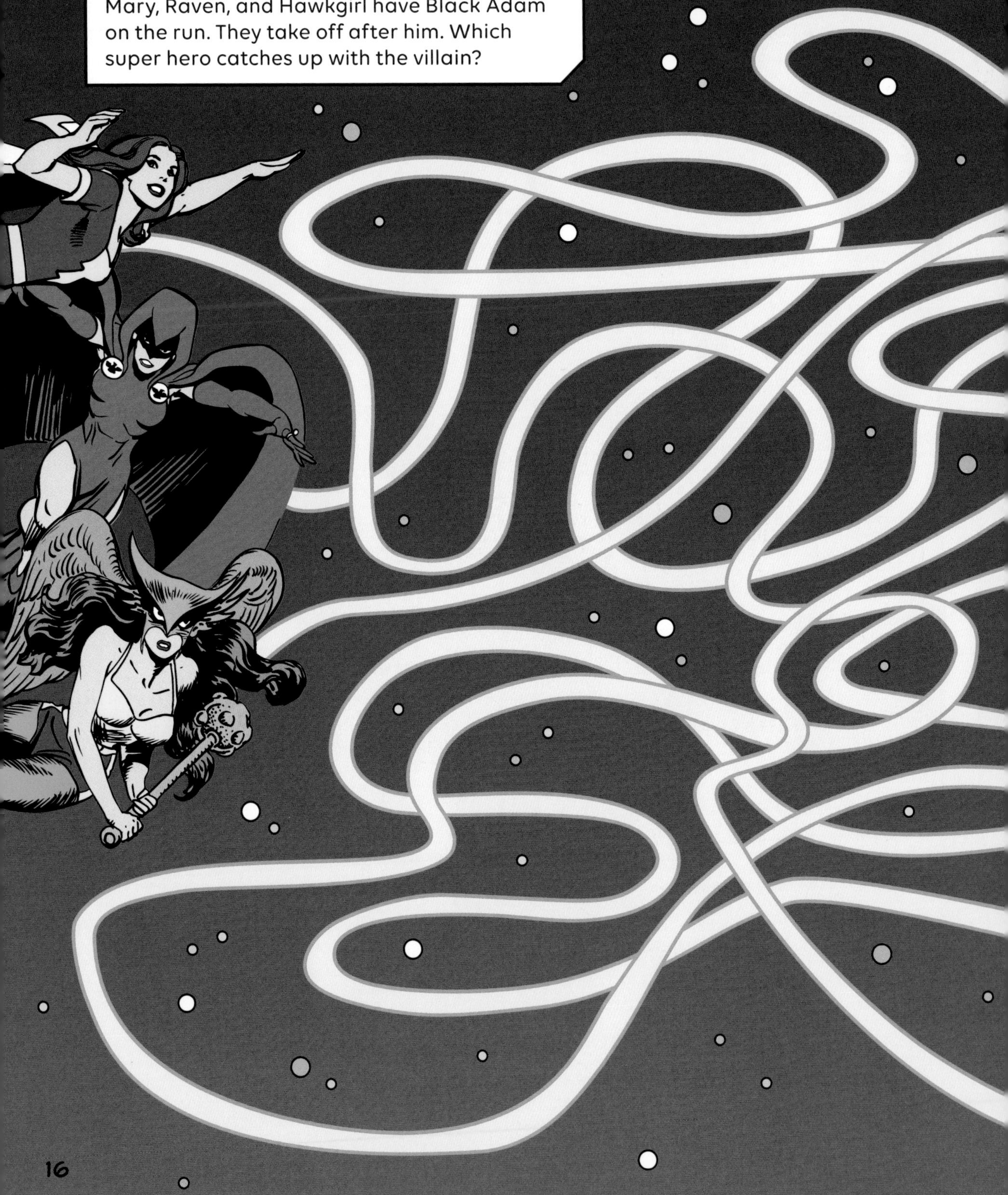

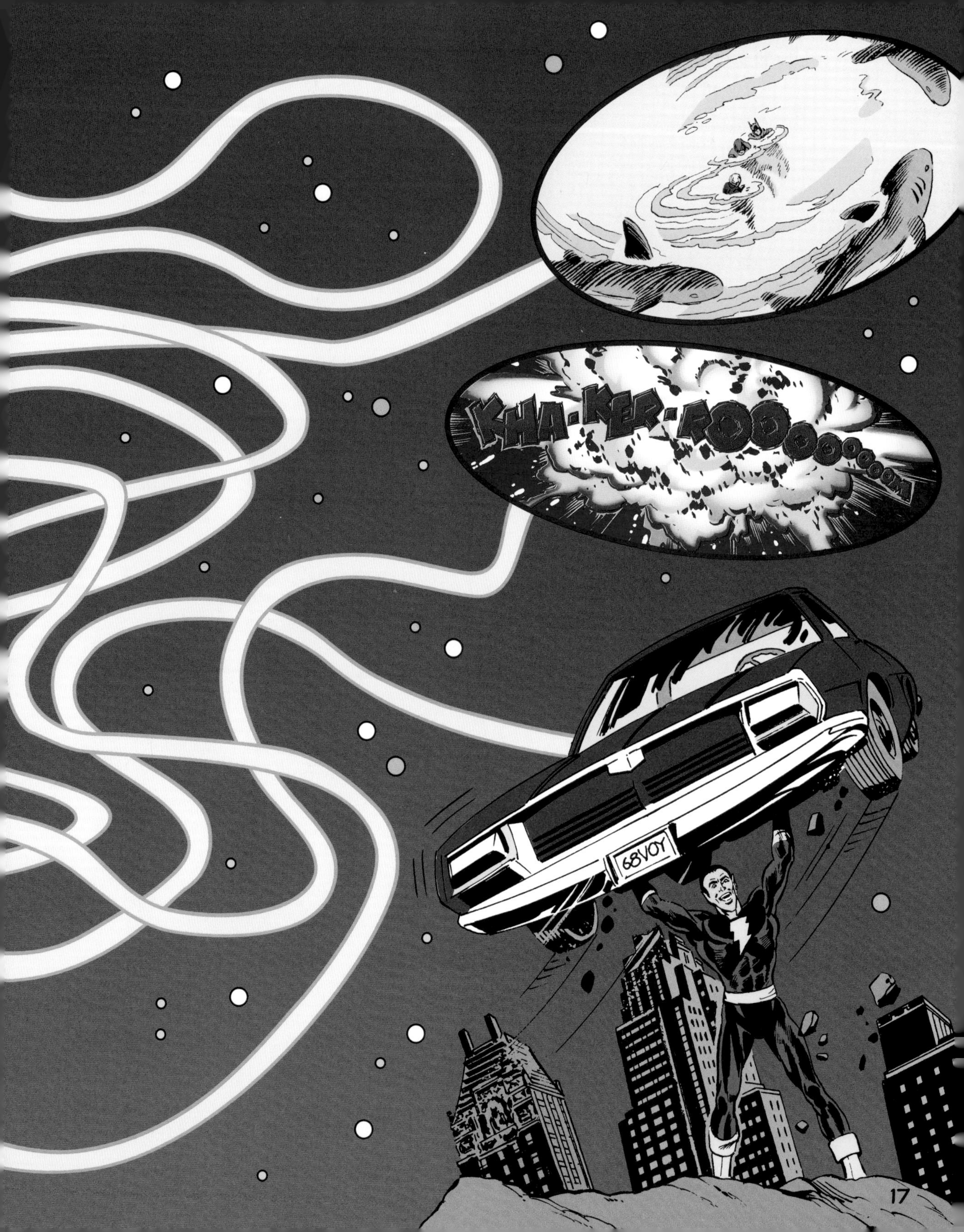
KHA-KER-ROOOOOOOOOM
68VOY

Crossword Showdown!

Fill in the blanks to complete this cunning crossword.

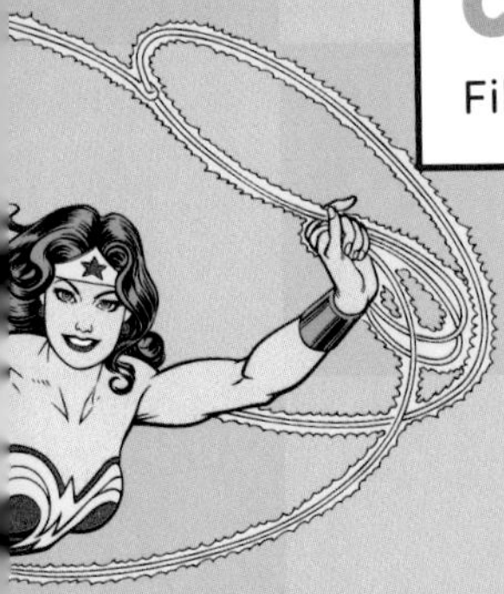

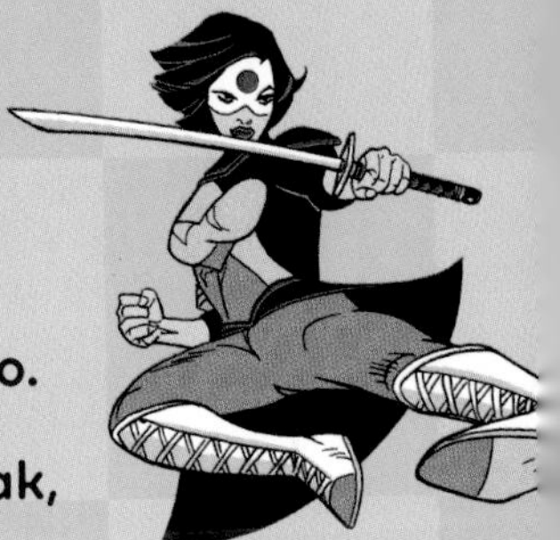

ACROSS

2 Wonder Woman's lasso makes people tell the ________.

5 Superman and Supergirl escaped their home planet before coming to ________.

6 Batgirl's cape is ________.

9 Katana and Batgirl both practice martial ________.

10 Batgirl rarely drives a car, but she has a speedy ________.

12 By day, Wonder Woman is known as ________ Prince.

13 ________ Quinn is the Joker's twisted partner in crime.

15 Superman and Supergirl are from the planet ________.

16 Batgirl carries her Batarangs and other awesome gadgets on her Utility ________.

17 When Black Canary rounds up a gang of troublemakers, she makes sure they end up behind ________.

DOWN

1 ________ is an unstoppable, sword-slinging Japanese super hero.

3 Wrapped in her cloak, ________ has many mysterious powers like healing, telekinesis, and teleportation.

4 Supergirl's fiery ________ vision can burn through walls if she needs it to!

7 Wonder Woman's gold ________ is unbreakable.

8 By day, Batman is known as Bruce ________.

11 The ________ is a super-villain who loves to leave puzzling clues at the scenes of his crimes.

14 Not every super hero has super________. Bumblebee and Batman have created special suits and gadgets that help them foil the bad guys.

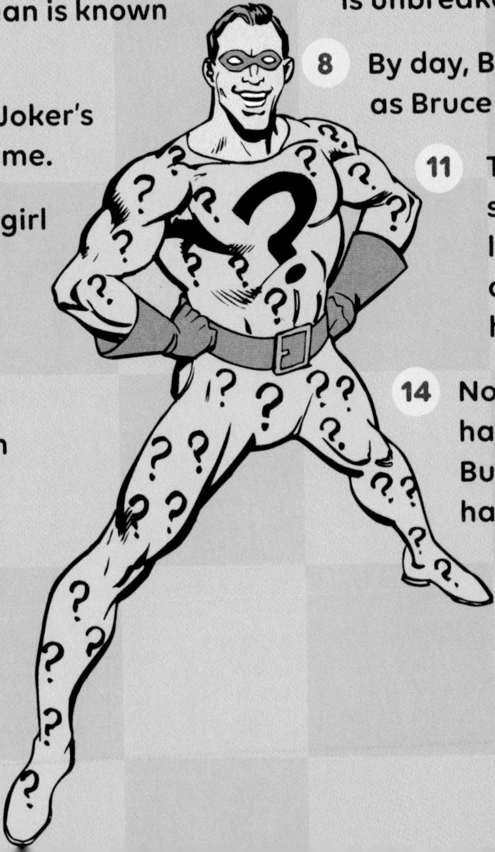

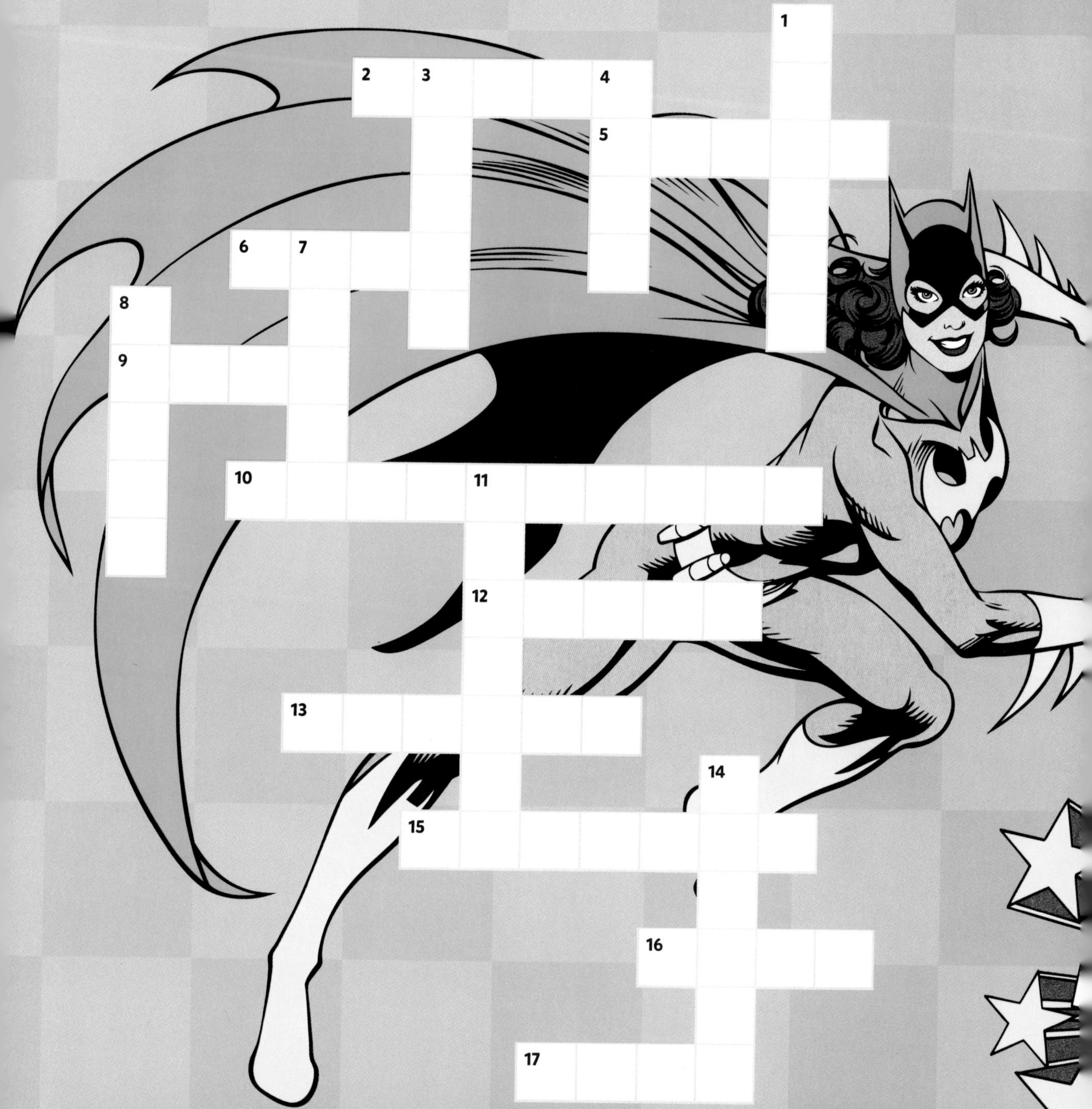

WORD LIST Need a hint? These are the words you'll need to fill in the blanks.

arts	blue	Harley	Krypton	powers	truth
bars	Diana	heat	lasso	Raven	Wayne
Belt	Earth	Katana	motorcycle	Riddler	

Decode the Jokes!

Use the key to fill in the blanks and uncover the punchlines.

KEY

A	B	C	D	E	F	G	H	I	J	K	L	M	N	O

P	Q	R	S	T	U	V	W	X	Y	Z

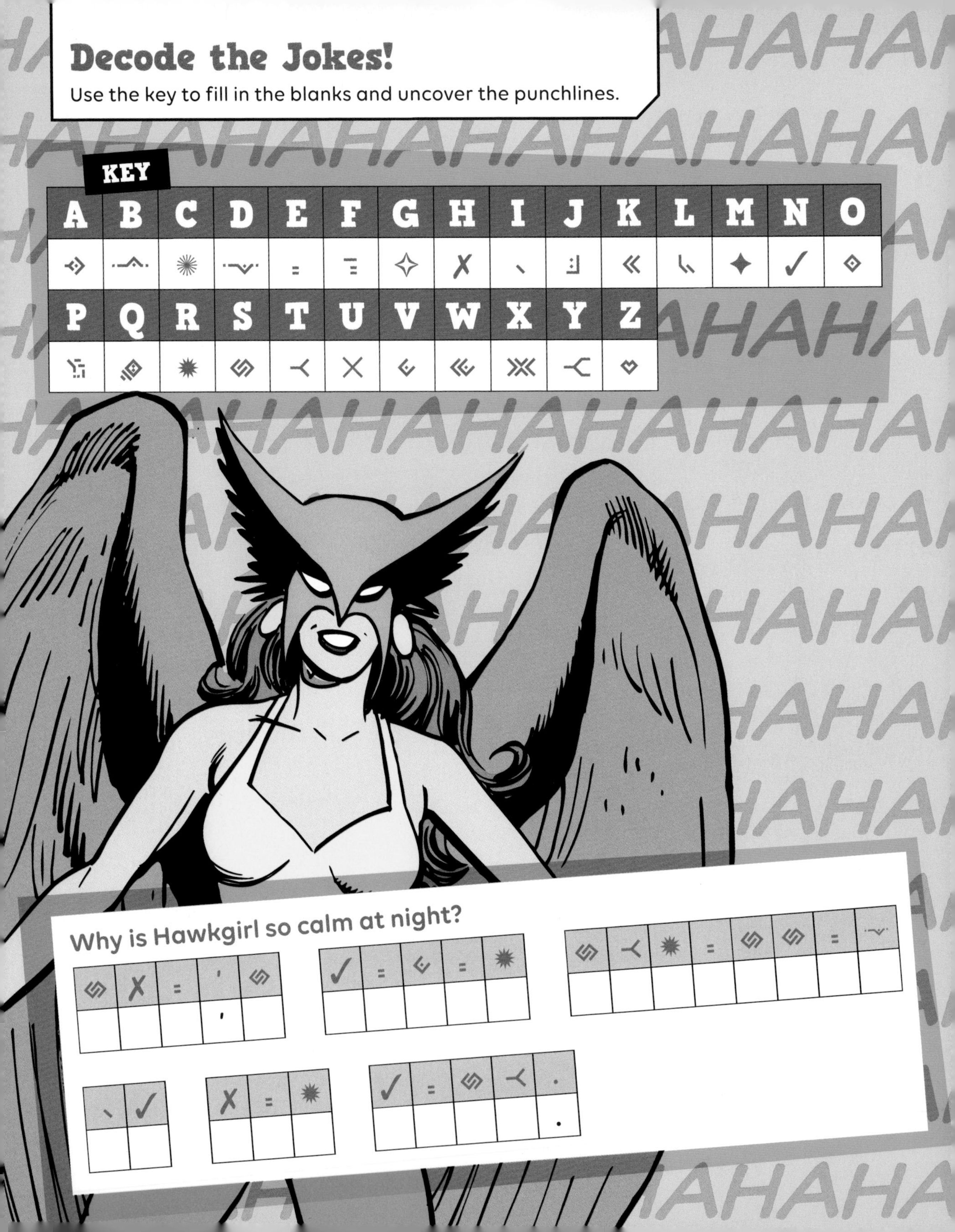

Why is Hawkgirl so calm at night?

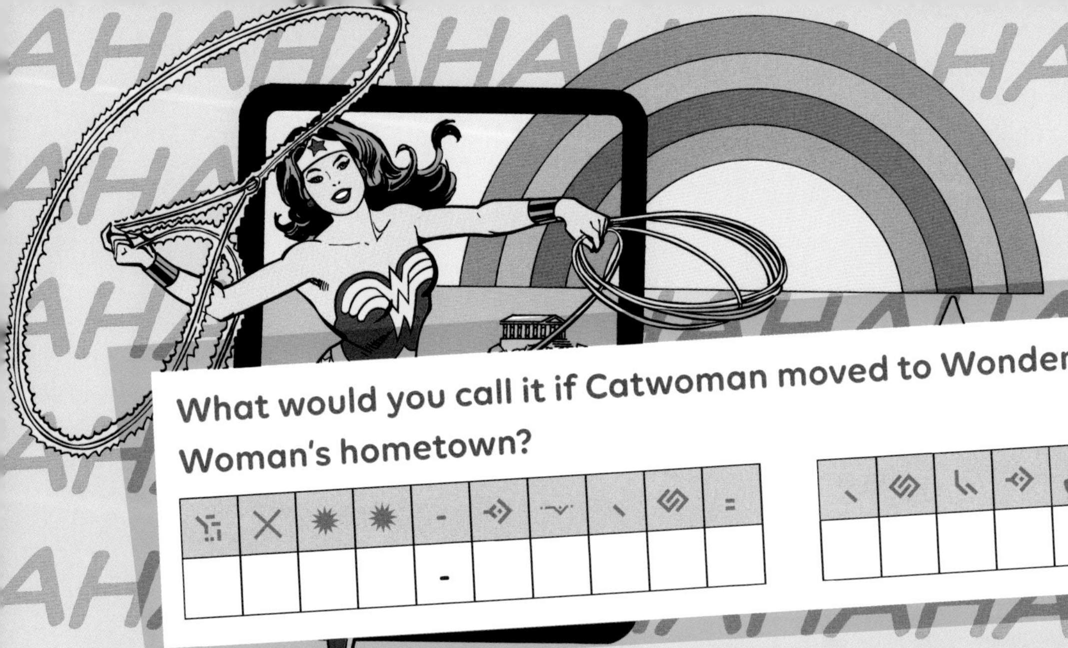

What would you call it if Catwoman moved to Wonder Woman's hometown?

What would you get if you crossed Raven with a frog?

Why did Krypto apologize to Bumblebee for woofing at her?

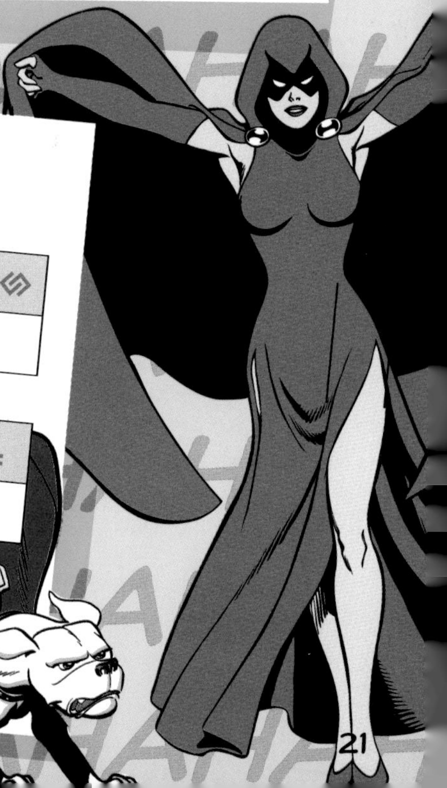

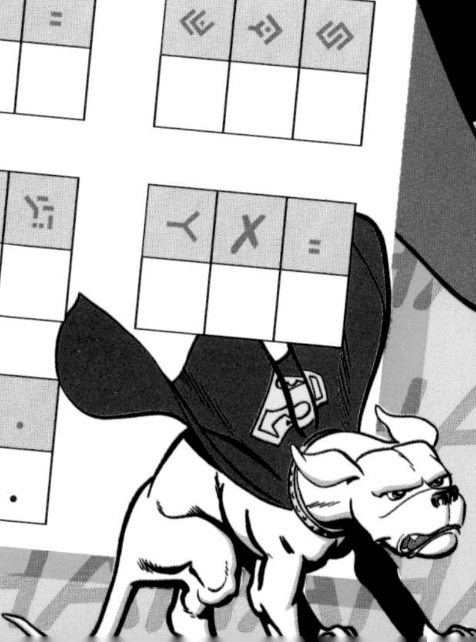

Symbol Strategy

Batgirl is an excellent detective. She uses her smarts and her instincts to solve riddles. Can you use your smarts and instincts to solve these picture puzzles?

PUZZLE 1

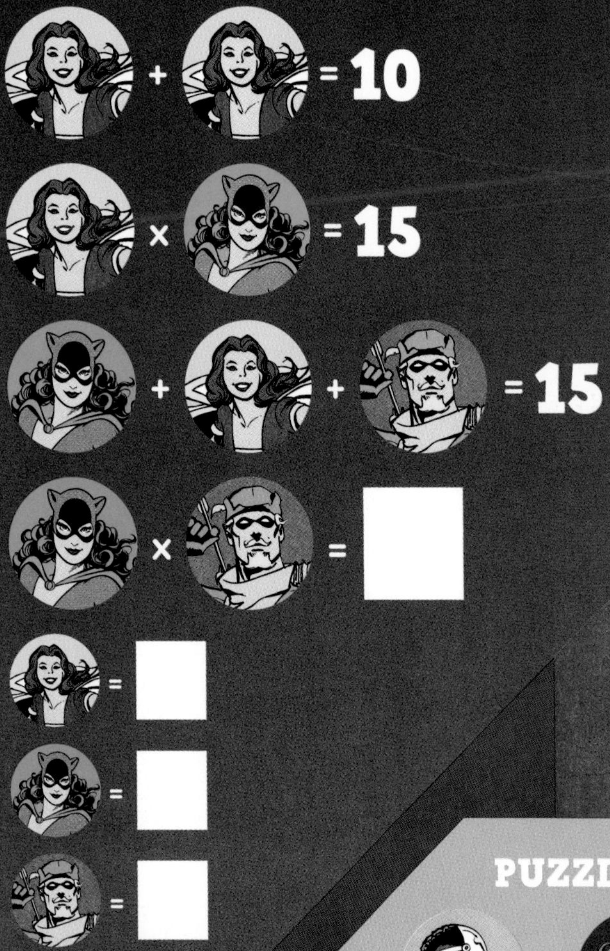

+ = 10
× = 15
+ + = 15
× =
=
=
=

PUZZLE 2

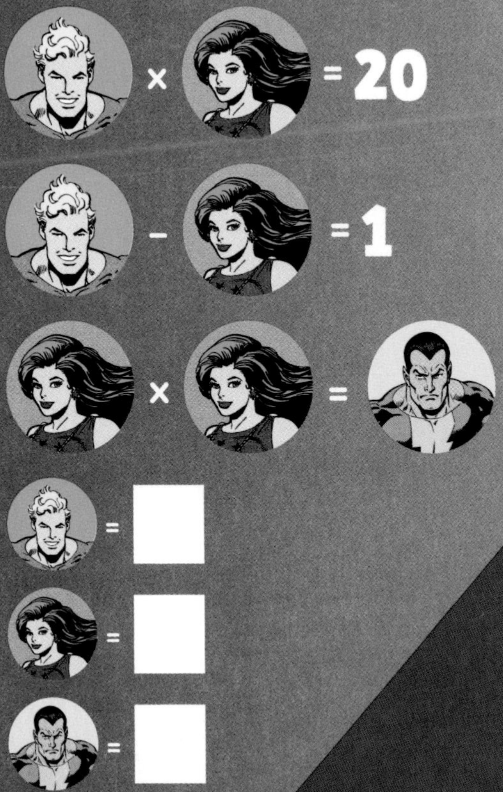

× = 20
- = 1
× =
=
=
=

PUZZLE 3

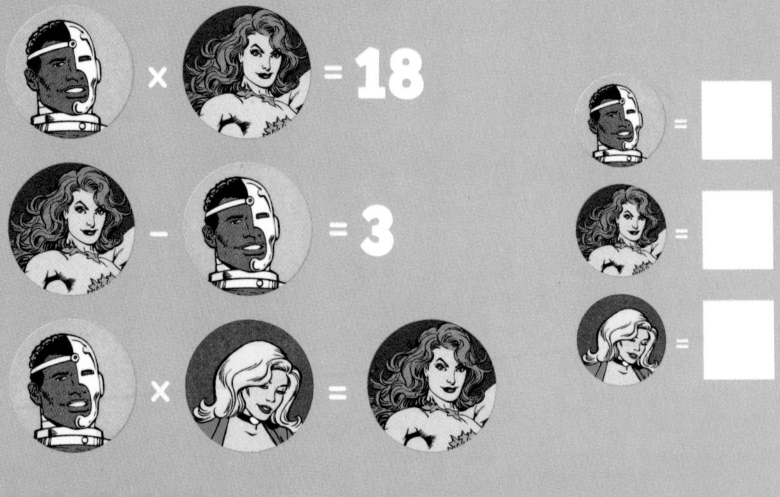

× = 18
- = 3
× =
=
=
=

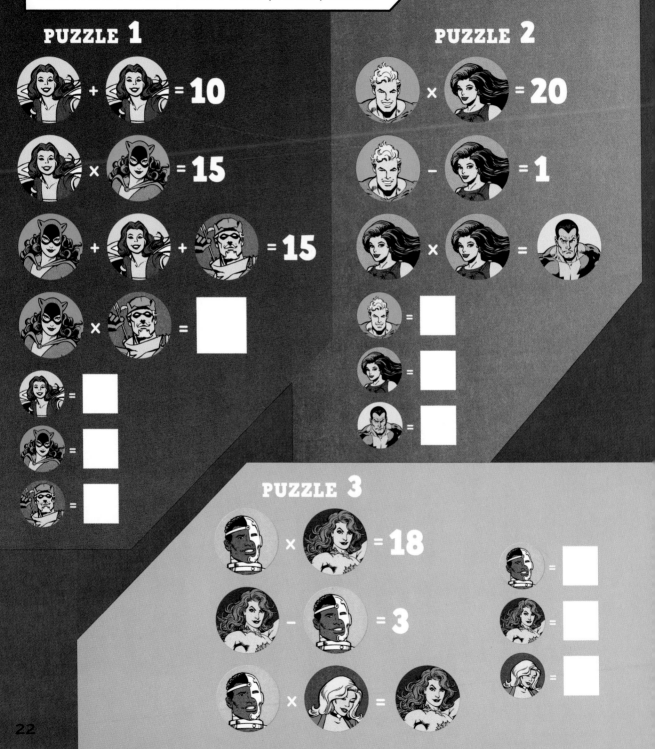

Test Your Memory

Study this comic cover for 30 seconds. Then turn the page and see how many questions you can answer correctly.

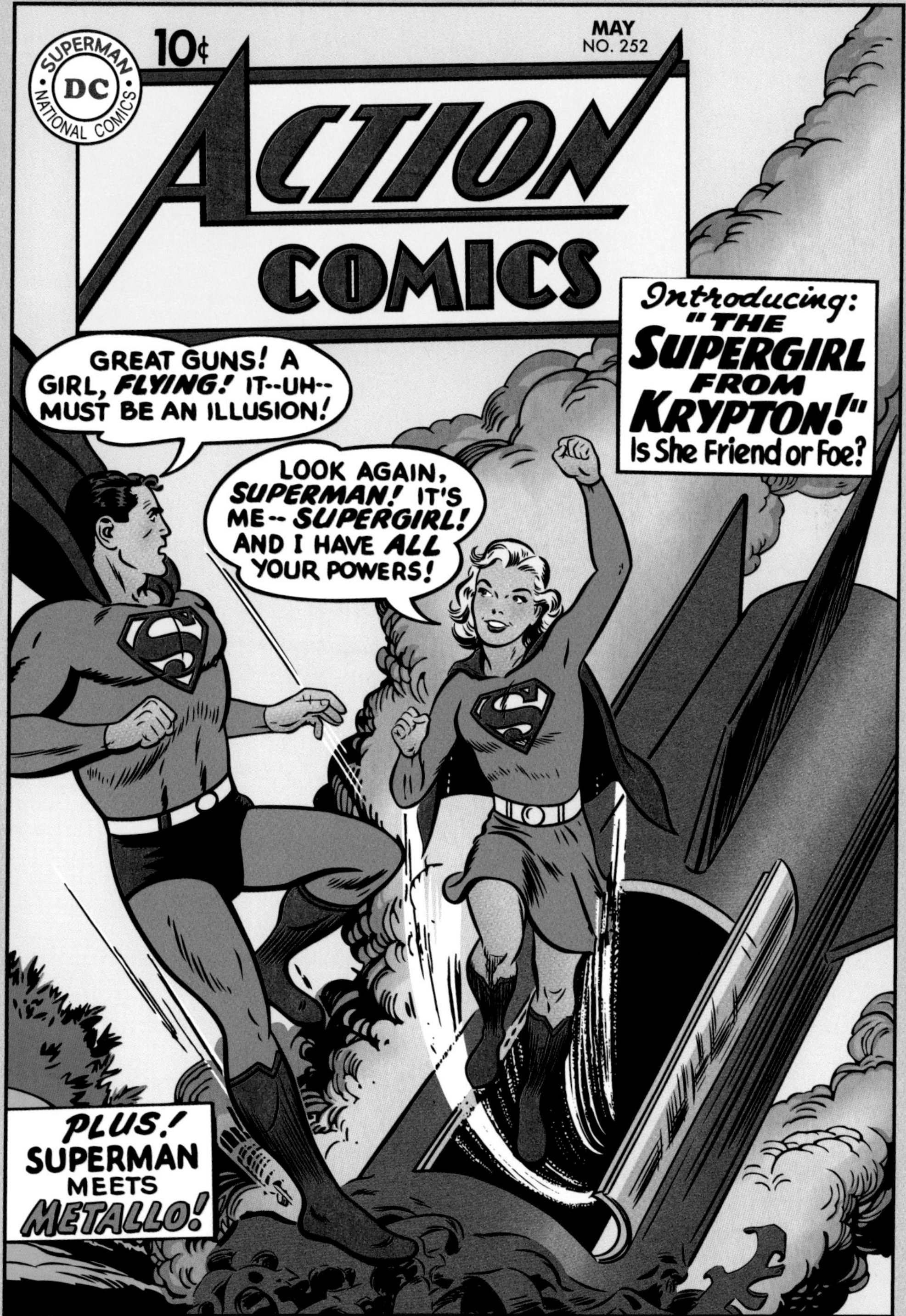
SUPERMAN DC NATIONAL COMICS
10¢
MAY NO. 252
ACTION COMICS
Introducing: "THE SUPERGIRL FROM KRYPTON!" Is She Friend or Foe?
GREAT GUNS! A GIRL, FLYING! IT--UH-- MUST BE AN ILLUSION!
LOOK AGAIN, SUPERMAN! IT'S ME-- SUPERGIRL! AND I HAVE ALL YOUR POWERS!
PLUS! SUPERMAN MEETS METALLO!

How Does Your Memory Stack Up?

Answer the questions below based on the picture on page 23.

1. How many people are in the picture?

a. One
b. Two
c. Three
d. Four

2. What color is Supergirl's rocket?

a. Red
b. Yellow
c. Purple
d. Black-and-white stripes

3. How many doors are on Supergirl's rocket?

a. One
b. Two
c. None
d. One door and two windows

4. How many planes are in the sky?

a. One
b. Two
c. Three
d. None

5. What else is in the sky?

a. A colorful bird
b. The sun
c. Fluffy white clouds
d. Smoke from the wreck

6. How does Superman react to seeing Supergirl?

a. He is surprised.
b. He is angry.
c. He gets the giggles.
d. He is scared.

7. Which super-villain is Superman going to meet?

a. Lex Luthor
b. Darkseid
c. Bizarro
d. Metallo

8. What color is Supergirl's belt?

a. Yellow
b. Brown
c. Green
d. Red

9. What question is posed on the cover?

a. How did she get here?
b. Is she friend or foe?
c. Would you like burgers or tacos for lunch?
d. Who is this Caped Crusader?

10. How much did this comic book cost?

a. 1 cent
b. 5 cents
c. 10 cents
d. 1 dollar

Climb the Word Ladder

Start at the bottom of this word ladder and climb to the top! Use the missing word in each clue to build the ladder. Each word in the ladder is just one letter different from the word below it.

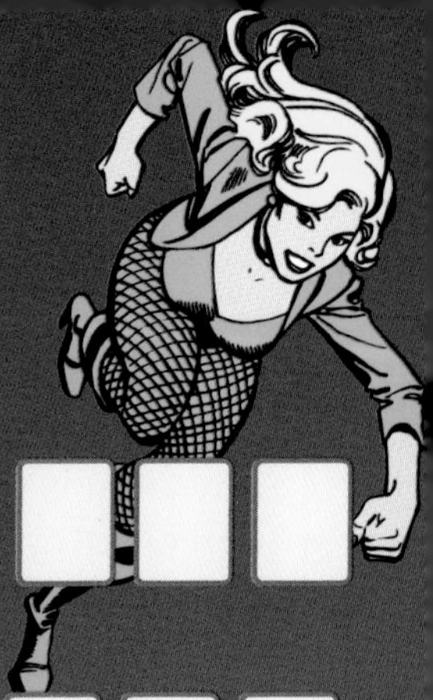

Black Canary was hot on the trail of two crooks who broke into a jewelry store and stole diamonds from the _____. ☐ ☐ ☐ ☐

Sometimes Lois Lane likes to interview people over coffee or hot chocolate at the _____. ☐ ☐ ☐ ☐

Batman and Robin exercise, practice using gadgets, and examine evidence in their secret lair, the Bat_____. ☐ ☐ ☐ ☐

Batgirl's long, flowing blue _____ flutters behind her when she swings through the air. ☐ ☐ ☐ ☐

Baseball players often wear _____ to keep the sun out of their eyes. ☐ ☐ ☐ ☐

_____ are Catwoman's favorite animals. ☐ ☐ ☐ ☐

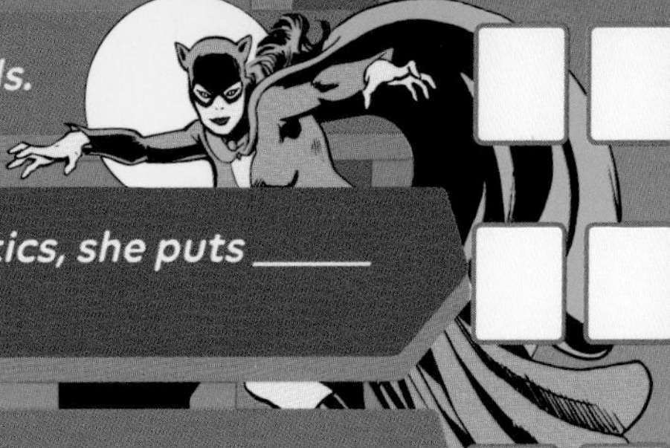

When Black Canary practices gymnastics, she puts _____ on the floor. ☐ ☐ ☐ ☐

In _____ class, Supergirl practices addition, subtraction, multiplication, and more. ☐ ☐ ☐ ☐

After a tough day battling super-villains, Batgirl takes a _____ to soothe her aching muscles. ☐ ☐ ☐ ☐

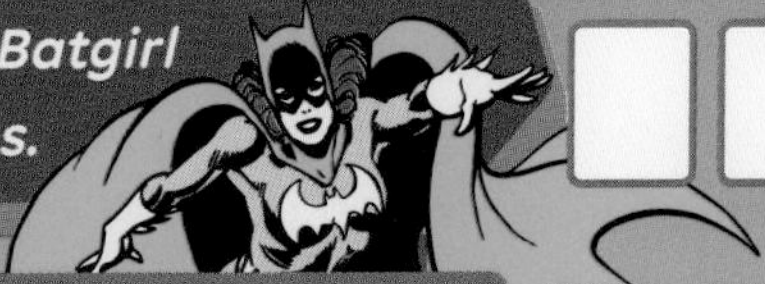

_____ Supergirl and Superman are from the planet Krypton. B O T H

Meet Mera!

Find each of the bold words in the word search on the right. They appear forward, backward, up, down, or diagonally.

Mera is an amazing **underwater** super hero. Some people think she is a **mermaid**, but she is so much more. **Queen** of **Atlantis**, she rules the **Seven Seas** with her husband **Aquaman**. Together, they battle any villains who **dive** deep to cause trouble, like **Black Manta**. Mera can breathe underwater, form water into objects, and **swim** like the strongest, fastest **fish**. Plus, she's got a serious **temper**! It's best to stay on her **good** side.

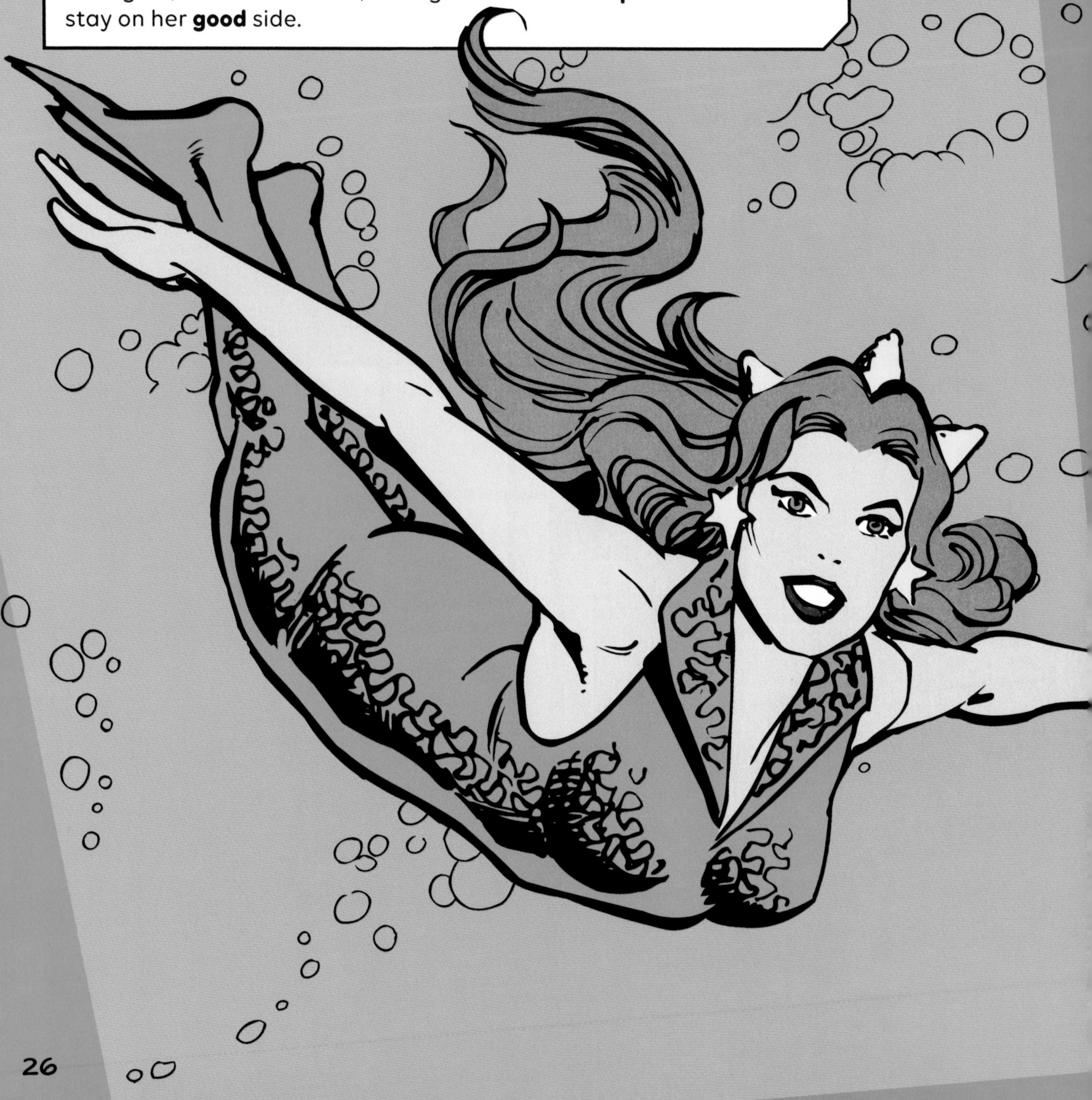

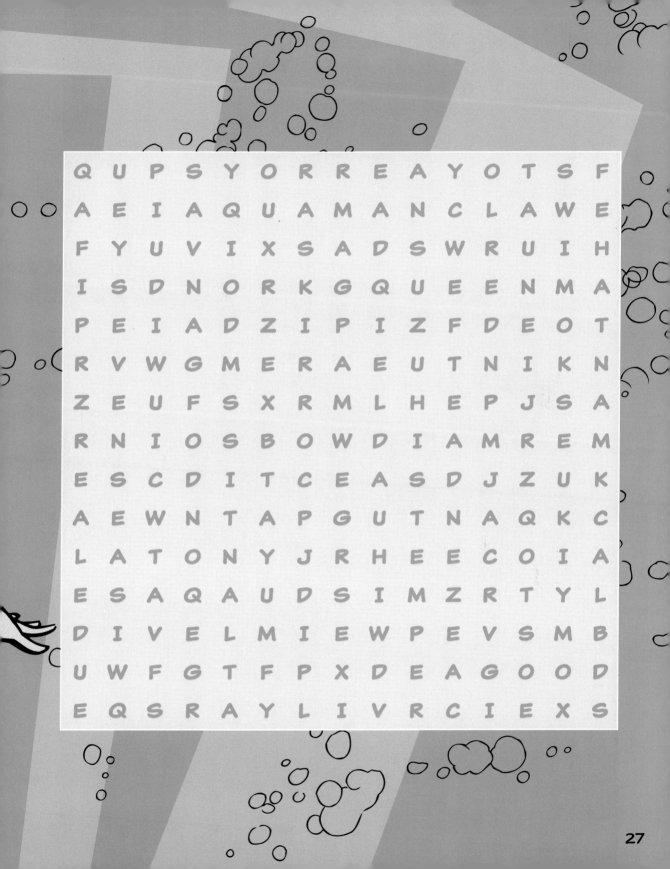

Q	U	P	S	Y	O	R	R	E	A	Y	O	T	S	F
A	E	I	A	Q	U	A	M	A	N	C	L	A	W	E
F	Y	U	V	I	X	S	A	D	S	W	R	U	I	H
I	S	D	N	O	R	K	G	Q	U	E	E	N	M	A
P	E	I	A	D	Z	I	P	I	Z	F	D	E	O	T
R	V	W	G	M	E	R	A	E	U	T	N	I	K	N
Z	E	U	F	S	X	R	M	L	H	E	P	J	S	A
R	N	I	O	S	B	O	W	D	I	A	M	R	E	M
E	S	C	D	I	T	C	E	A	S	D	J	Z	U	K
A	E	W	N	T	A	P	G	U	T	N	A	Q	K	C
L	A	T	O	N	Y	J	R	H	E	E	C	O	I	A
E	S	A	Q	A	U	D	S	I	M	Z	R	T	Y	L
D	I	V	E	L	M	I	E	W	P	E	V	S	M	B
U	W	F	G	T	F	P	X	D	E	A	G	O	O	D
E	Q	S	R	A	Y	L	I	V	R	C	I	E	X	S

What's in a Name?

In these acrostics, the first letter of each line spells out a word or message. Use some of your favorite super hero's names to make acrostics.

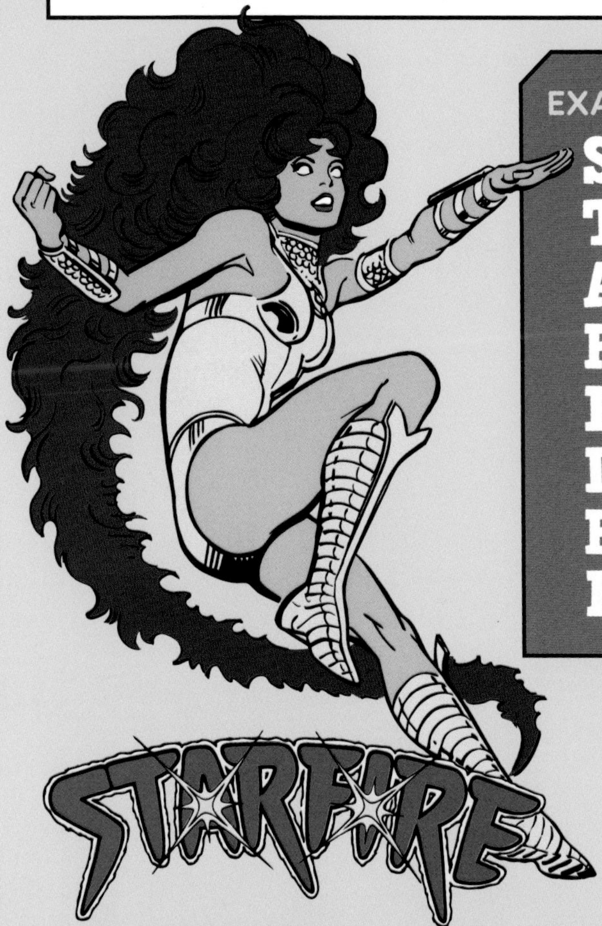
STARFIRE

EXAMPLE:

Smart
Trusted member of the Teen Titans
A princess from the planet Tamaran
Ready to fight for what's right
Flight is one of her many powers
Impressive warrior
Rebellious and strong
Energetic

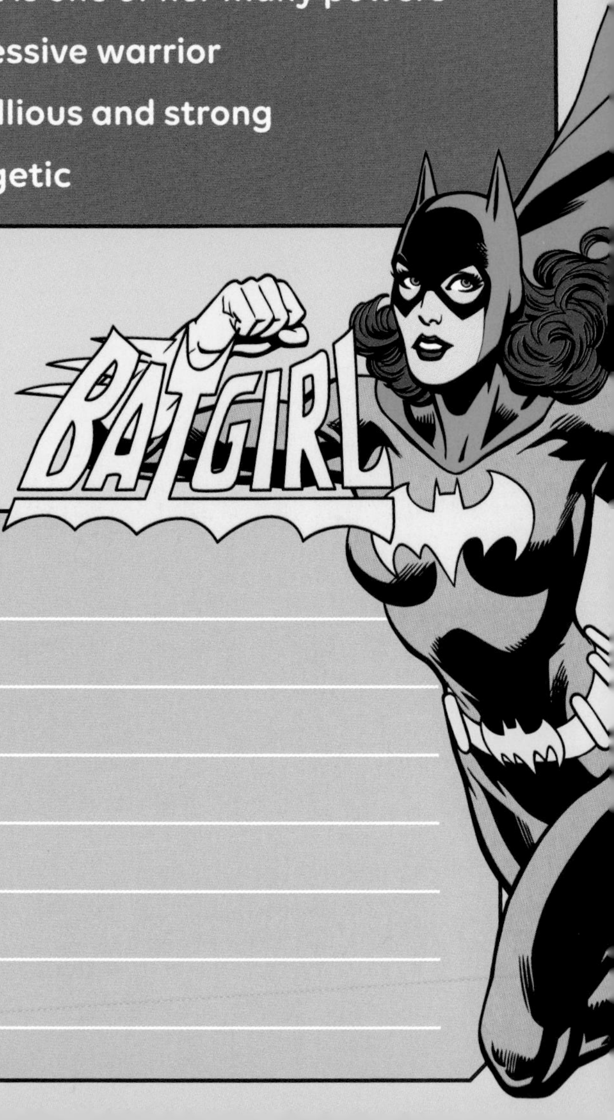
BATGIRL

B ________________________________

A ________________________________

T ________________________________

G ________________________________

I ________________________________

R ________________________________

L ________________________________

MERA

M
E
R
A

Write an acrostic using your name. Try out the name of a sibling or friend too.

Let's Make Magic!

Follow the grid to re-create the image. "Ward!" says Zatanna! (That's a spell to make you "draw.")

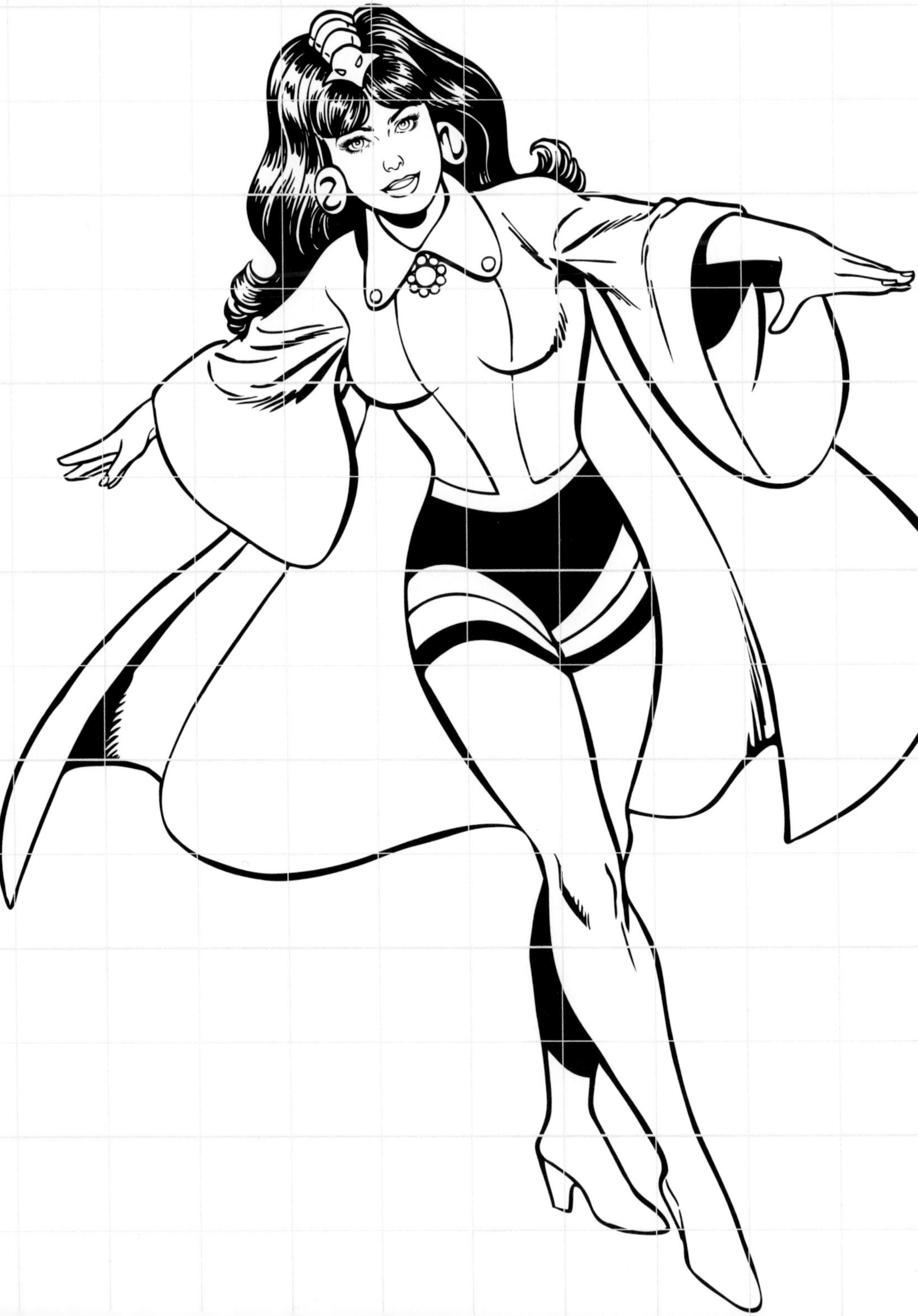

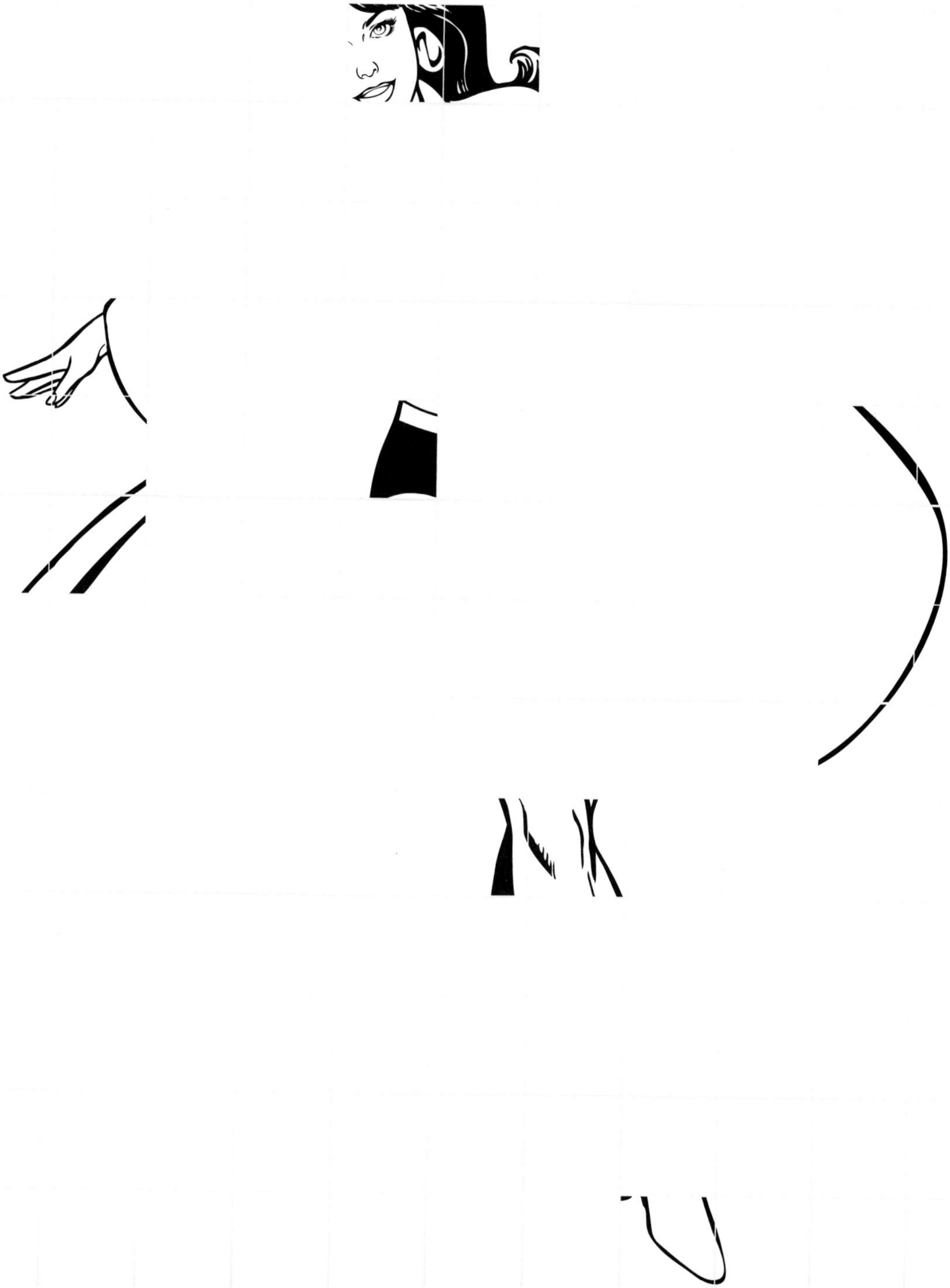

The Real Catwoman

Catwoman is a mystery. Is she Batman's friend or enemy? Is she a cunning super-villain, or is she helping the police? It sure is tough to figure her out. But you can start with this picture. Can you find 9 things that have changed from one pic to the next?

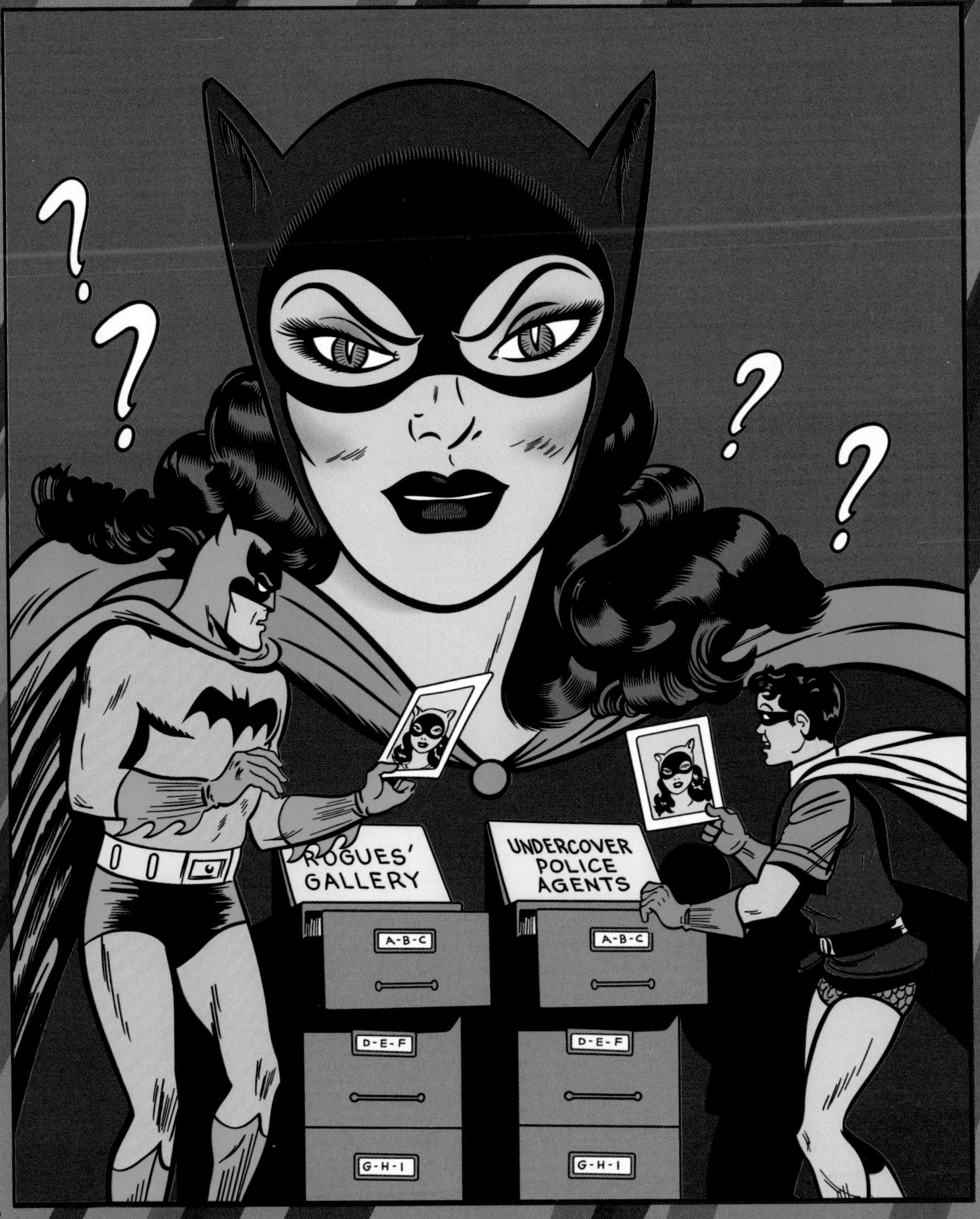
ROGUES' GALLERY
UNDERCOVER POLICE AGENTS
A-B-C
A-B-C
D-E-F
D-E-F
G-H-I
G-H-I

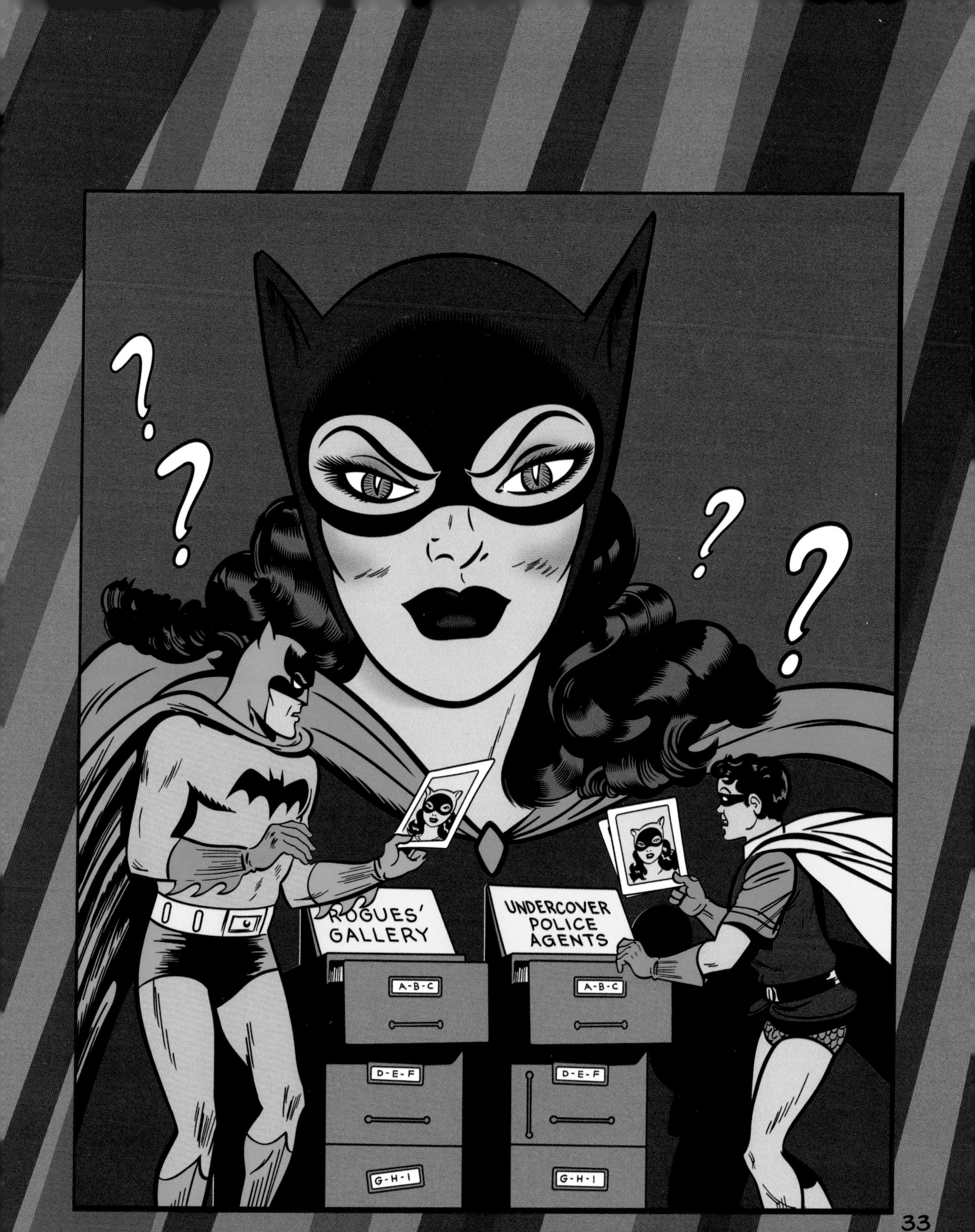
ROGUES' GALLERY
UNDERCOVER POLICE AGENTS
A-B-C
D-E-F
G-H-I
A-B-C
D-E-F
G-H-I

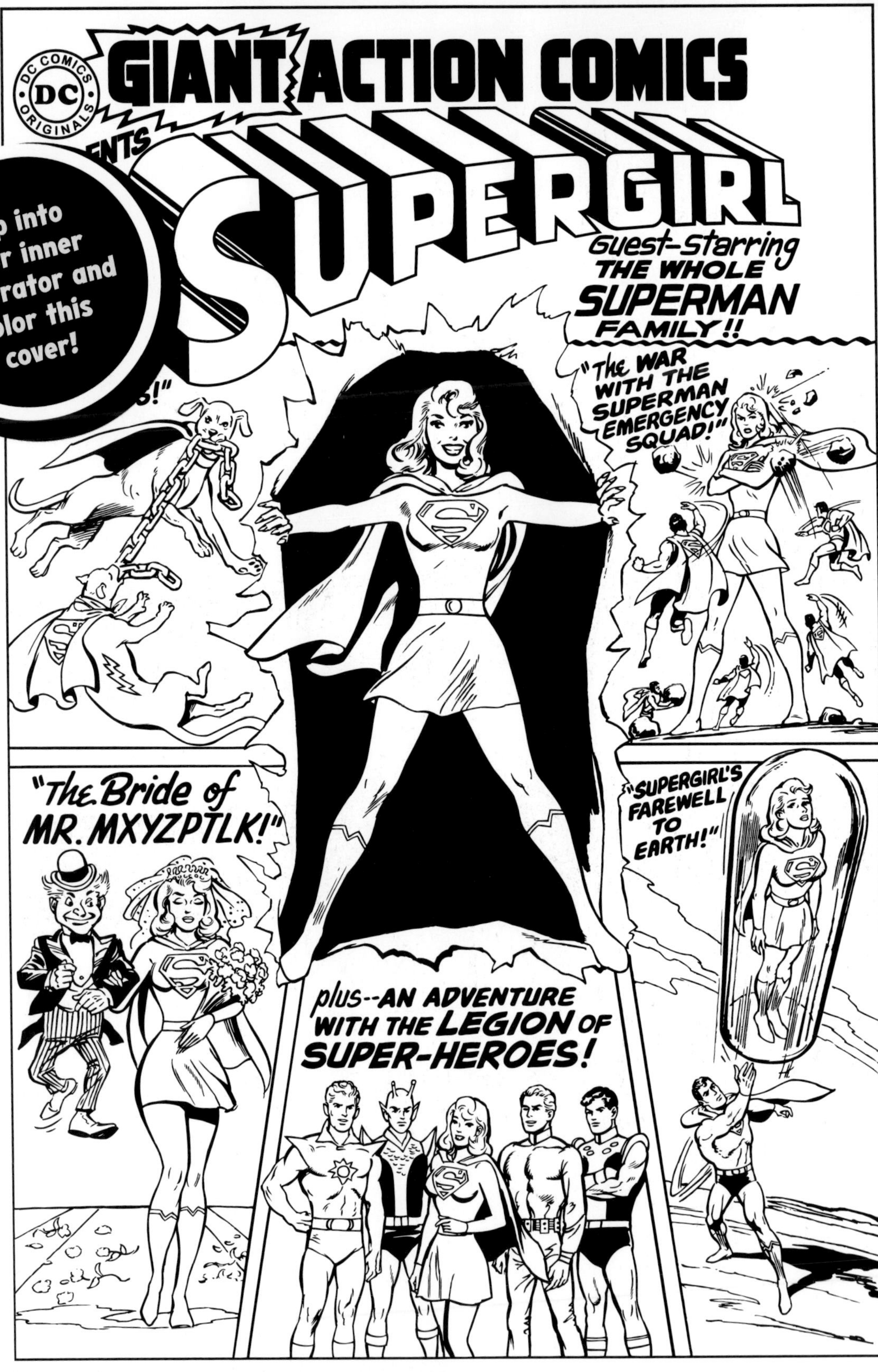
DC COMICS ORIGINALS
DC
GIANT ACTION COMICS
SUPERGIRL
Guest-Starring THE WHOLE SUPERMAN FAMILY!!
"The WAR WITH THE SUPERMAN EMERGENCY SQUAD!"
"The Bride of MR. MXYZPTLK!"
"SUPERGIRL'S FAREWELL TO EARTH!"
plus--AN ADVENTURE WITH THE LEGION OF SUPER-HEROES!

Tap into your inner illustrator and color this cover!

Supergirl to the Rescue!

Supergirl used her incredible vision to locate Superman. And good thing she did! Because it looks like the Man of Steel could use a hand. But Supergirl isn't sure how to get to Superman. Which path should she take?

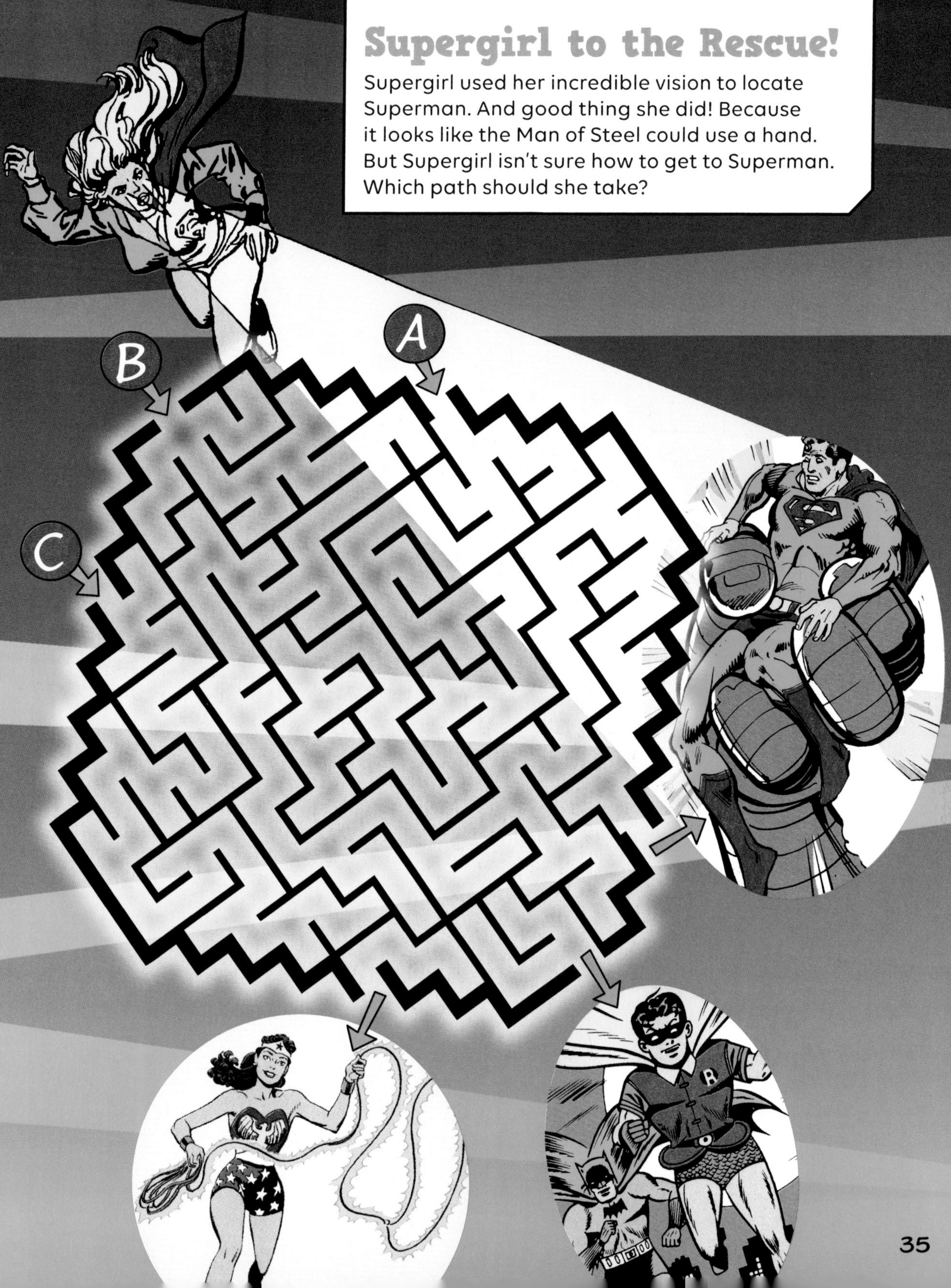

A
B
C

Let Loose Your Imagination!

Write a story about the picture you see.

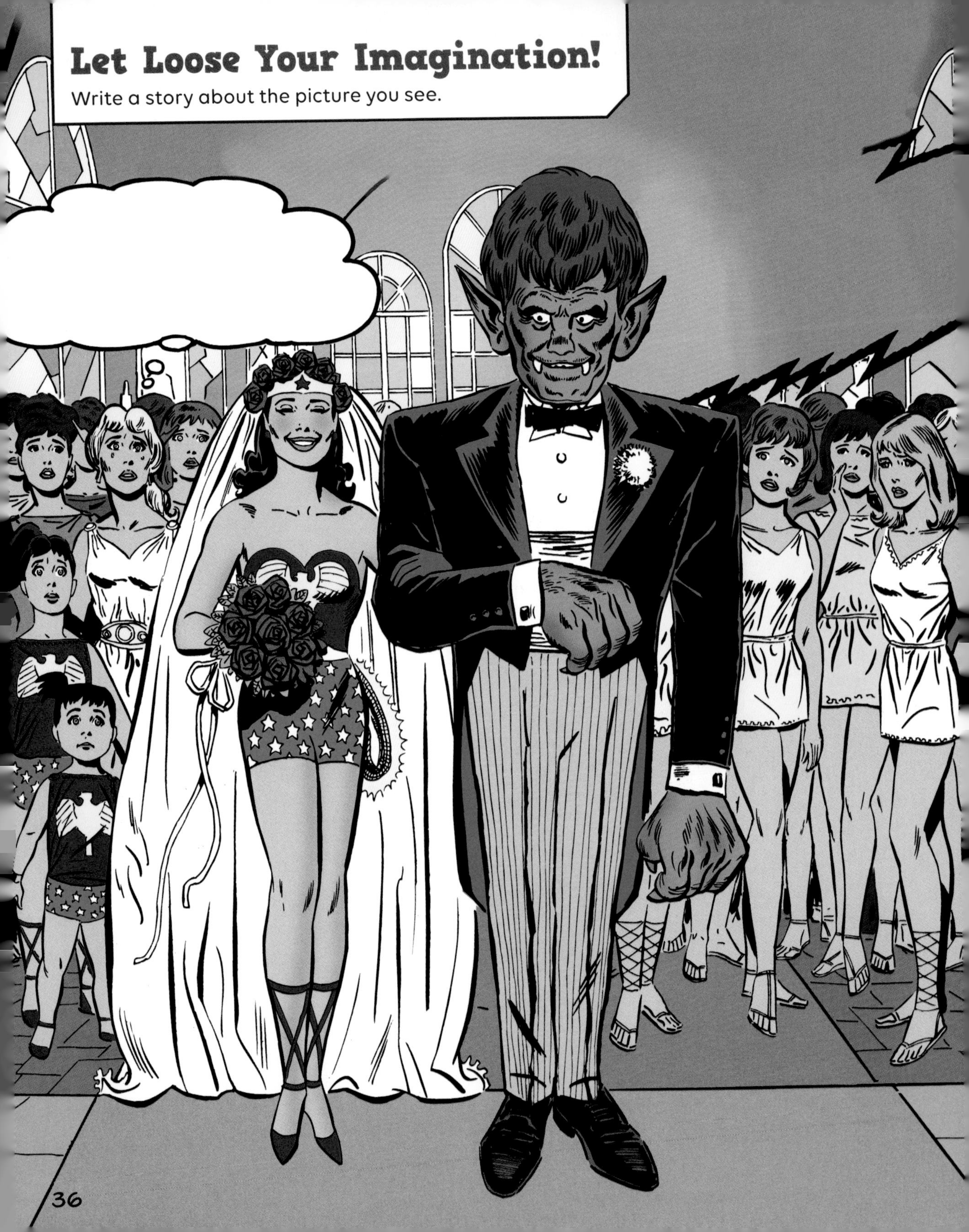

Connect the Matches!

Draw a line that connects each pair of identical pictures. You can draw lines horizontally and vertically, but not diagonally. Make sure no lines cross. When you are done, every box in the grid will have either a line or a picture in it.

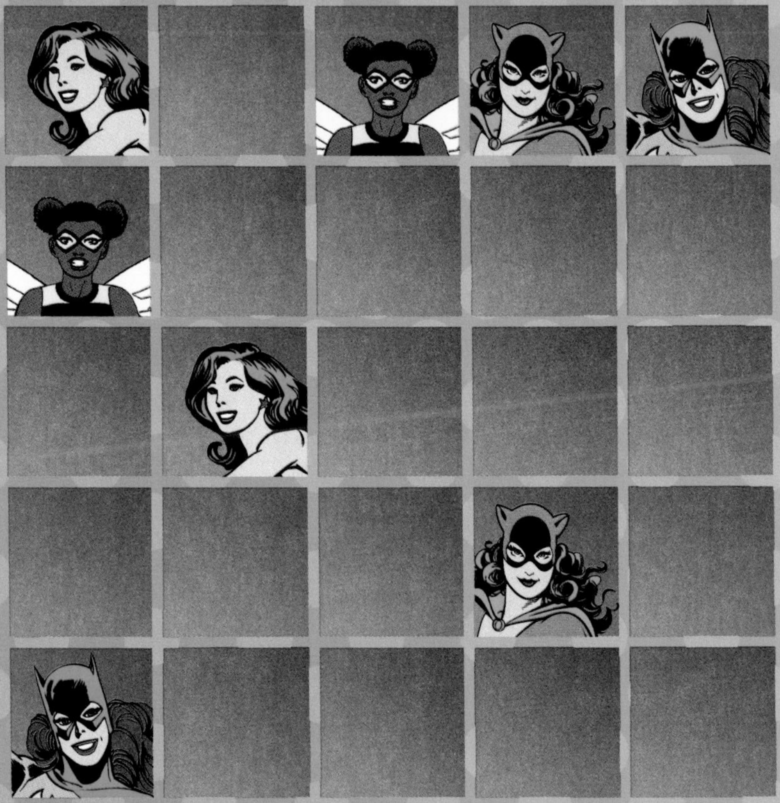

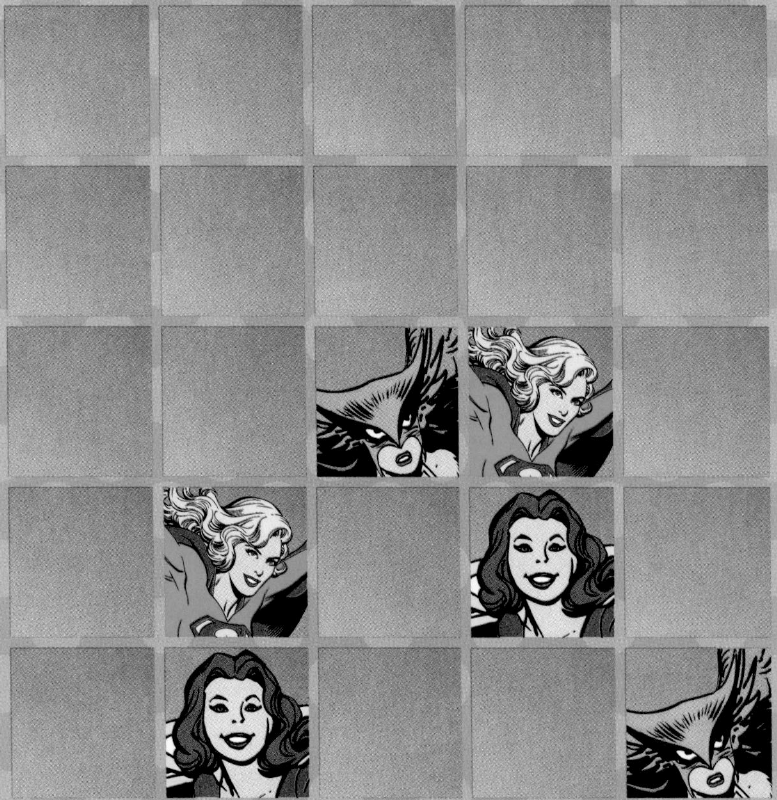

Which Letters Are Missing?

Supergirl needs your help to figure out which super-villain is trying to hatch a new plot. See which letters of the alphabet are missing from the page, then rearrange the letters to reveal the culprit's name.

C S Y I X P
B L
N F G S
X H A I W
M H A D C F H
X Y C Q
L U P X N
L A Z F I
I A D
W U Q S M V A
D C U
Z M
T T S
D G L Y V

MISSING LETTERS:

_____

SUPER-VILLAIN NAME:

_____

Funny Fill-Ins

Match the symbols in the key to the letters they represent to uncover the answers to these riddles.

KEY

A	B	C	D	E	F	G	H	I	J	K	L	M	N	O
Ω	π	/	Δ	Σ	≈	ƒ	#	∞	÷	~	@	∫	»	©

P	Q	R	S	T	U	V	W	X	Y	Z
®	%	§	*	¿	ø	…	✓	¬	-	\

Is Batgirl a good fighter?

-	Σ	*	,
			,

*	#	Σ

®	ø	¿	*

¿	#	Σ

π	Ω	¿

∞	»

/	©	∫	π	Ω	¿	.
						.

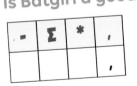

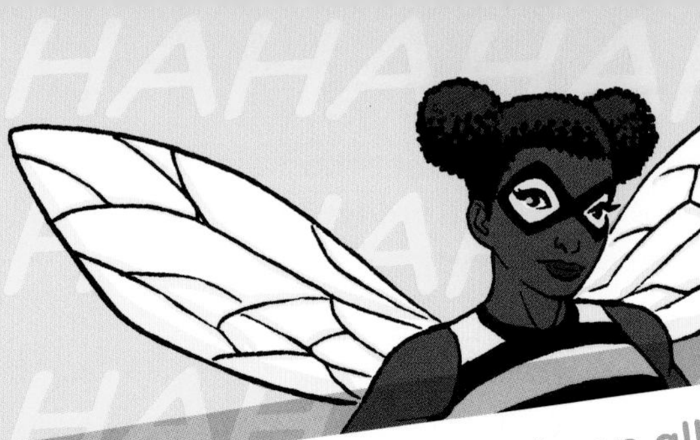

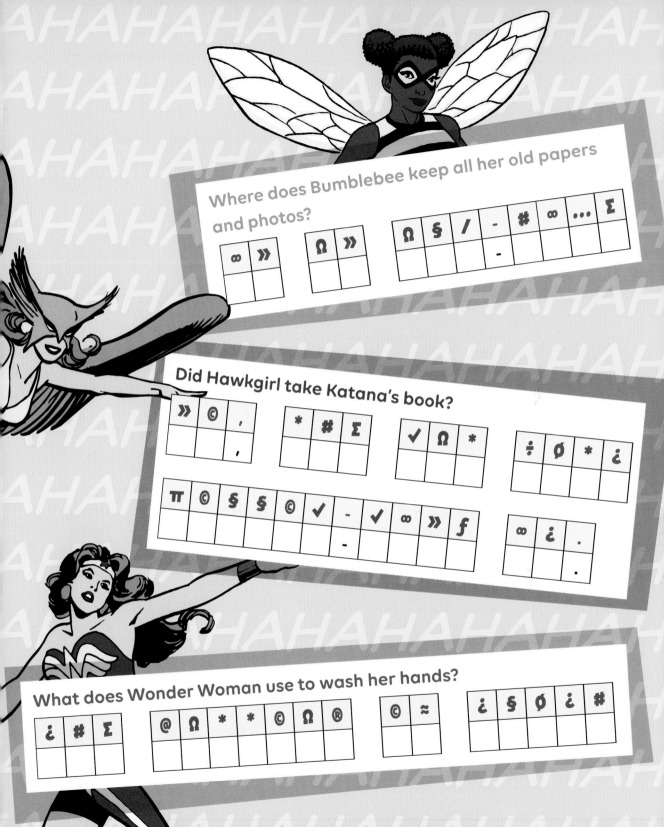

Where does Bumblebee keep all her old papers and photos?

∞	»

Ω	»

Ω	§	/	-	#	∞	…	Σ
			-				

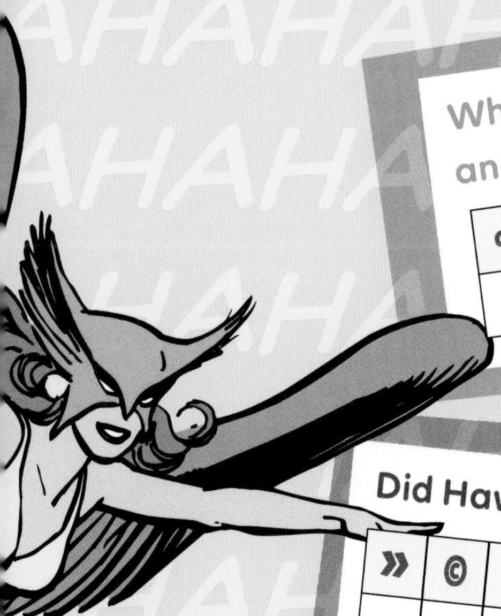

Did Hawkgirl take Katana's book?

»	©	,
		,

*	#	Σ

✓	Ω	*

÷	ø	*	¿

π	©	§	§	©	✓	-	✓	∞	»	ƒ
						-				

∞	¿	.
		.

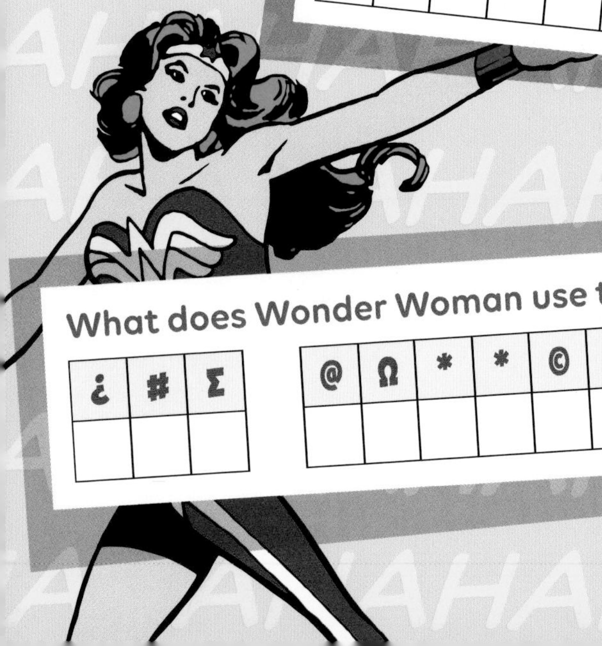

What does Wonder Woman use to wash her hands?

¿	#	Σ

@	Ω	*	*	©	Ω	®

©	≈

¿	§	ø	¿	#

One Wondrous Change

One of these Wonder Girls looks different than the rest. Use your superpowers to spot the difference.

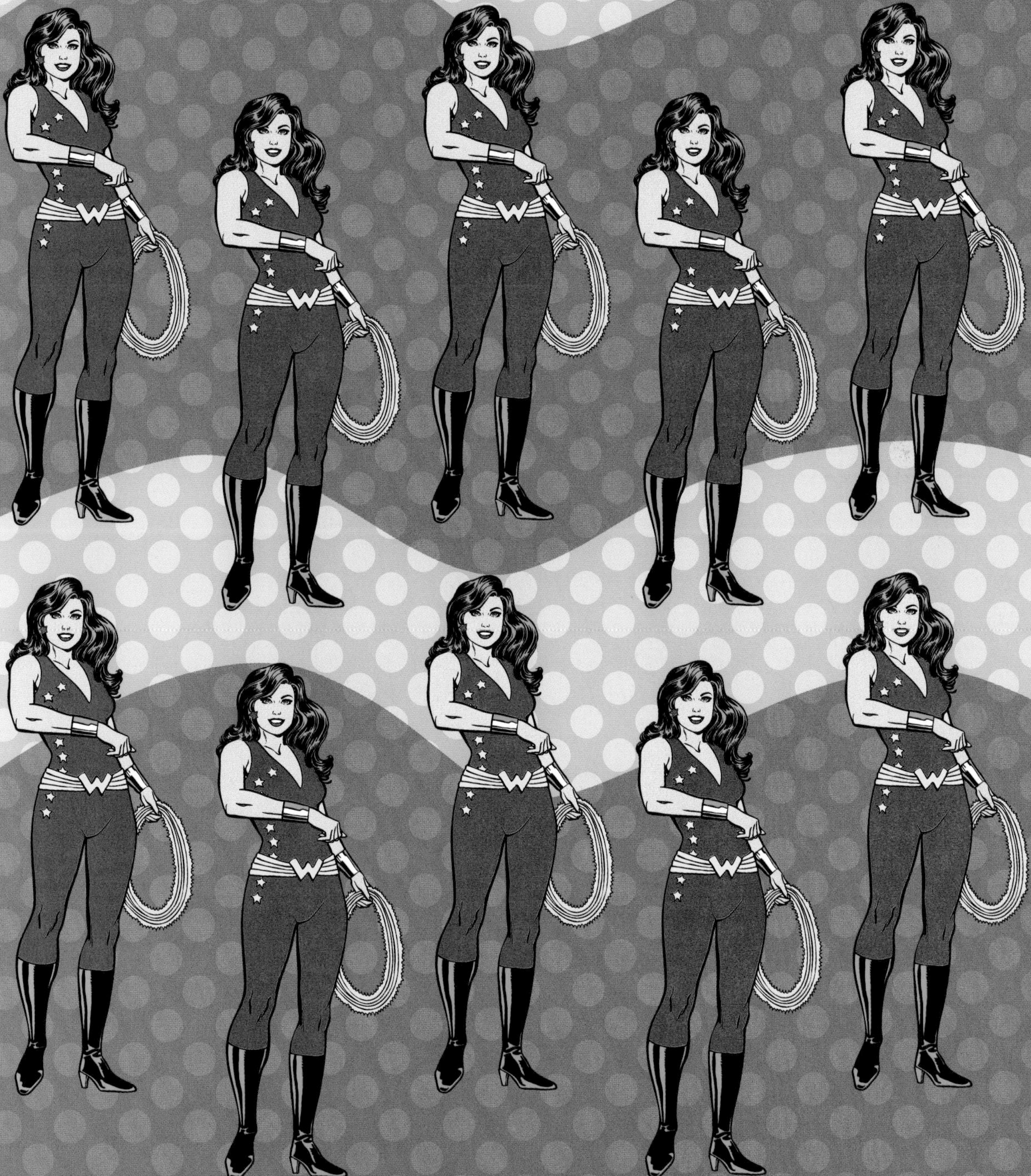

Add 'Em Up!

Use your math powers to unravel these puzzles.

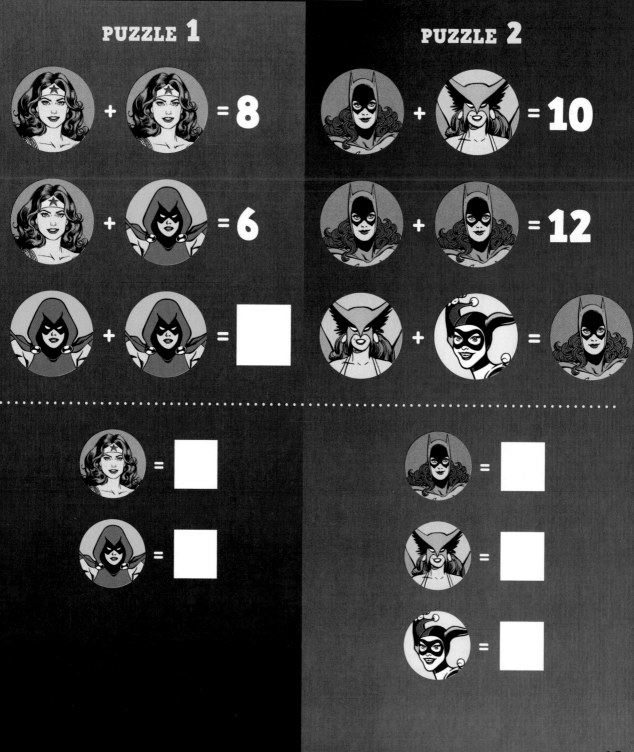

PUZZLE 1

Wonder Woman + Wonder Woman = 8

Wonder Woman + Raven = 6

Raven + Raven = ☐

Wonder Woman = ☐

Raven = ☐

PUZZLE 2

Batgirl + Hawkgirl = 10

Batgirl + Batgirl = 12

Hawkgirl + Harley Quinn = Batgirl

Batgirl = ☐

Hawkgirl = ☐

Harley Quinn = ☐

Watch Out for Dead Ends!

Uh oh! It looks like Green Lantern is in trouble. Guide Black Canary through the maze so she can help Green Lantern subdue Mantis and prevent him from committing any more crimes!

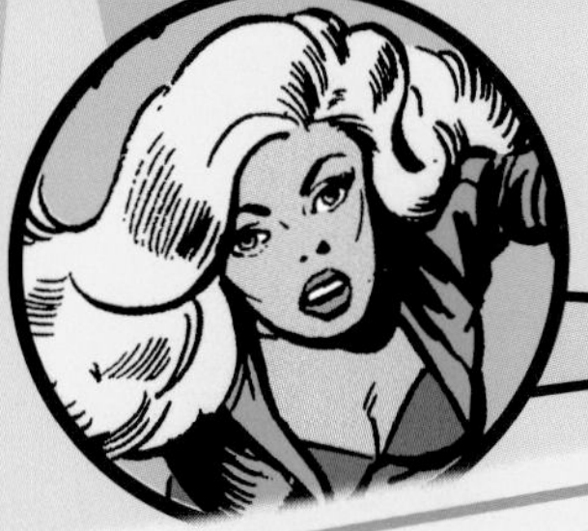

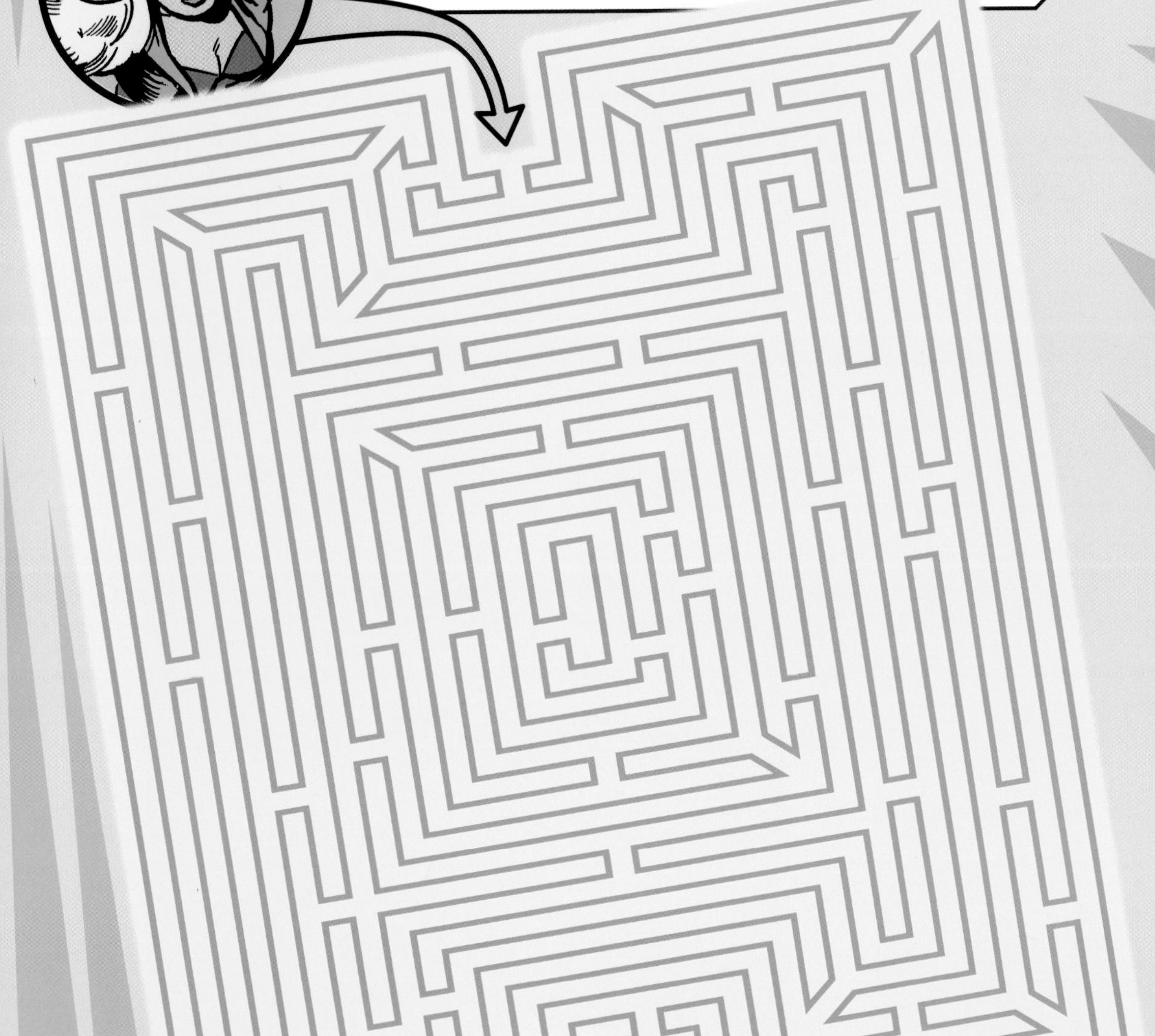

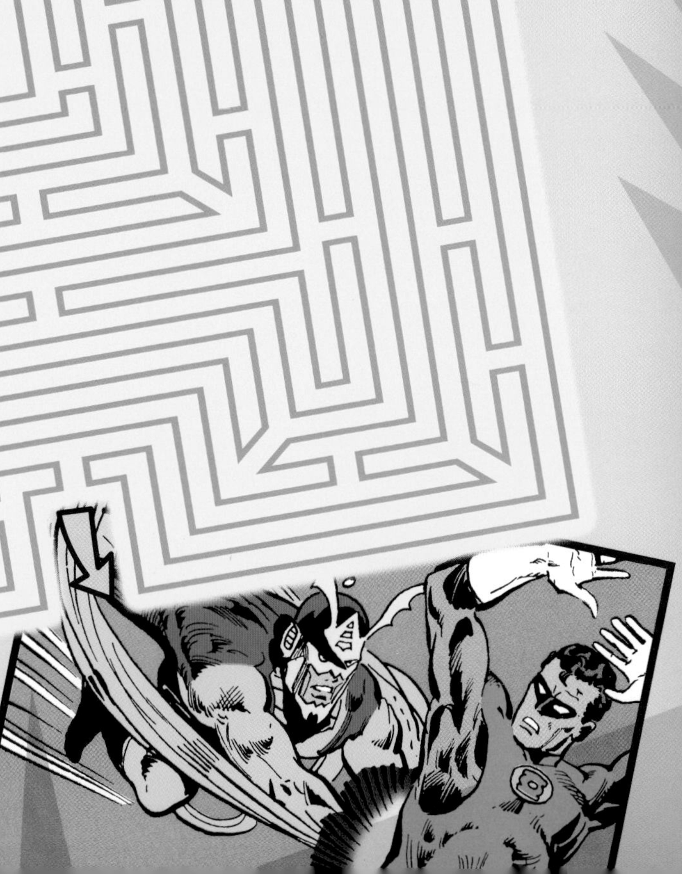

A Trip Down Memory Lane

Study this comic book cover for 30 seconds, then turn the page and test your memory.

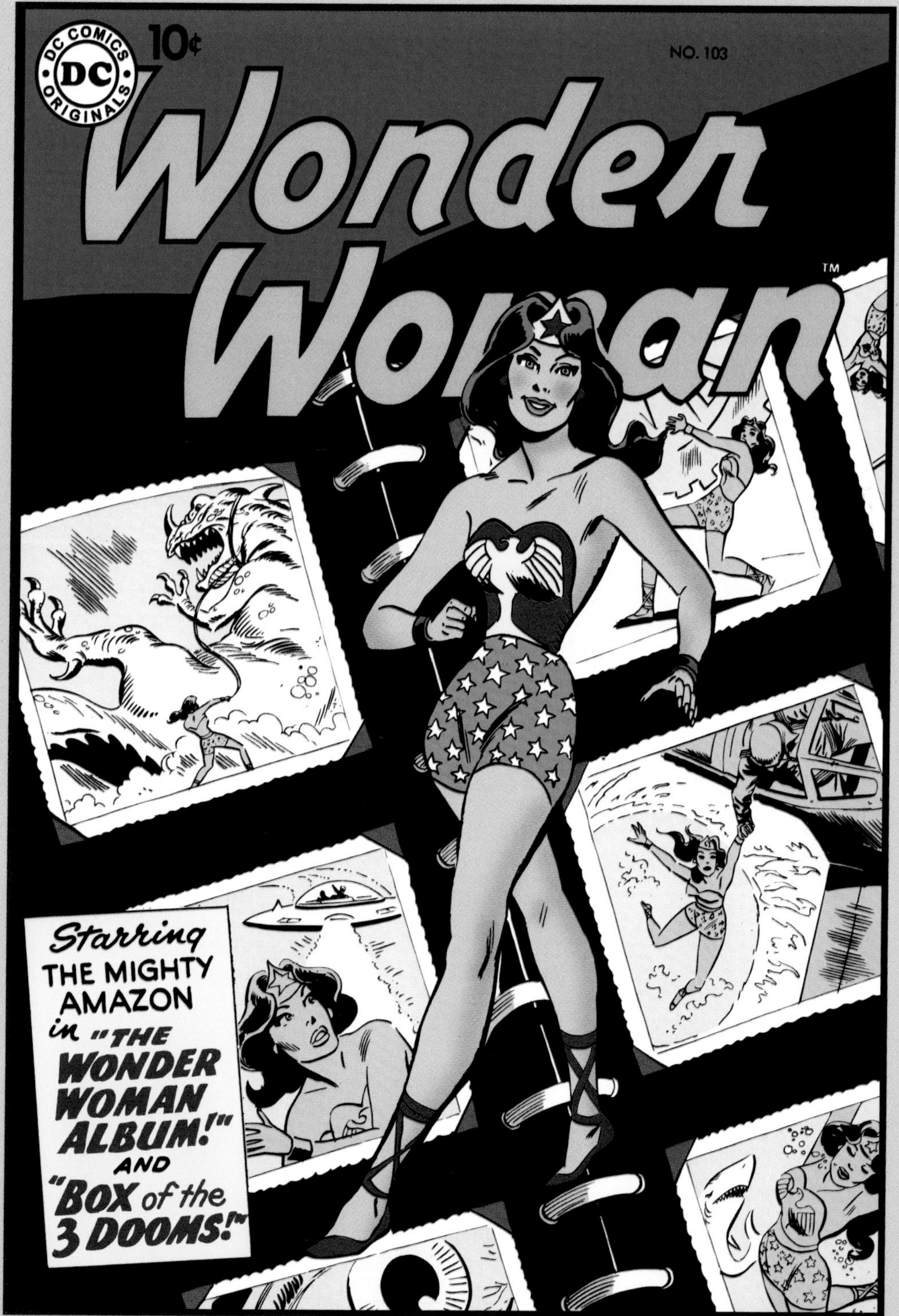
DC COMICS ORIGINALS
DC
10¢
NO. 103
Wonder Woman
TM
Starring THE MIGHTY AMAZON in "THE WONDER WOMAN ALBUM!" AND "BOX of the 3 DOOMS!"

Do You Have a Photographic Memory?

Answer the questions below based on the comic book cover on page 45.

1. Which of these is NOT on the comic book cover?

a. A dinosaur

b. A giant eyeball

c. A UFO

d. A crocodile

2. How many snapshots are visible on the cover (even if you can't see the whole picture):

a. Four

b. Five

c. Six

d. Seven

3. What sea creature is in the water with Woman Woman?

a. A dolphin

b. A shark

c. A giant sea turtle

d. A manta ray

4. How much is the comic book?

a. 10 cents

b. 15 cents

c. 50 cents

d. 1 dollar

5. What is the name of the comic book?

a. The Adventures of Wonder Woman

b. Wonder Woman

c. Wonder Woman and Friends

d. The Amazing Wonder Woman

6. What color is the title of the comic book?

a. Green

b. White

c. Orange

d. Pink

7. In one picture, Wonder Woman is hanging from a ________.

a. Window

b. Airplane

c. UFO

d. Bridge

8. Which phrase does NOT appear on the comic book?

a. "Box of the 3 Dooms!"

b. "The Wonder Woman Album!"

c. "Wonder Woman's Scrapbook!"

d. "The Mighty Amazon!"

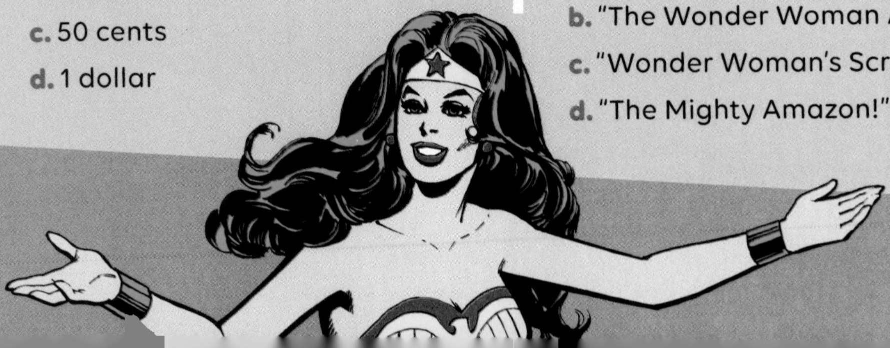

Change a Letter, Build a Word

Use the missing word in each clue to build the ladder. Each word in the ladder is just one letter different from the words above and below.

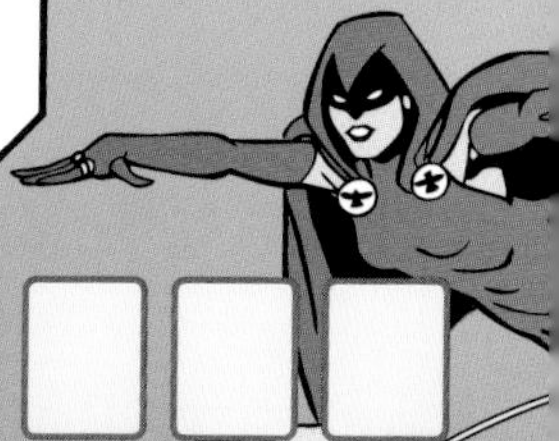

When super heroes hear rumors about crooks planning crimes, they have to figure out which stories are fake and which stories are ______.

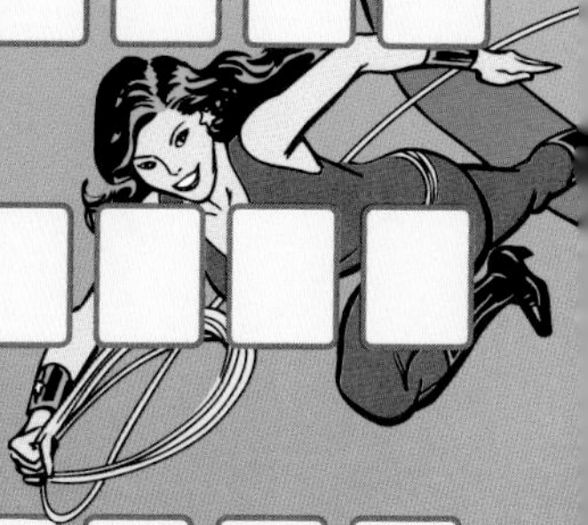

Raven has the power to make injured people feel better. She can help ______ them.

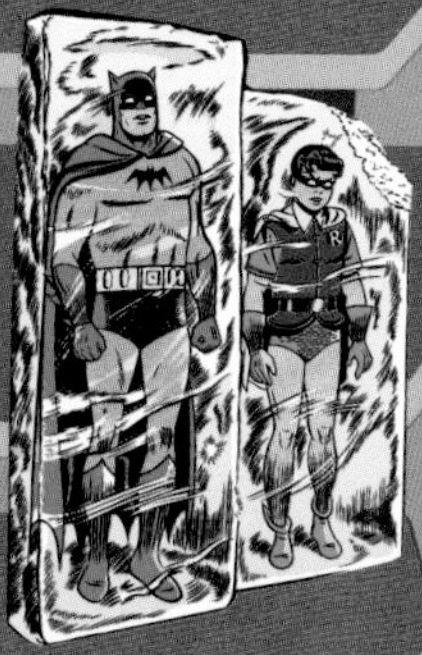

After a visit from Captain Cold, Batman and Robin need Supergirl to use her ______ vision to thaw them out.

Supergirl has super senses. Make a noise 10 miles away, and she can still ______ you.

Scarecrow uses a terrible concoction to make people live their worst nightmares. He likes to make people feel ______.

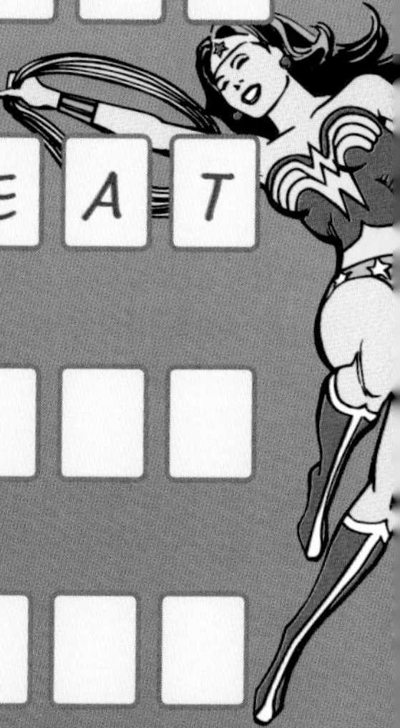

Wonder Woman has so many astounding achievements. Defeating Ares was an incredible ______!

F E A T

Plastic Man can change his shape. To slip through a closed door, he can even make himself ______.

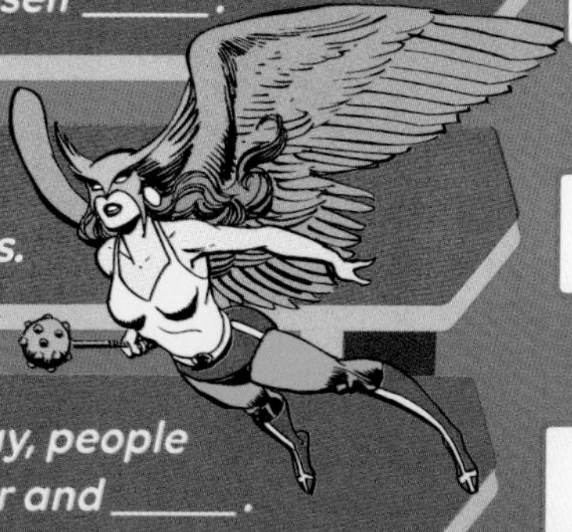

To fly through the sky, Hawkgirl only needs to ______ her giant wings.

When Wonder Woman saves the day, people are so happy and grateful they cheer and ______.

Portrait of Power

Use your enhanced vision to perfect your drawing skills. Let the grid be your guide as you recreate this powerful portrait of Supergirl.

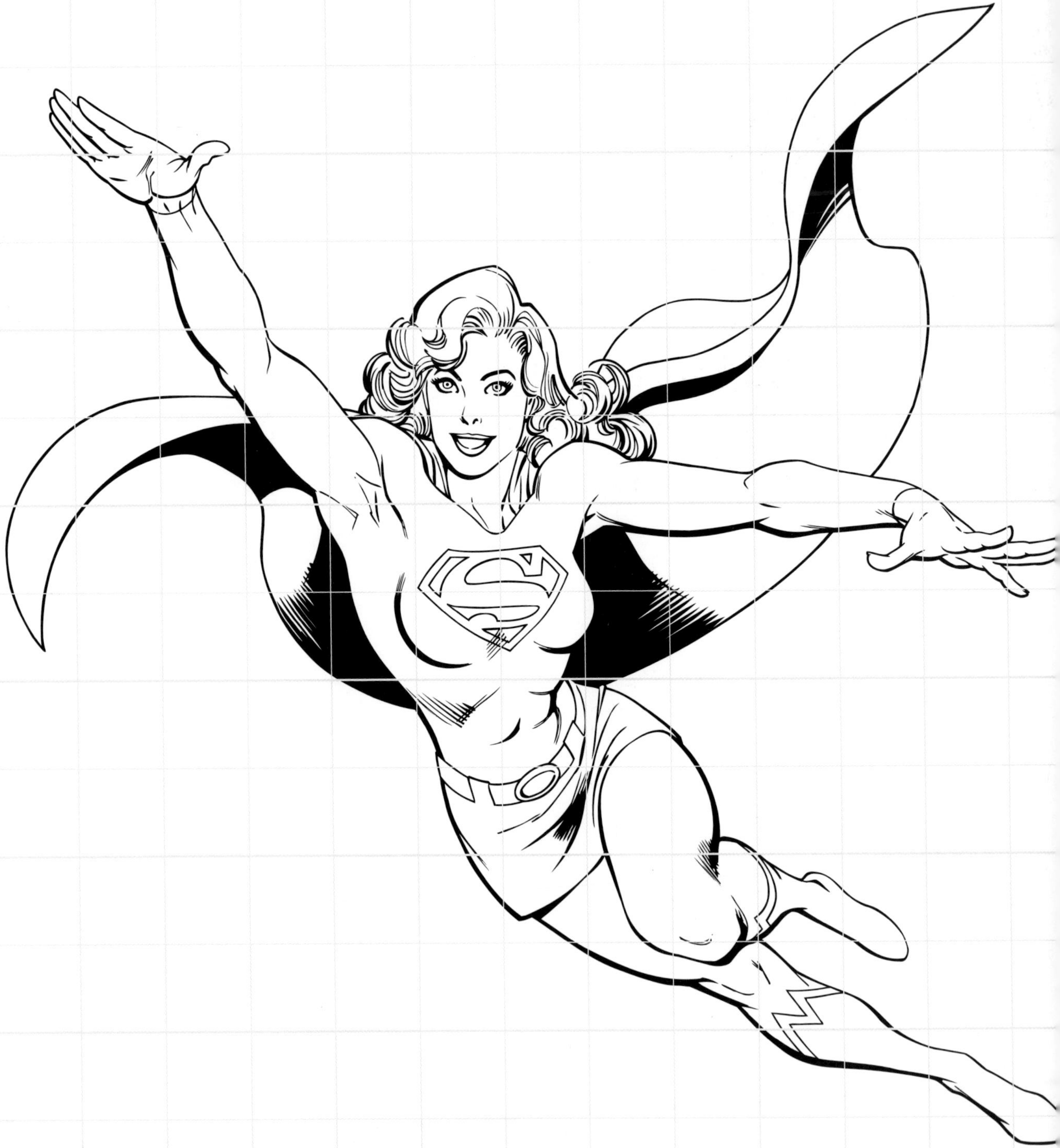

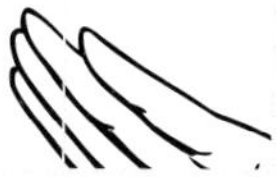

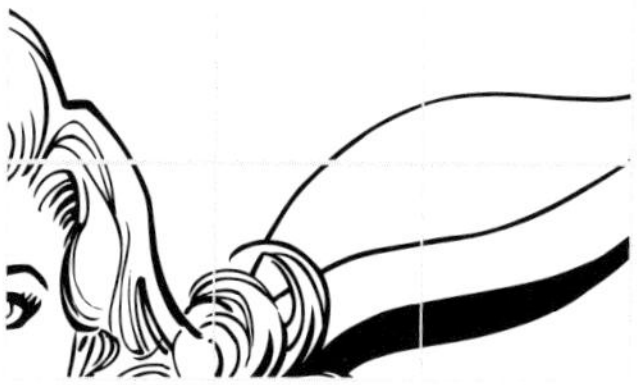

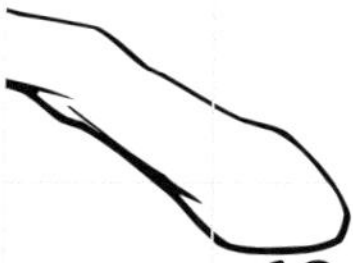

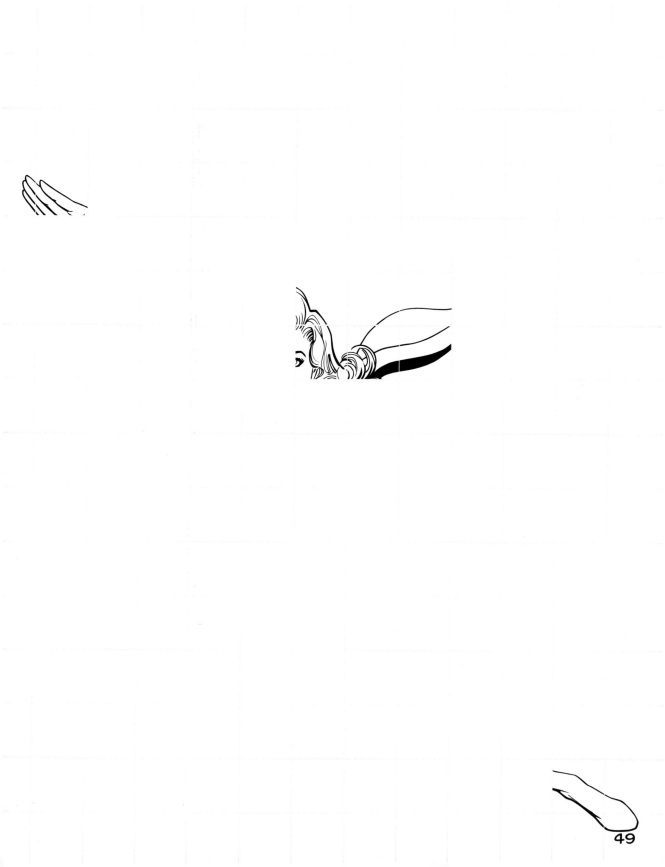

One Letter at a Time!

Use your brainpower to fill in this challenging word ladder. Change one letter in each line to get from the top word to the bottom word.

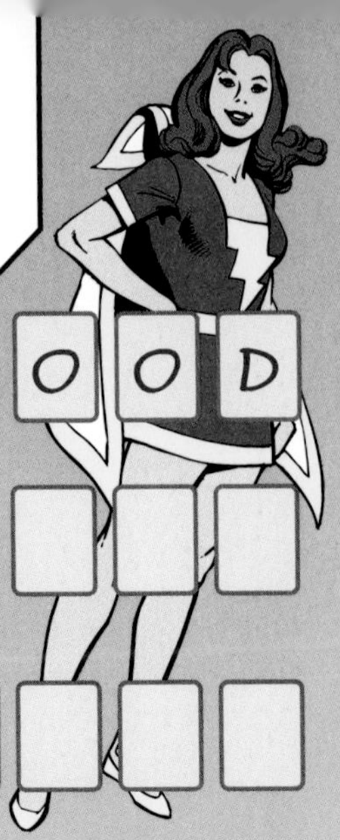

Super heroes often join battles of ______ against evil. G O O D

Robots do not eat ______.

After doing laundry, even heroes have to ______ their super hero suits.

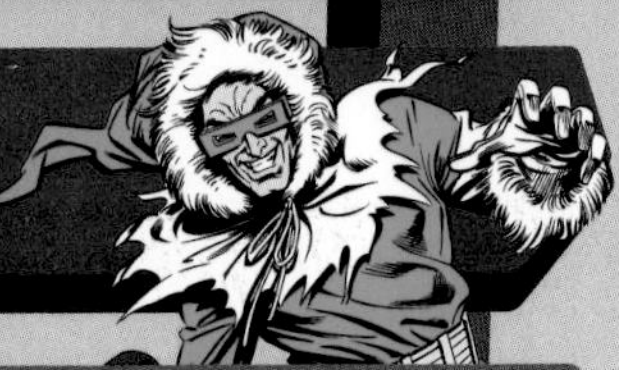

Captain ______ uses a special weapon to stun people so he can commit crimes.

A young male horse is a ______.

The symbol across Mary's chest is a lightning ______.

Batman carries many helpful gadgets on his Utility ______.

"Ding, ding, ding" is the sound of a ______.

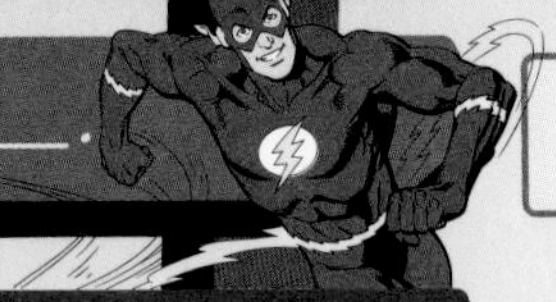

The Flash can hit and catch the same fast ______.

Giganta can grow and grow and grow until she is as ______ as a skyscraper.

When Krypto is happy, he wags his ______.

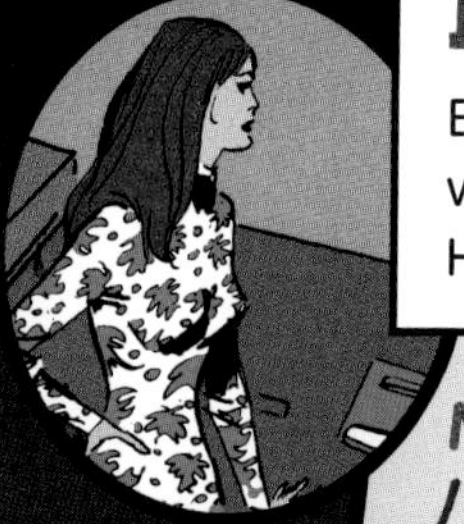

Letter by Letter

By day, Batgirl is the librarian Barbara Gordon. She loves to read and play word games. Don't you? Below are four phrases that are related to Batgirl. How many words can you make out of the letters in each phrase?

M-A-R-T-I-A-L A-R-T-I-S-T

IT

SIT

MAT

C-R-I-M-E F-I-G-H-T-E-R

G-O-T-H-A-M C-I-T-Y

B-A-R-B-A-R-A G-O-R-D-O-N

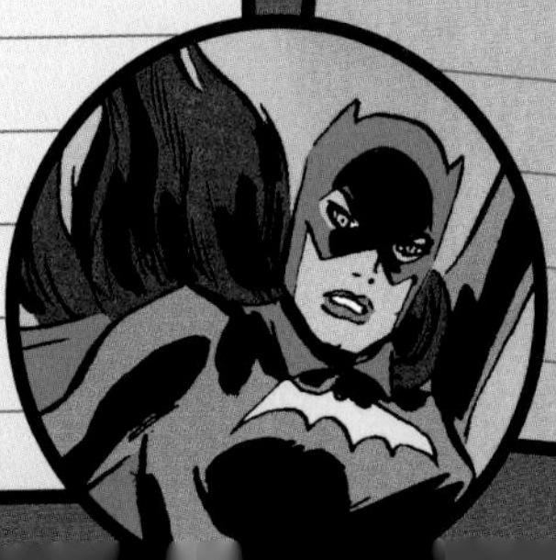

How Many?

Each face corresponds to a number. Match these heroes to a number that makes the equations add up.

PUZZLE 1

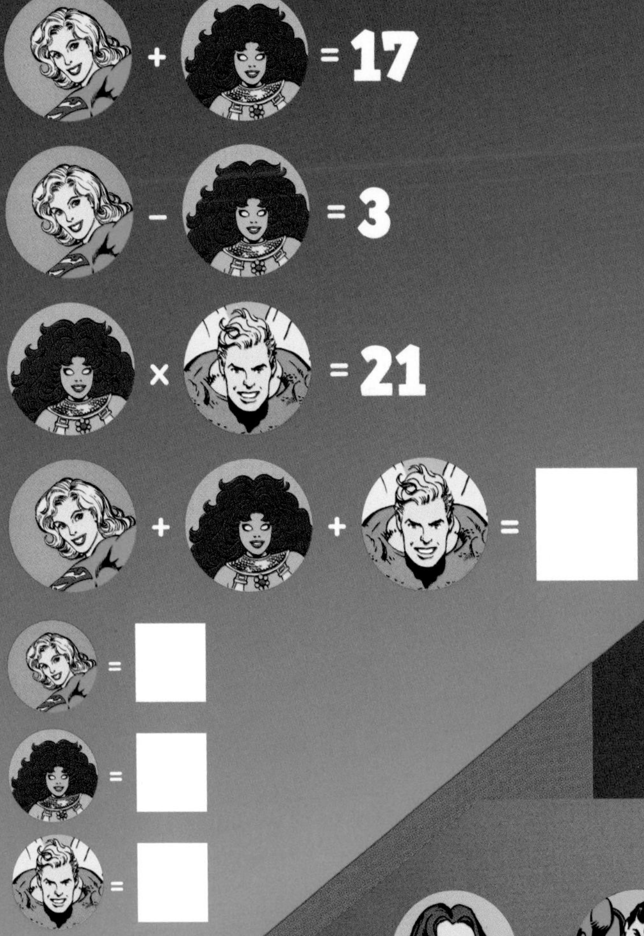
+ = 17
– = 3
× = 21
+ + =
=
=
=

PUZZLE 2

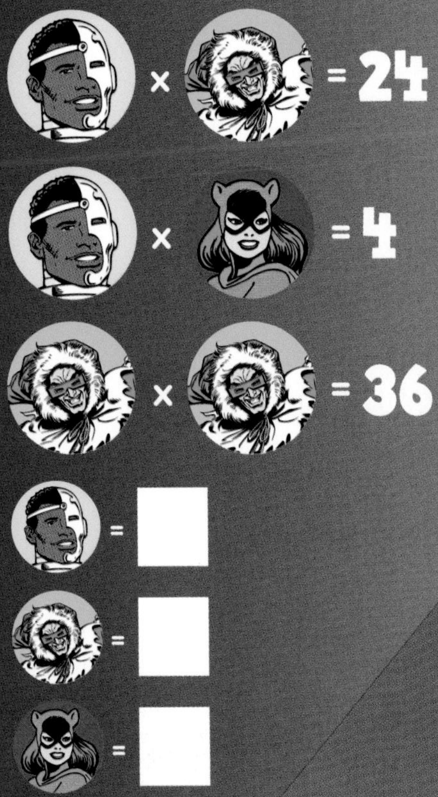
× = 24
× = 4
× = 36
=
=
=

PUZZLE 3

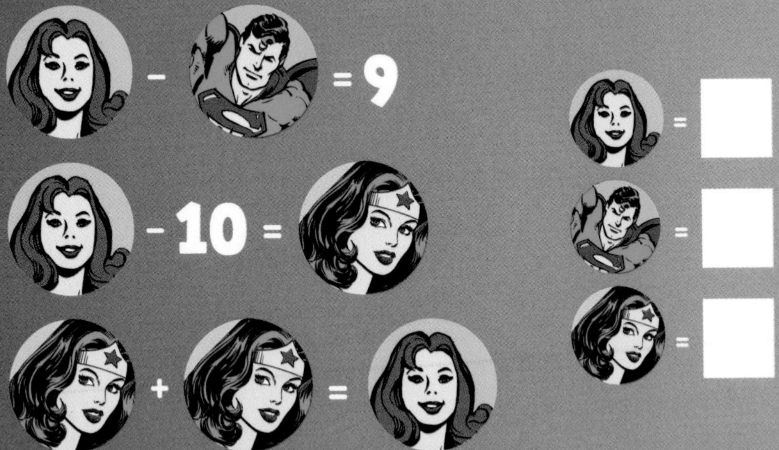
– = 9
– 10 =
+ =
=
=
=

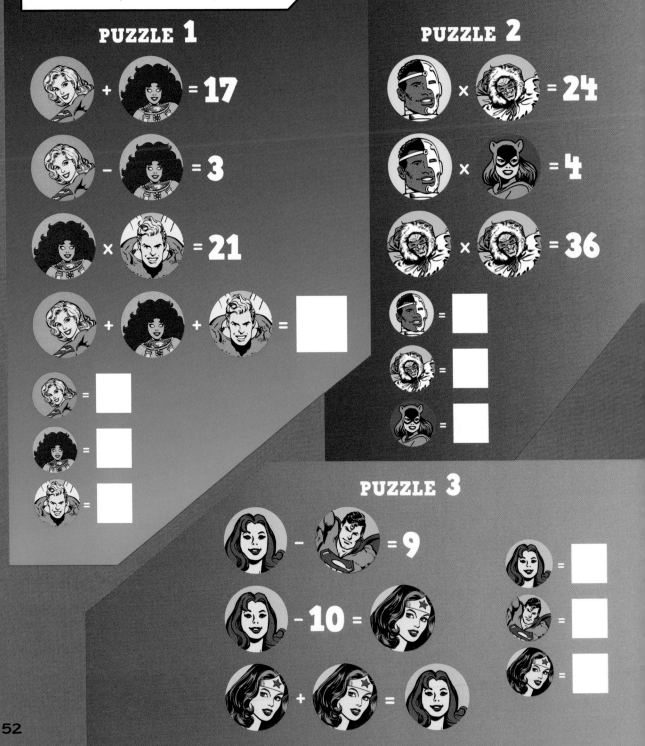

Spot the Standout

Seven Supergirls are identical. One is a little different. Which one is it?

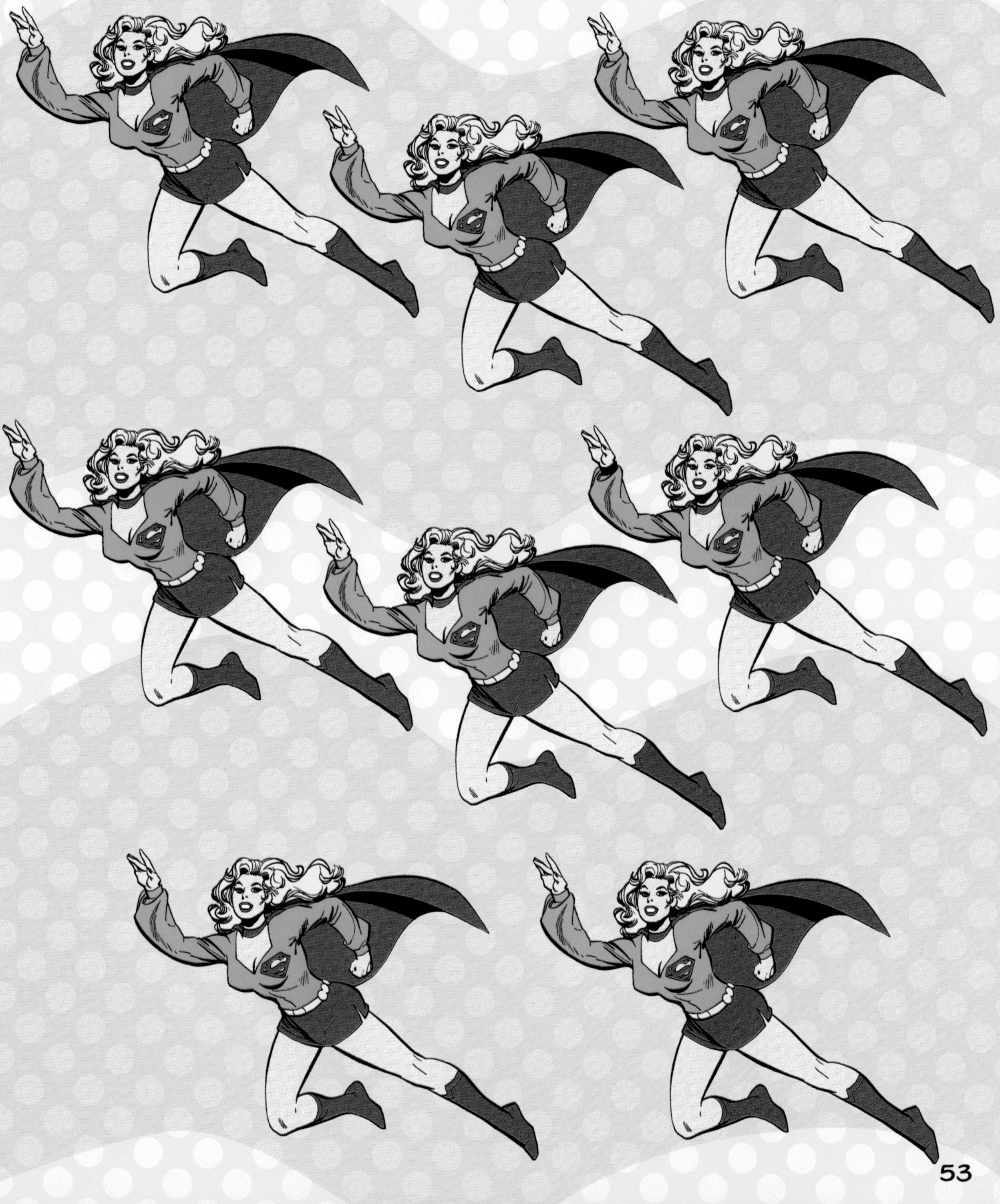

Batgirl Stands Up for What's Right!

Did something happen to send Batgirl into the streets with a sign? What is Batgirl protesting? What does her sign say? Describe this demonstration.

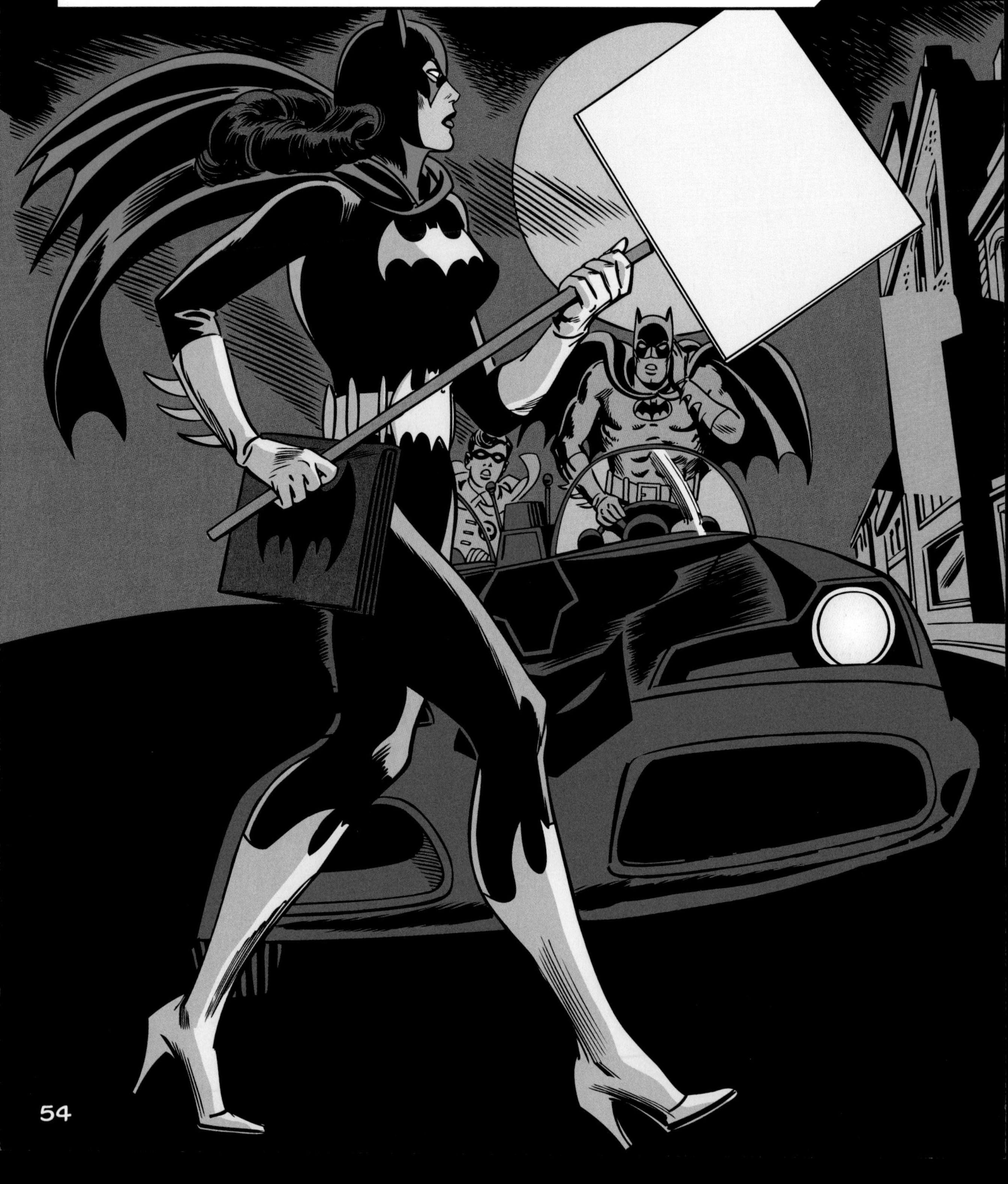

Conquer this Crossword!

Use these clues to complete this clever crossword.

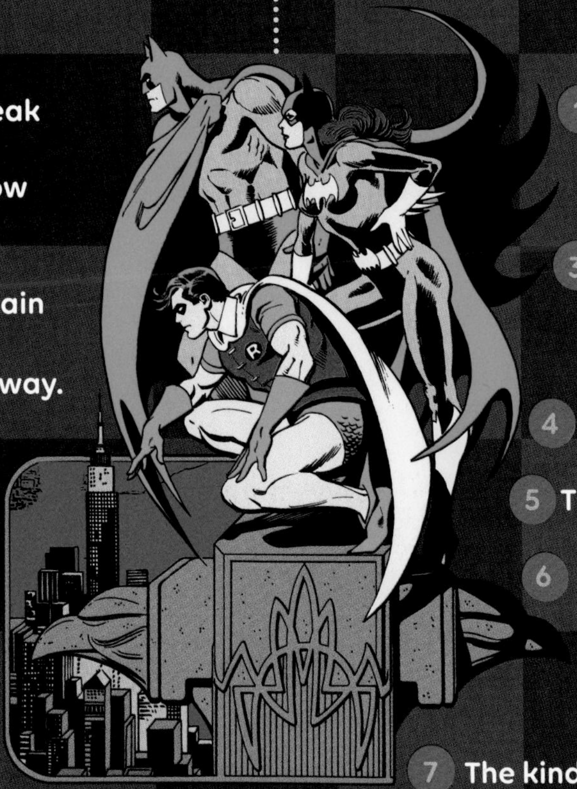

ACROSS

2 The opposite of weak

5 The opposite of slow

7 The ________ is a spotted catlike villain who is often in Wonder Woman's way.

8 Batman and Robin's tricked-out, gadget-filled car

10 What Wonder Woman wears on her head

11 Where the Bat-Signal shines

13 Wonder Woman has an invisible one

DOWN

1 What Wonder Woman wears on her wrists

3 Batgirl and Batman live in this city

4 Zatanna's power

5 The opposite of foes

6 Members of the Justice League work together as a ________ .

7 The kinds of books that tell super hero stories

9 Wonder Woman's tribe

12 Birds, planes, and some super heroes can do this

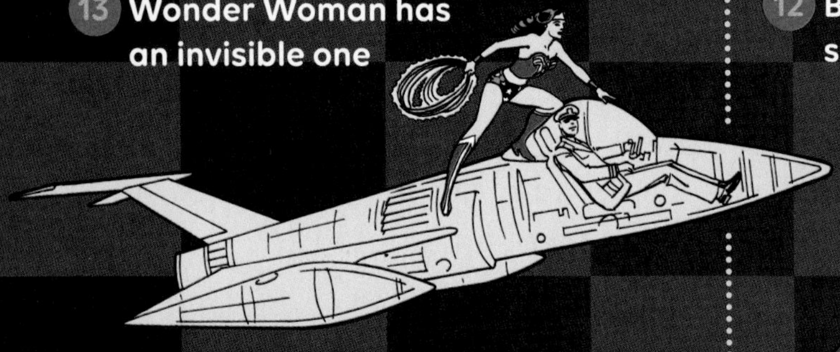

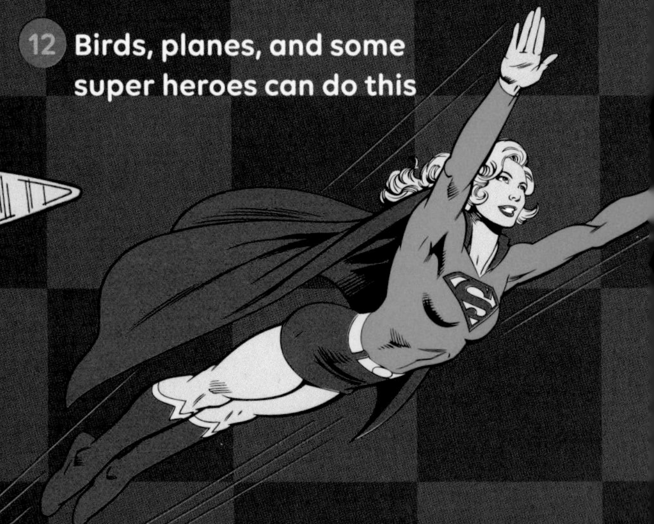

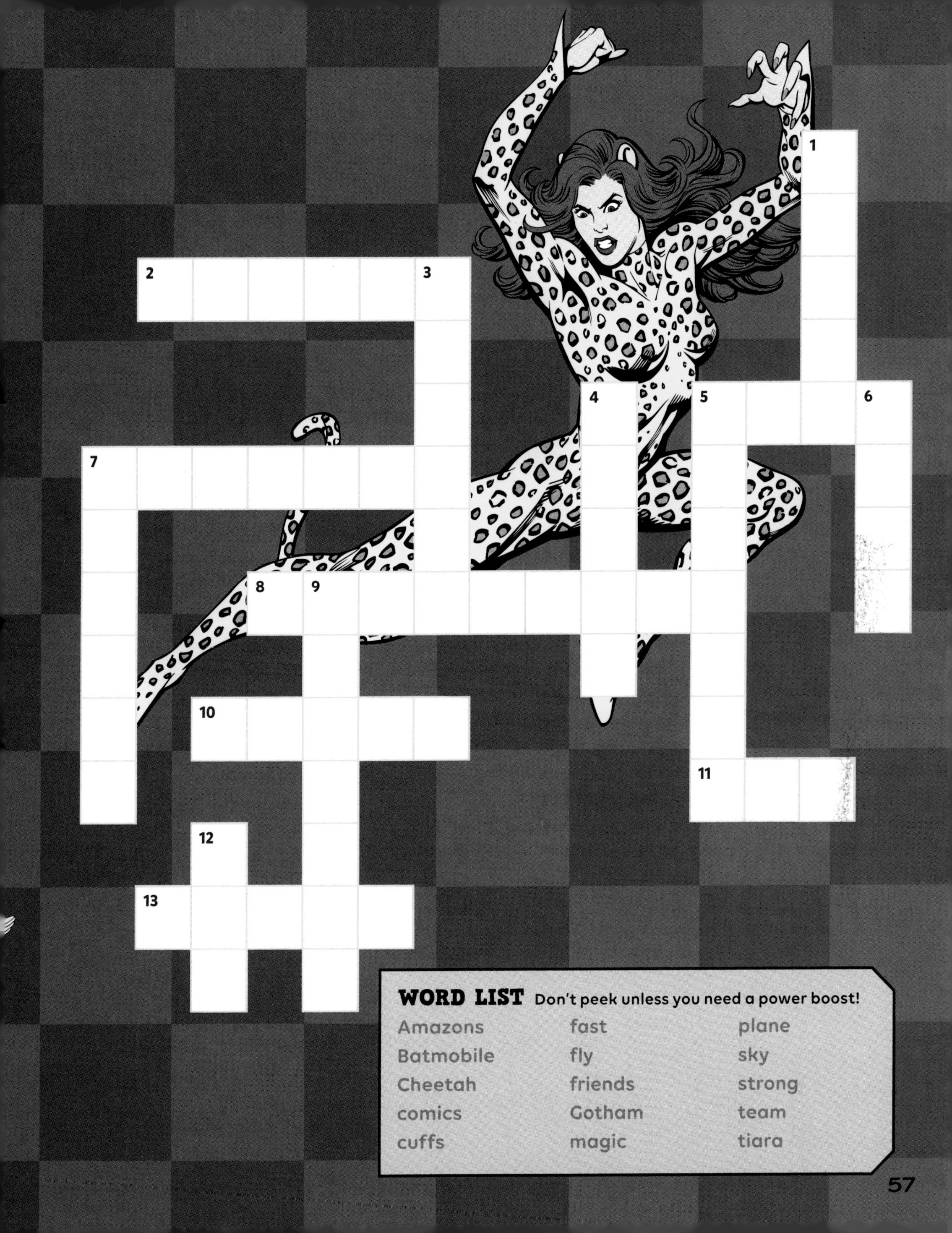
1
2
3
4
5
6
7
8
9
10
11
12
13

WORD LIST Don't peek unless you need a power boost!

Amazons	fast	plane
Batmobile	fly	sky
Cheetah	friends	strong
comics	Gotham	team
cuffs	magic	tiara

Count the Clues and You'll Know Who!

The Riddler set up a trap for Wonder Woman. But he left her a cheeky note. Now she must collect keys to figure out which super-villain is on her tail. How many keys can you find on these pages?

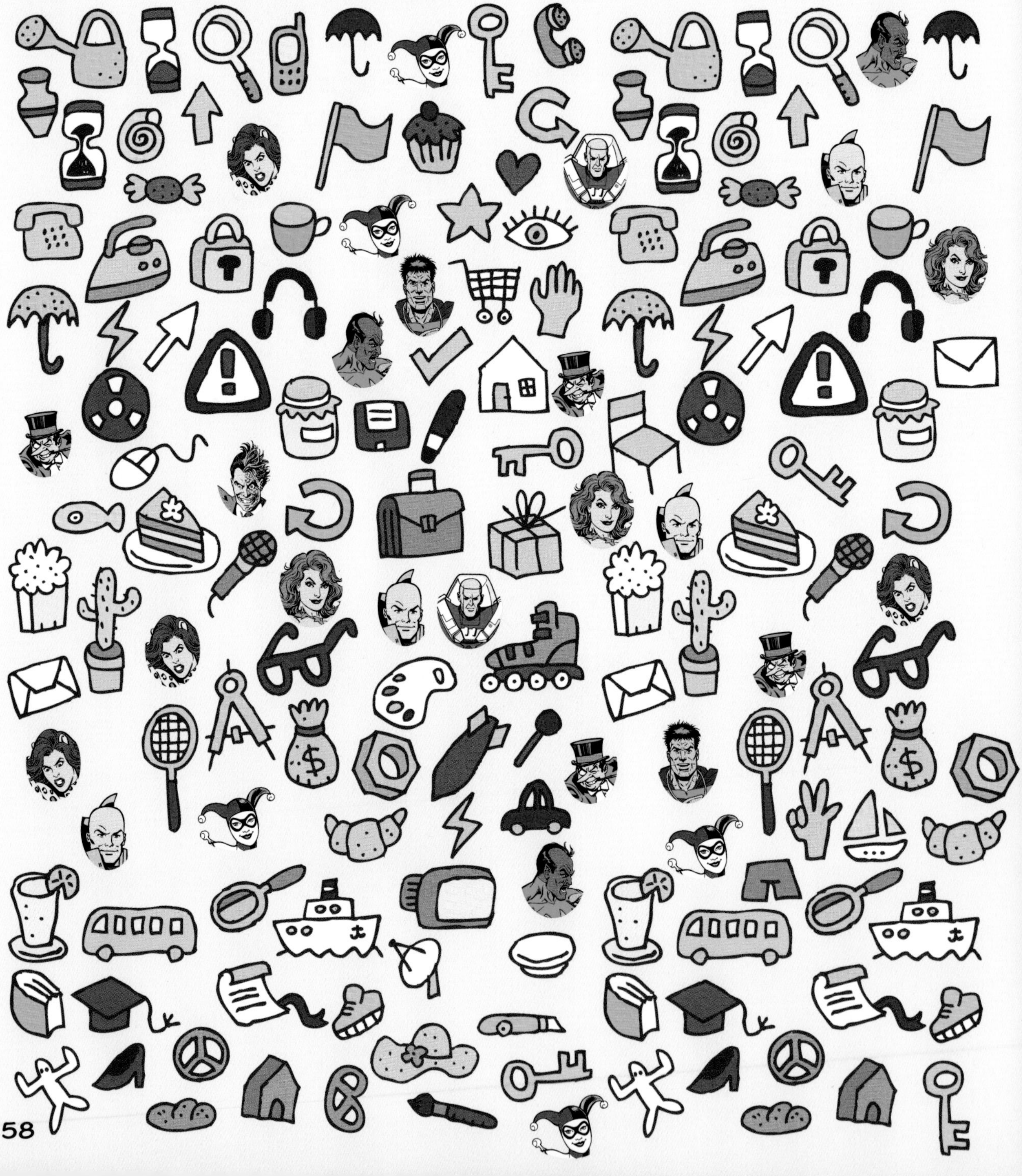

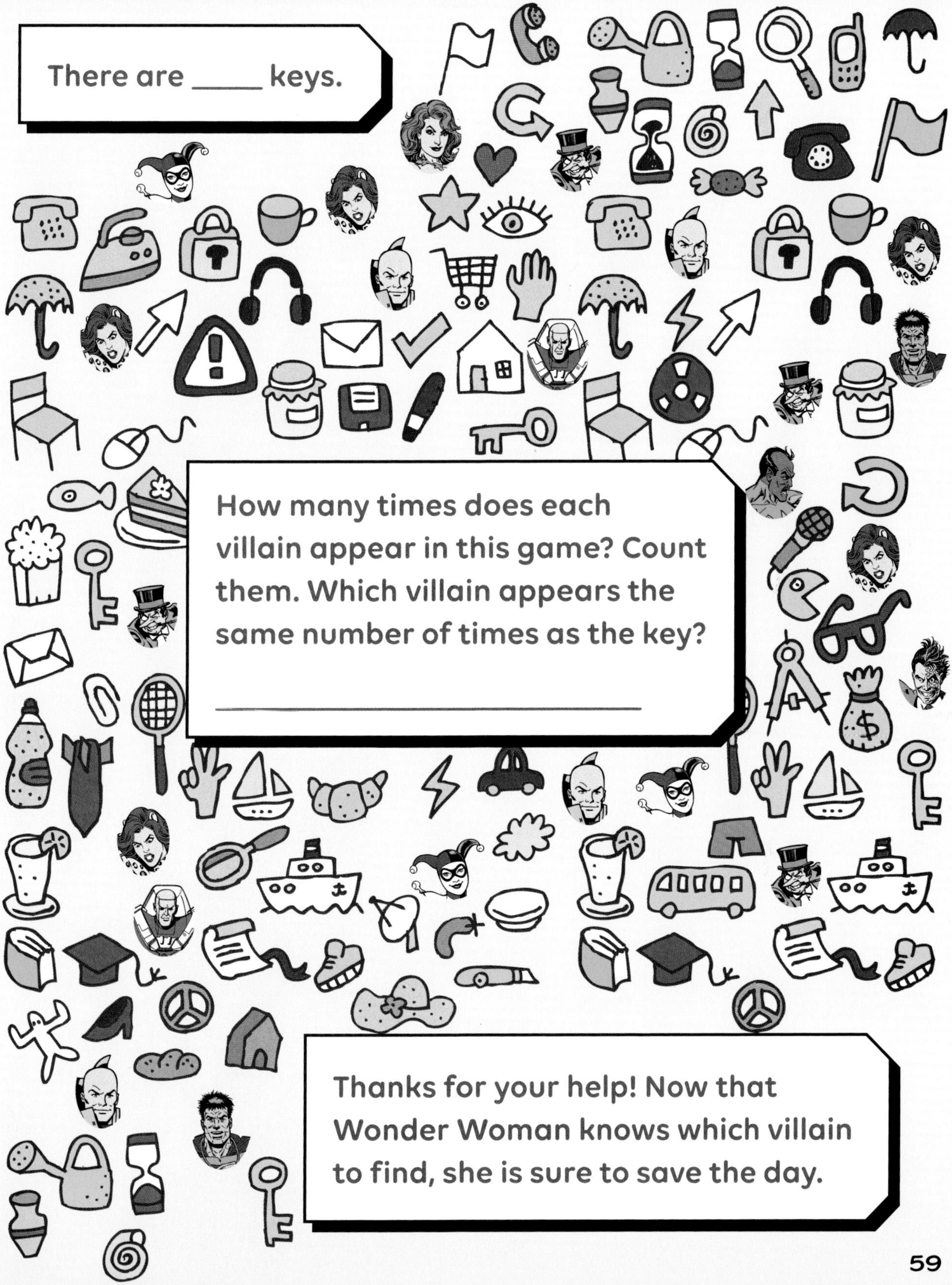

There are _____ keys.

How many times does each villain appear in this game? Count them. Which villain appears the same number of times as the key?

____

Thanks for your help! Now that Wonder Woman knows which villain to find, she is sure to save the day.

Arrows Ahoy!

Robin Hood stole from the rich to give to the poor—and Wonder Woman saved his hide! The arrows are flying. What else is moving? Find 10 things that have changed.

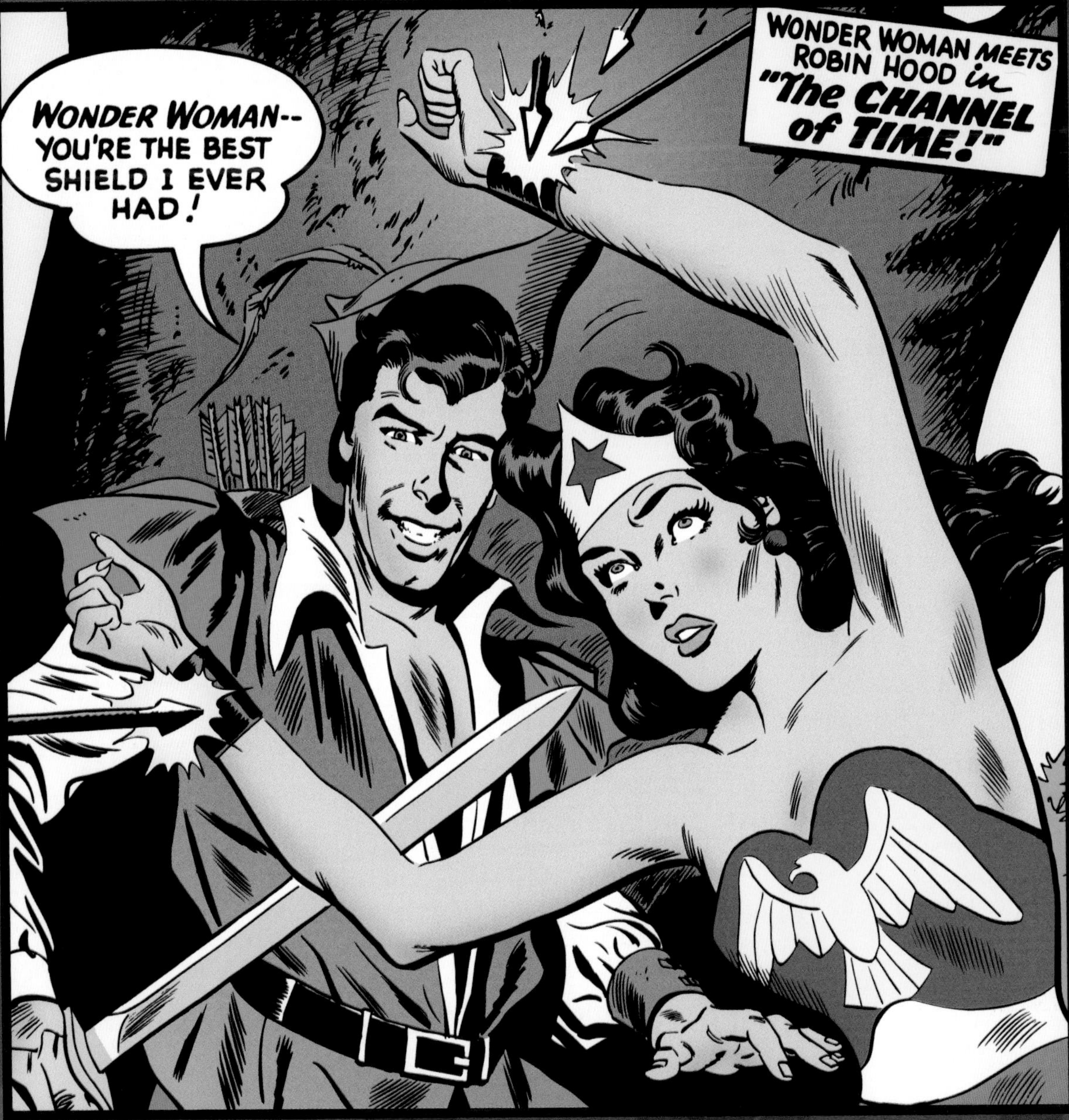
WONDER WOMAN MEETS ROBIN HOOD in "The CHANNEL of TIME!"
WONDER WOMAN-- YOU'RE THE BEST SHIELD I EVER HAD!

Which Way Should She Go?

Wonder Woman wants to take a shortcut to get back to Paradise Island. Which path gets her where she wants to go?

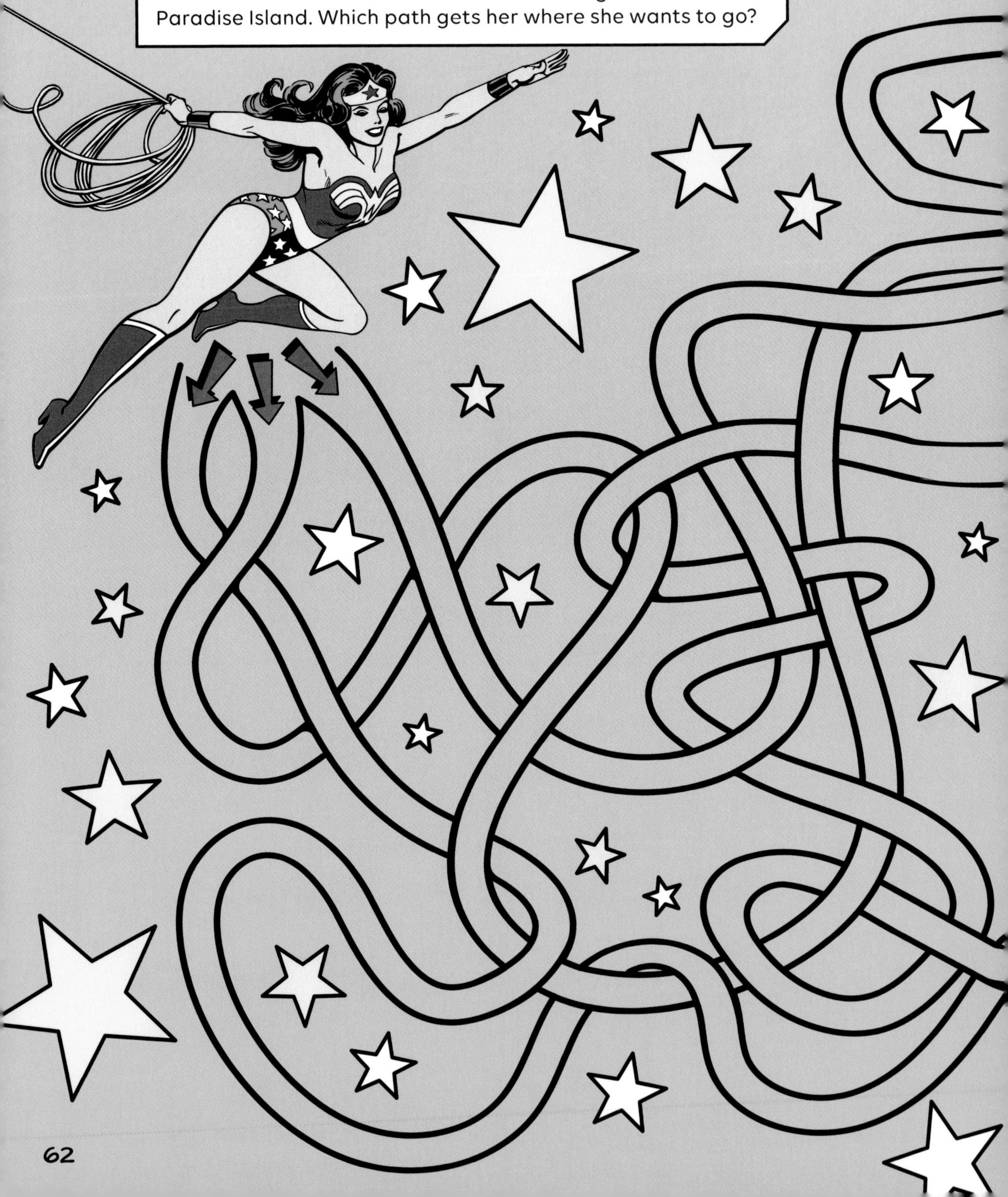

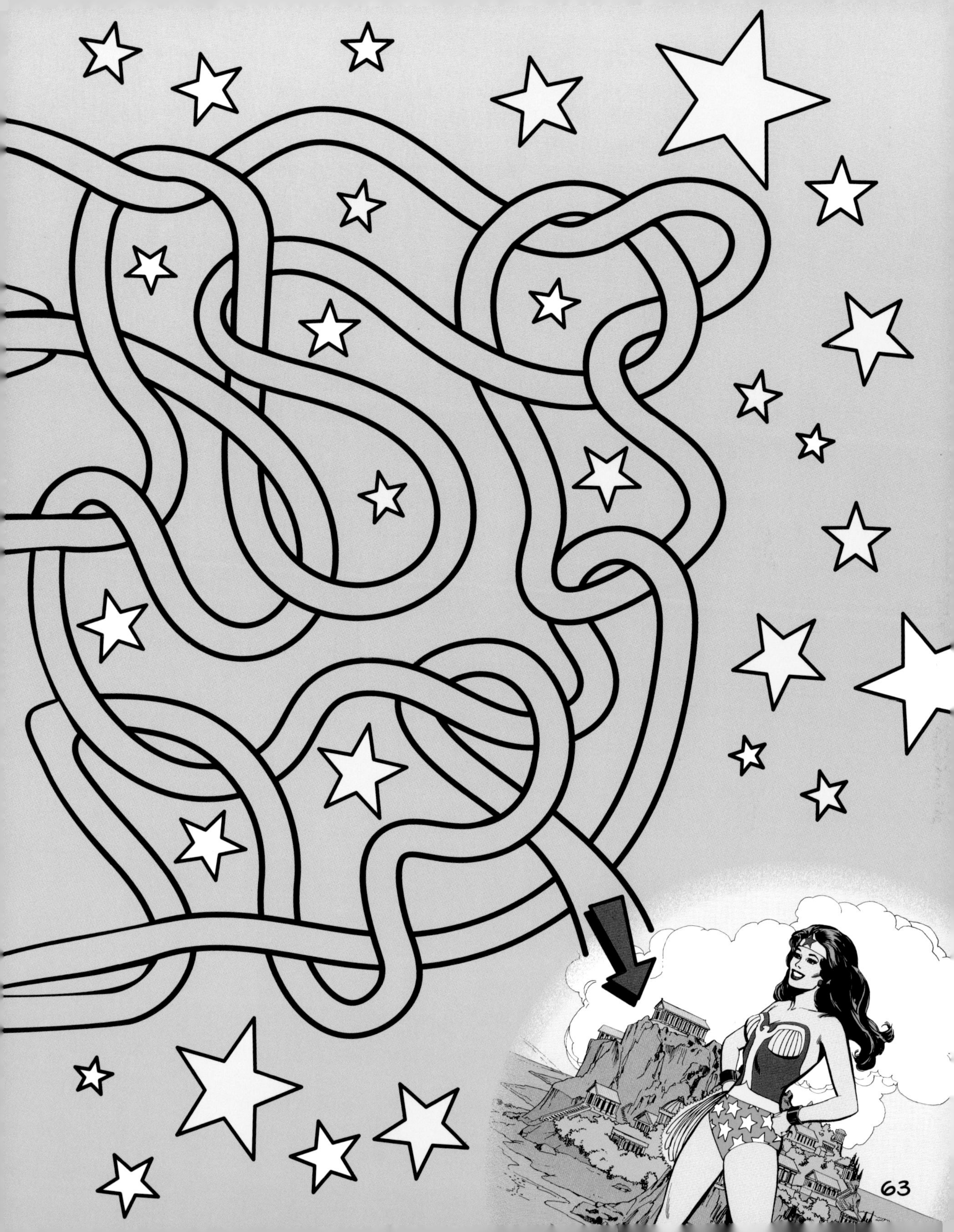

Pick the Lucky Path

The Riddler created a labyrinth to trip up the super heroes who were after him. Three heroes went in, but only one will come out on the other side. Which hero will it be? Batgirl, Katana, or Starfire?

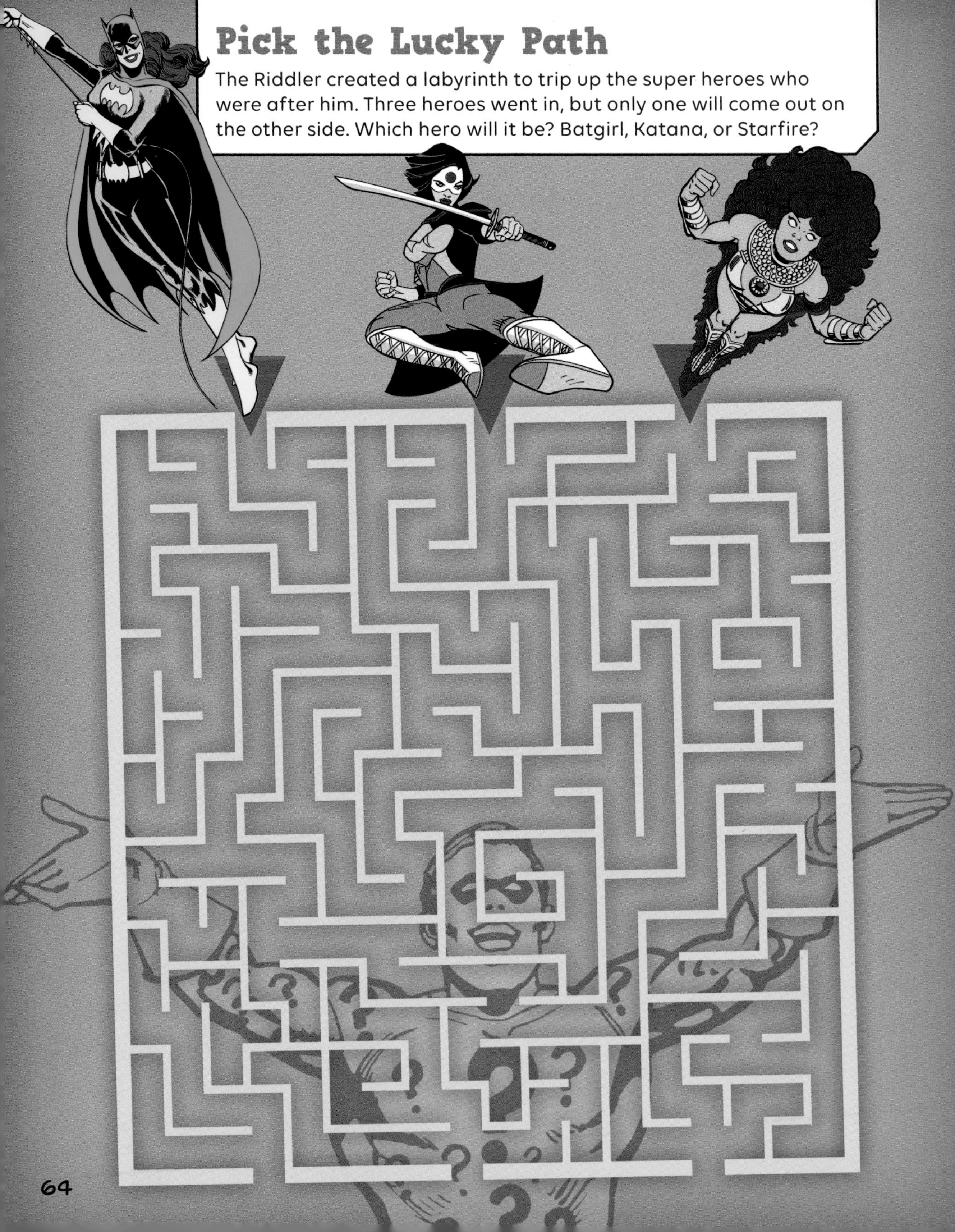

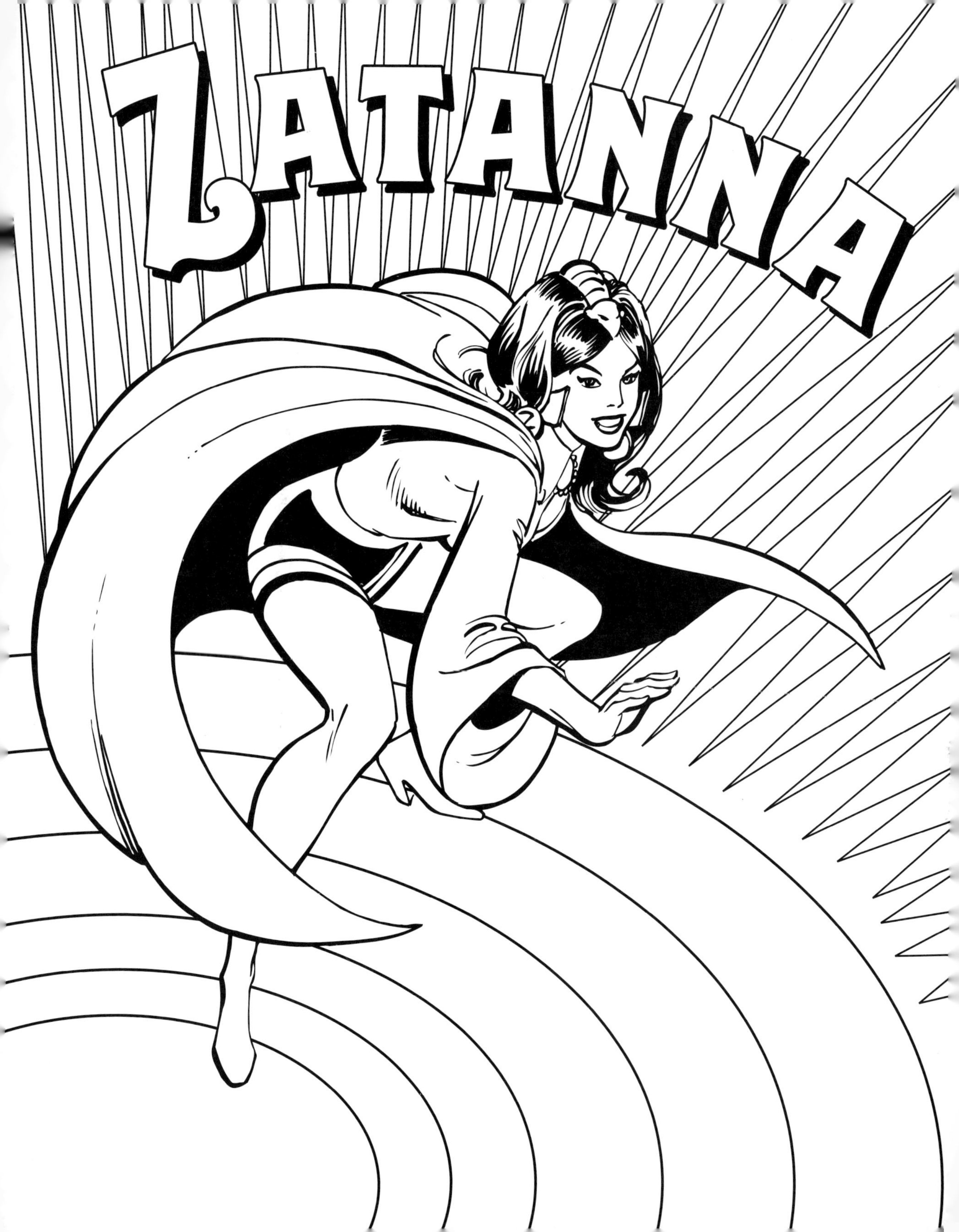
ZATANNA

Identify the Mystery Hero

One magnificent super hero rescued a bus full of kids from a flash flood. But she was gone before the reporters arrived. Can you help Lois Lane figure out who it was? Use the clues below to reveal which hero saved the day.

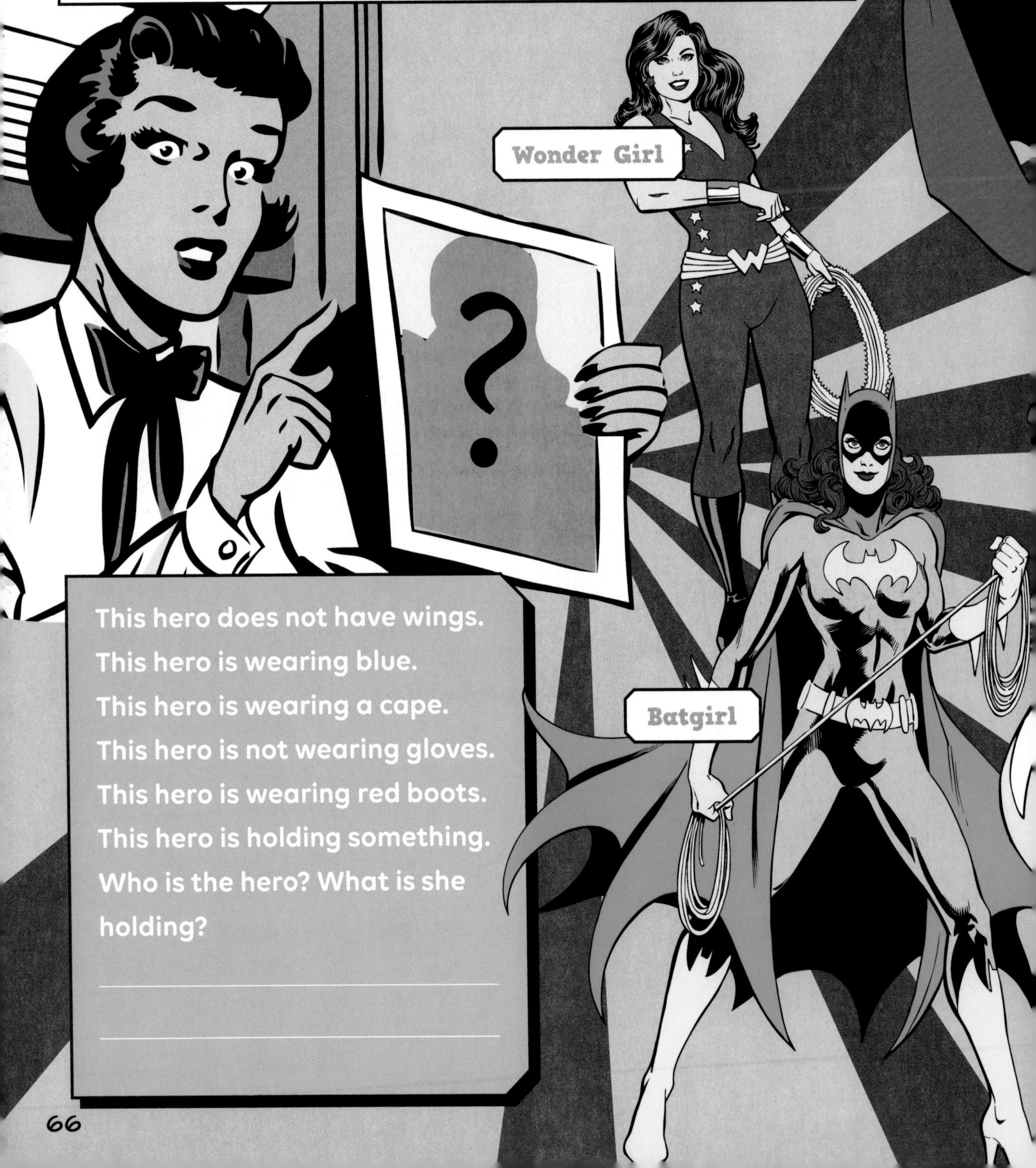

Wonder Girl
Batgirl

This hero does not have wings.
This hero is wearing blue.
This hero is wearing a cape.
This hero is not wearing gloves.
This hero is wearing red boots.
This hero is holding something.
Who is the hero? What is she holding?

____

____

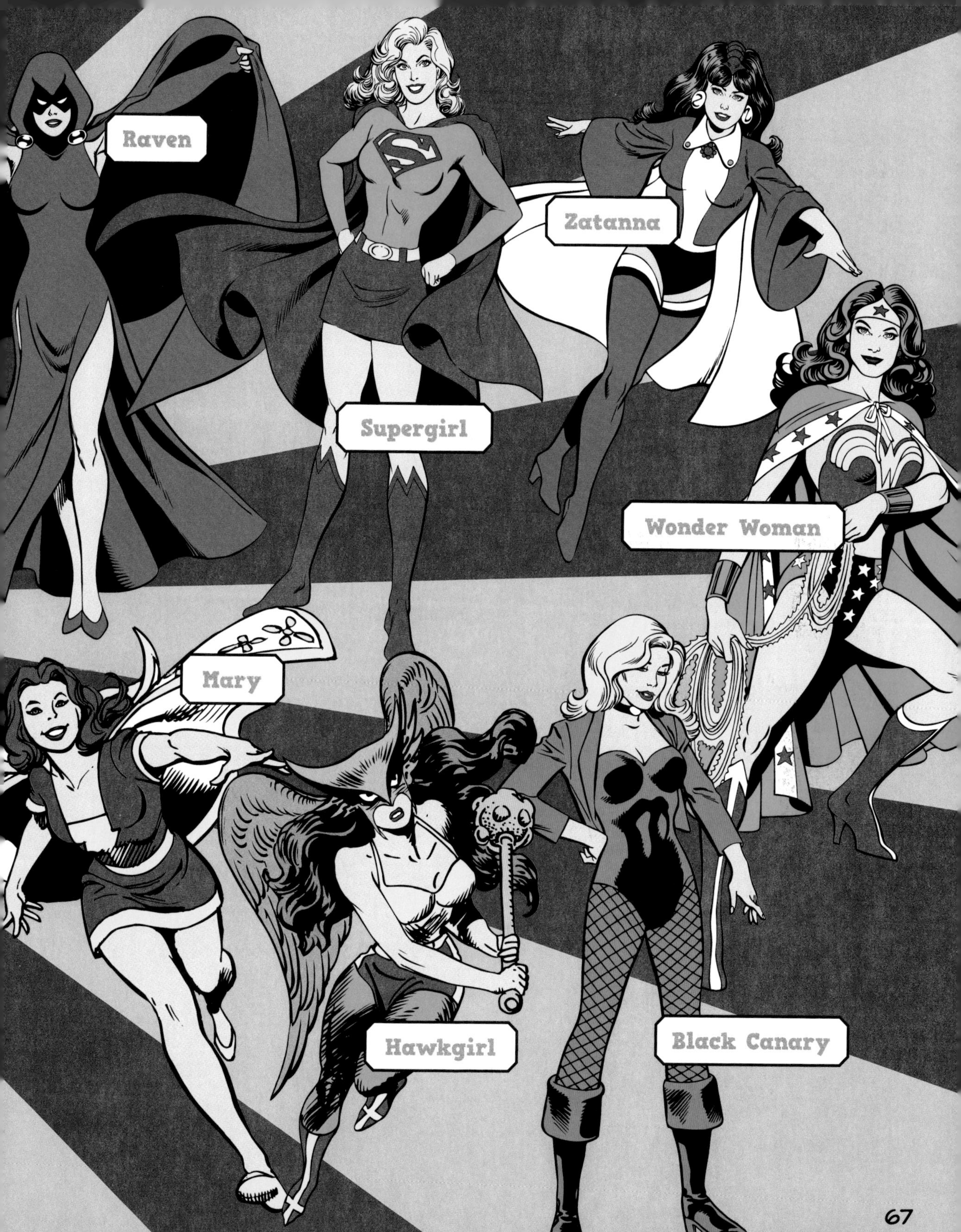
Raven
Supergirl
Zatanna
Wonder Woman
Mary
Hawkgirl
Black Canary

Comedy Code

Use the key below to help to reveal the punchlines to these out-of-this-world jokes.

KEY

A	B	C	D	E	F	G	H
▲	π	/	Δ	Σ	≈	f	#

I	J	K	L	M	N	O	P
∞	÷	~	@	■	»	●	И

Q	R	S	T	U	V	W	X
Π	√	★	¿	Ø	…	□	¬

Y	Z
—	↑

Knock, knock.
Who's there?
Ro.
Ro-who?

✓	●	■	▲	∞	»	Σ

/	▲	@	■		▲	»	Δ

@	Σ	¿	¿	Ø	/	Σ

#	▲	»	Δ	@	Σ		¿	#	Σ

★	∞	¿	Ø	▲	¿	∞	●	»	.

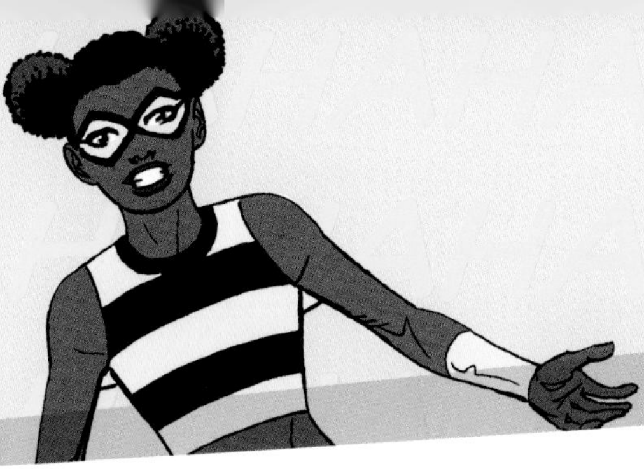

Why does Bumblebee buzz?

π	Σ	/	▲	Ø	★	Σ

★	#	Σ

Δ	●	Σ	★	»	'	¿
					,	

~	»	●	□

#	●	□

¿	●

□	#	∞	★	¿	@	Σ

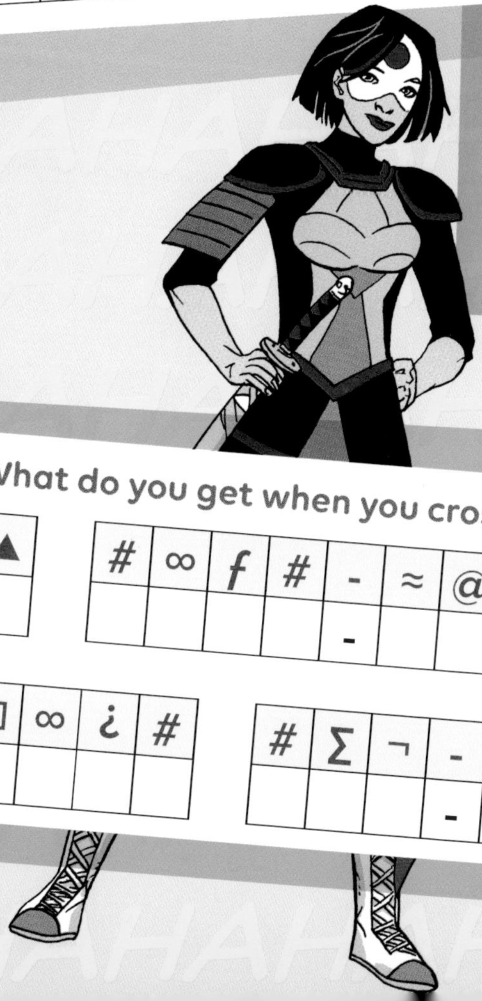

What is Katana's favorite food?

★	□	●	✓	Δ	≈	∞	★	#

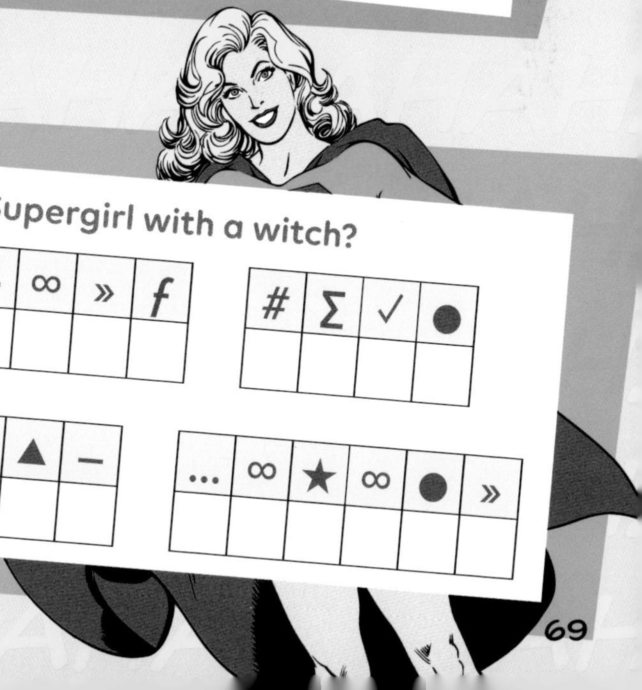

What do you get when you cross Supergirl with a witch?

▲

#	∞	f	#	-	≈	@	–	∞	»	f
				-						

#	Σ	✓	●

□	∞	¿	#

#	Σ	¬	-	✓	▲	–
			-			

…	∞	★	∞	●	»

A Capitol Crime

Batgirl and Robin tussle with a time-traveling troublemaker. But he's not the only thing up to no good. This picture keeps changing too! Use your keen senses to spot 9 things that have changed.

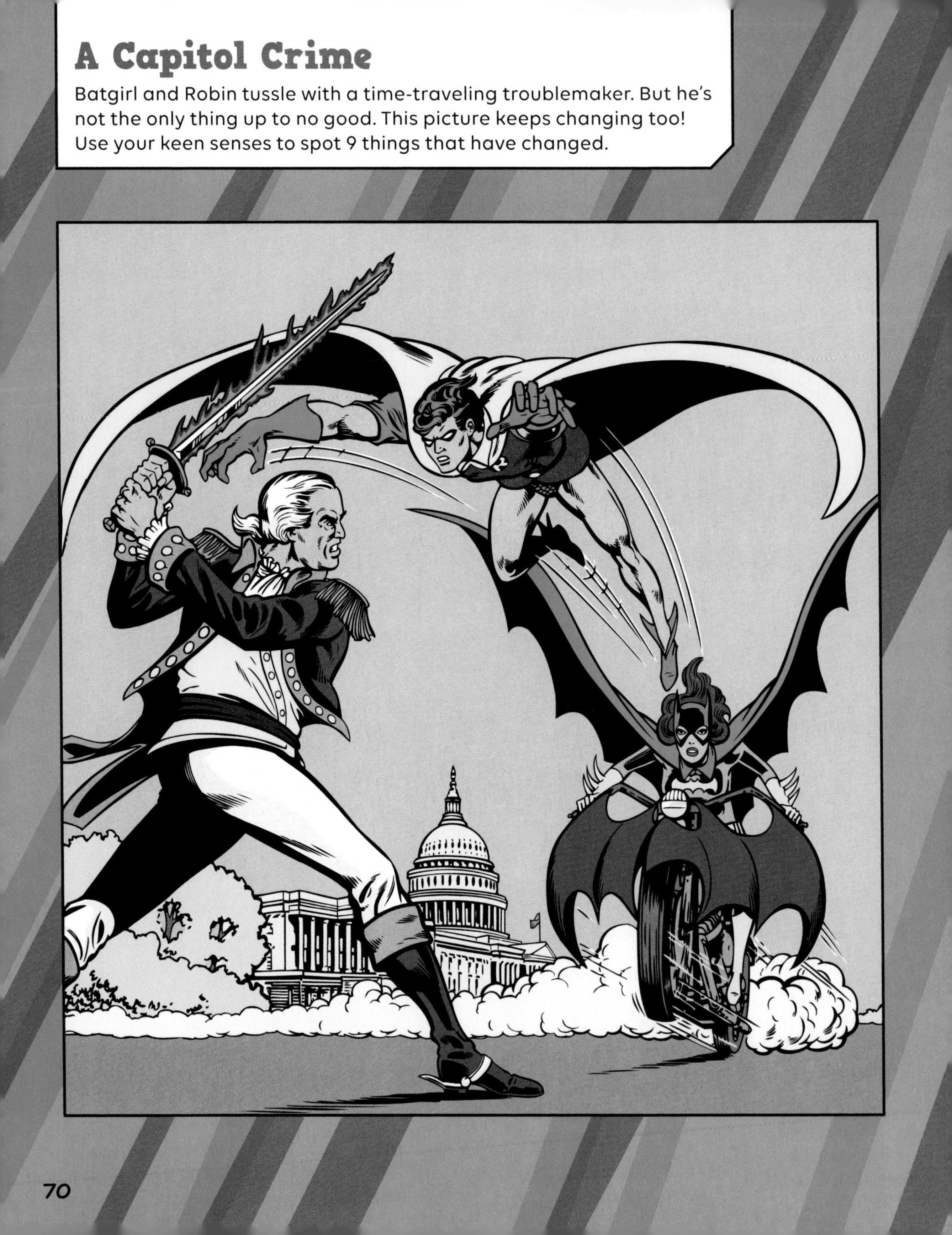

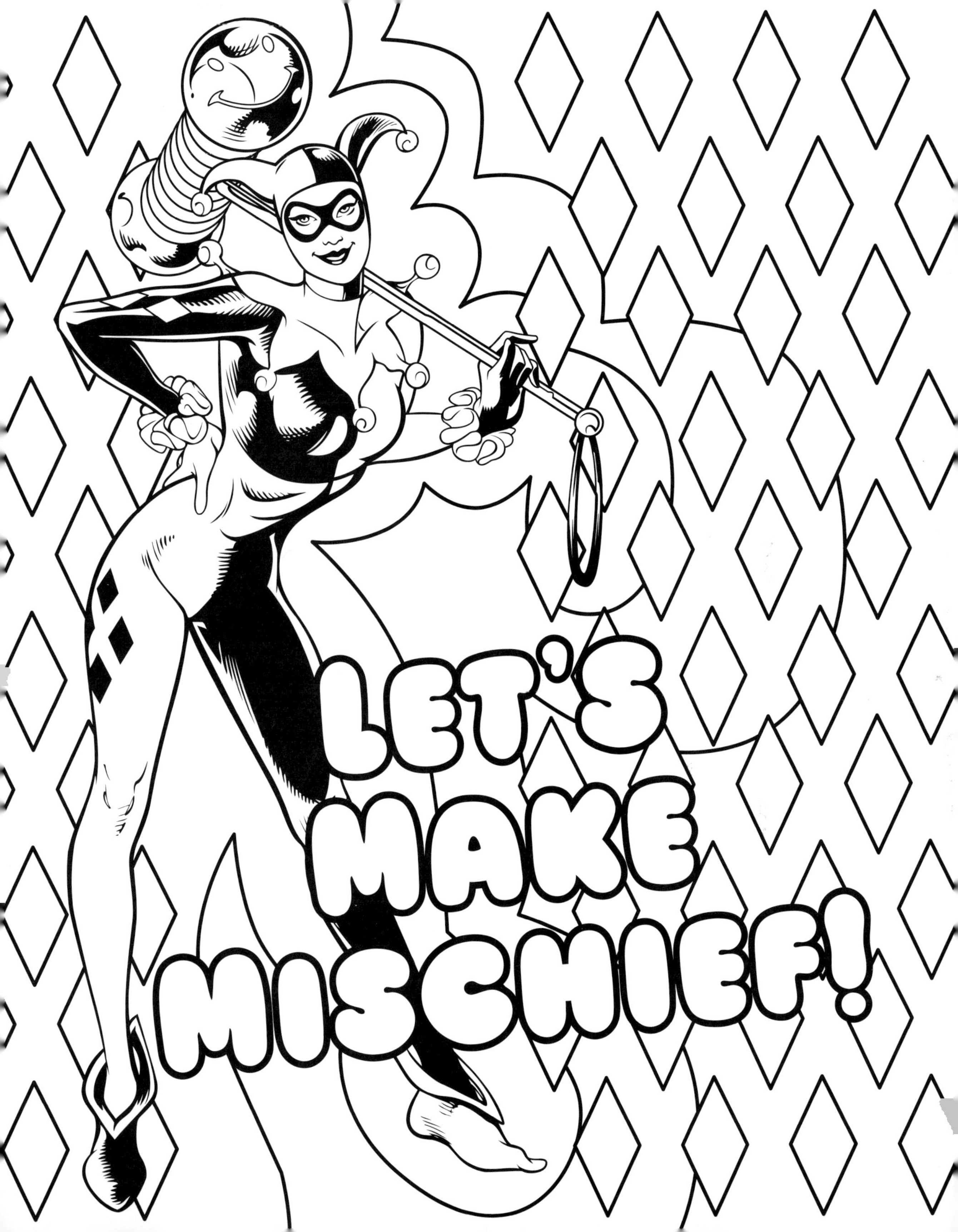
LET'S MAKE MISCHIEF!

Paw-Some Kitten Maze

Streaky has caught Lex Luthor's scent. She'll follow him through this maze, no problem. Can you?

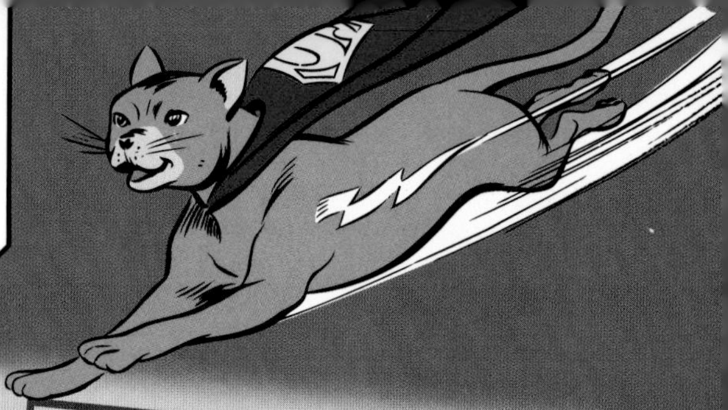

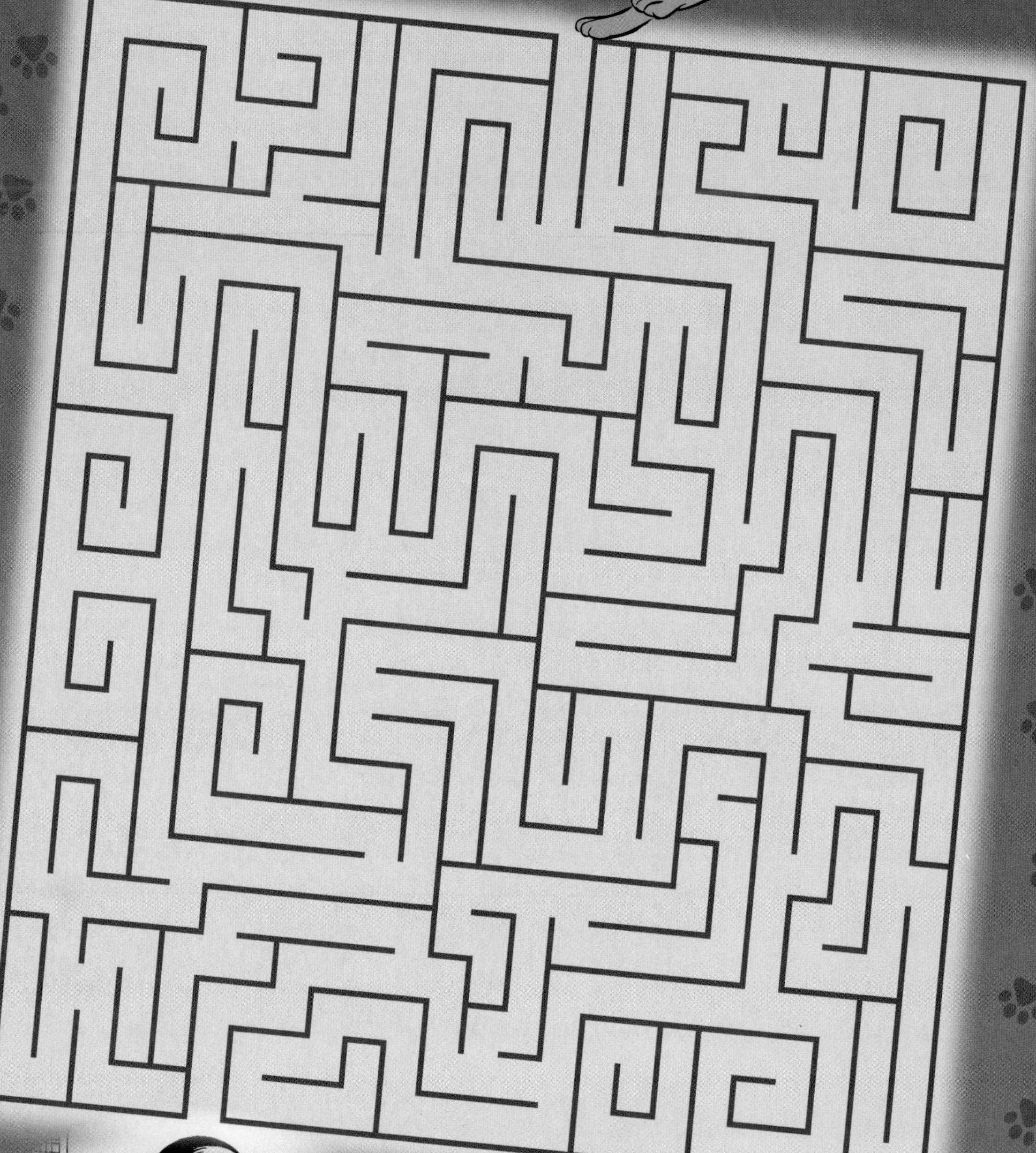

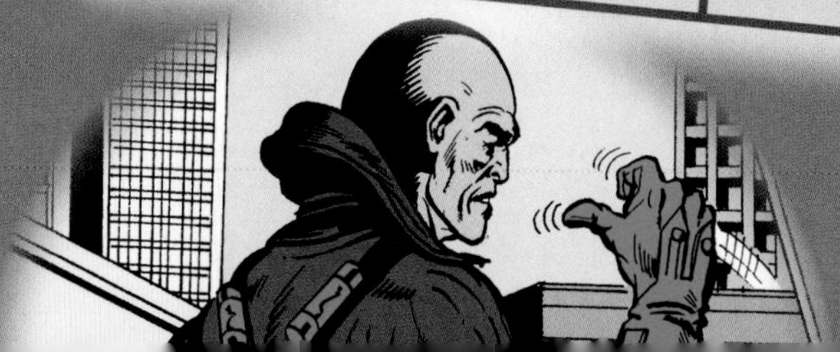

Crossword Challenge

Solve these clues to complete this crossword.

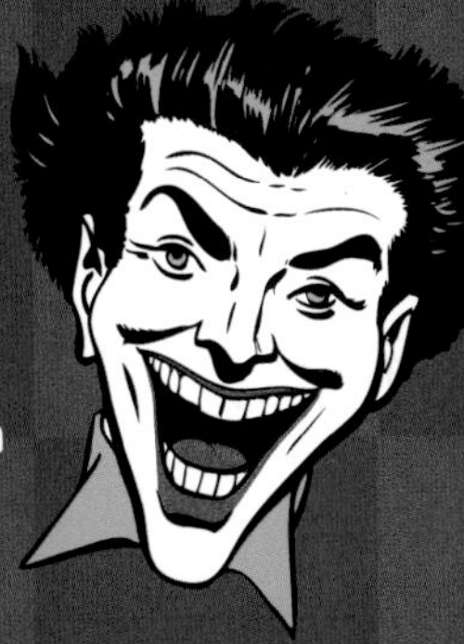

ACROSS

1 Where crooks go when they're arrested

4 Supergirl's cousin

7 A short, stout, bird-loving super-villain with a monocle

8 Commissioner Gordon is in charge of the ________ .

10 Bumblebee can shrink down tiny when she wears her super hero ________ .

11 The sound a bumblebee makes

12 What Batgirl loves to read

15 What Supergirl wears on her back

16 Super heroes come in all shapes and ________ .

DOWN

1 A grinning super-villain who likes a good punchline

2 Hackers can release a virus using this

3 Lois Lane works at a ________ .

5 The God of War (and a foe of Wonder Woman)

6 Black Canary's power is in raising her ________ .

9 What makes Wonder Woman's jet so special? It's ________ .

11 Animals Hawkgirl flies among

13 Tools that help heroes open locked doors

14 Batgirl wears a ________ to cover her face.

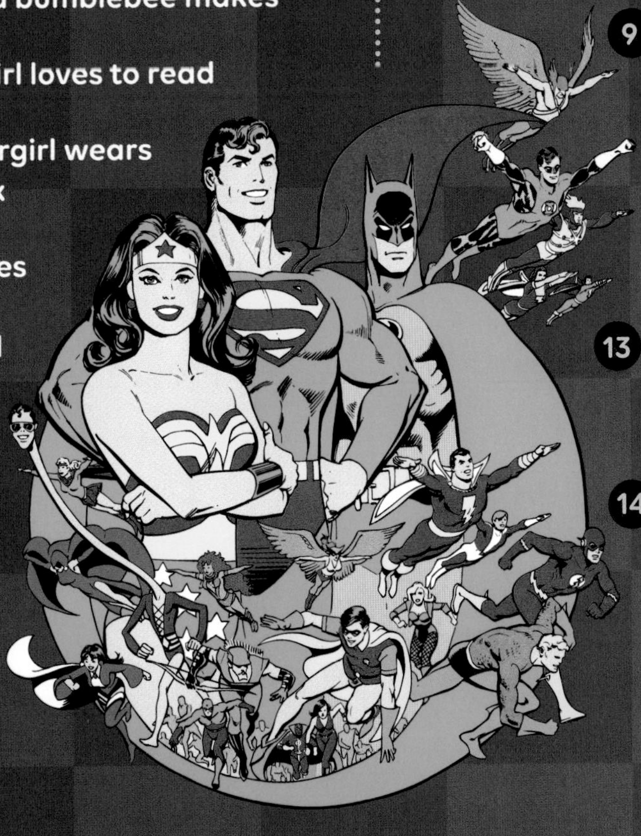

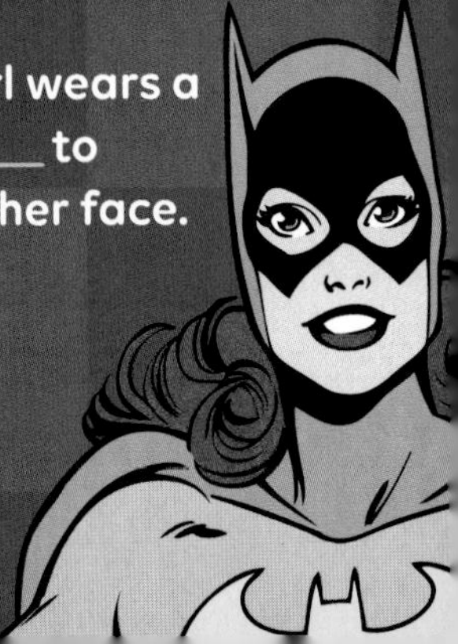

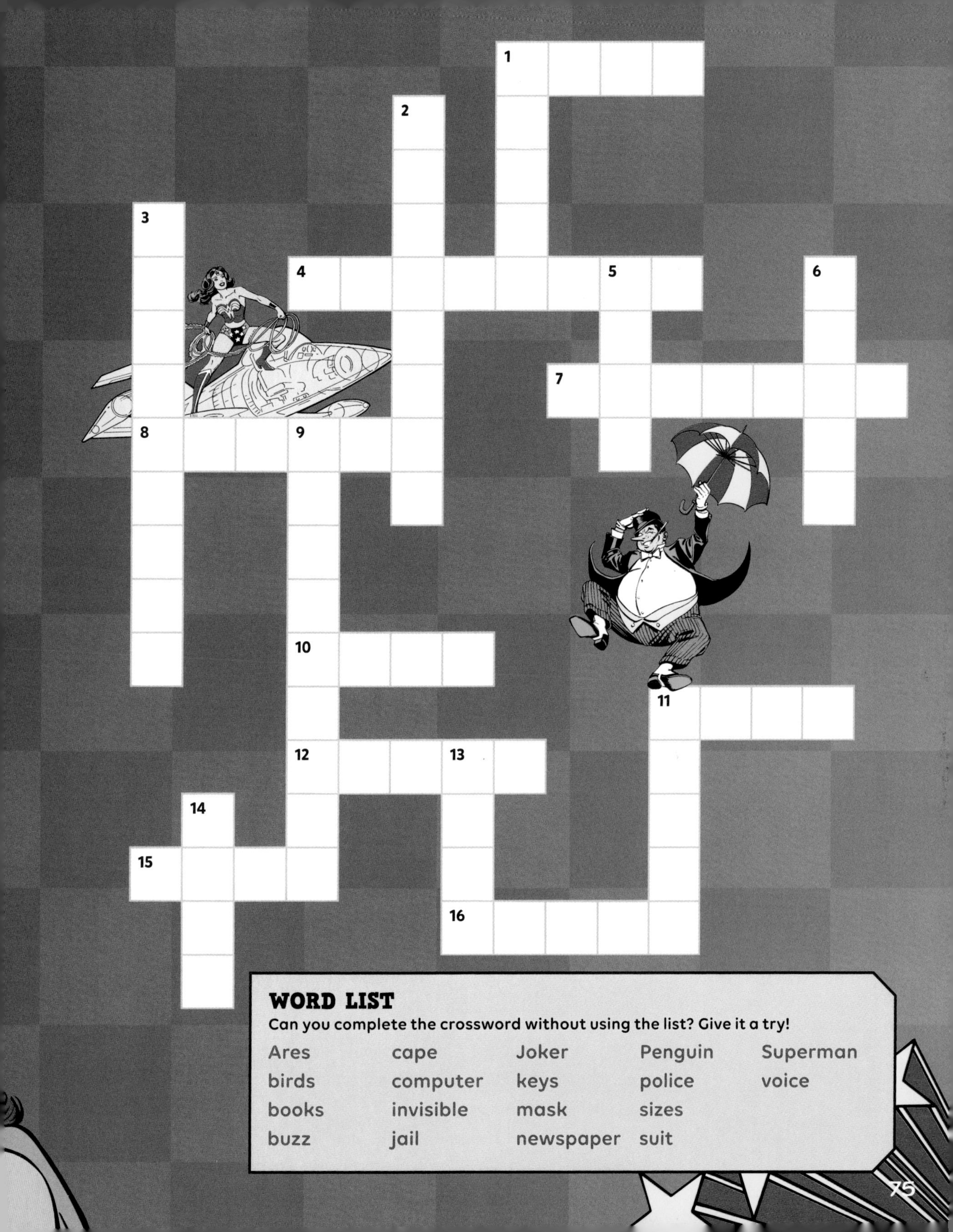
1
2
3
4
5
6
7
8
9
10
11
12
13
14
15
16

WORD LIST

Can you complete the crossword without using the list? Give it a try!

Ares
birds
books
buzz
cape
computer
invisible
jail
Joker
keys
mask
newspaper
Penguin
police
sizes
suit
Superman
voice

Ready to Rhyme?

Let's test your rhyming powers!
What rhymes with FIRE?

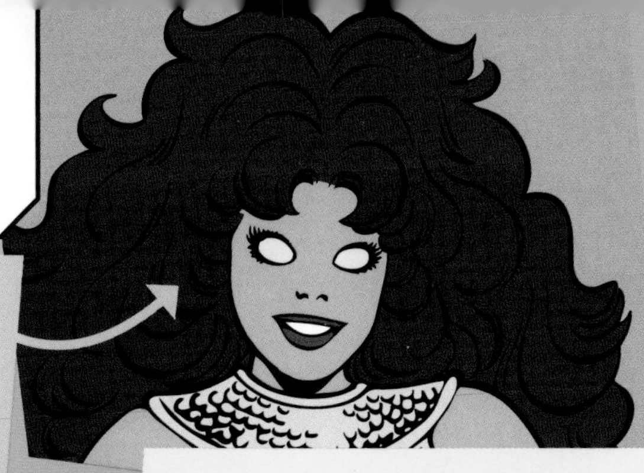

This is Starfire. She likes to sing. Maybe she should join the c h _ _ _ .

A s _ _ _ _ _ _ _ is a beautiful, blue jewel.

Once she fought against a villain who liked to suck people's blood. This fanged bad guy was a _ _ _ p _ _ _ .

One of the four rubber wheels on a car is a _ _ r _ .

Someone you look up to is someone you _ d _ _ _ _ .

The perfect person for a job is the one you want to _ _ _ e .

Someone who tells fibs is a _ _ _ r .

At the top of a church is a tall pointy structure called a s _ _ _ _ .

To make potatoes crispy, you put them in the _ _ y _ _ .

Circus workers with a great sense of balance sometimes walk the _ _ _ h - _ _ _ _ .

After clothes are done in the washing machine, they go in the _ r _ _ _ .

During a baseball game, the person who judges disputes and makes sure everyone follows the rules is the _ m _ _ _ _ .

In any transaction, there is a seller and a b _ _ _ _ .

One escalator takes you lower, the other takes you _ _ _ _ e _ .

Spot the Bogus Batgirl

One of these heroes has been altered. Which Batgirl is different from the rest?

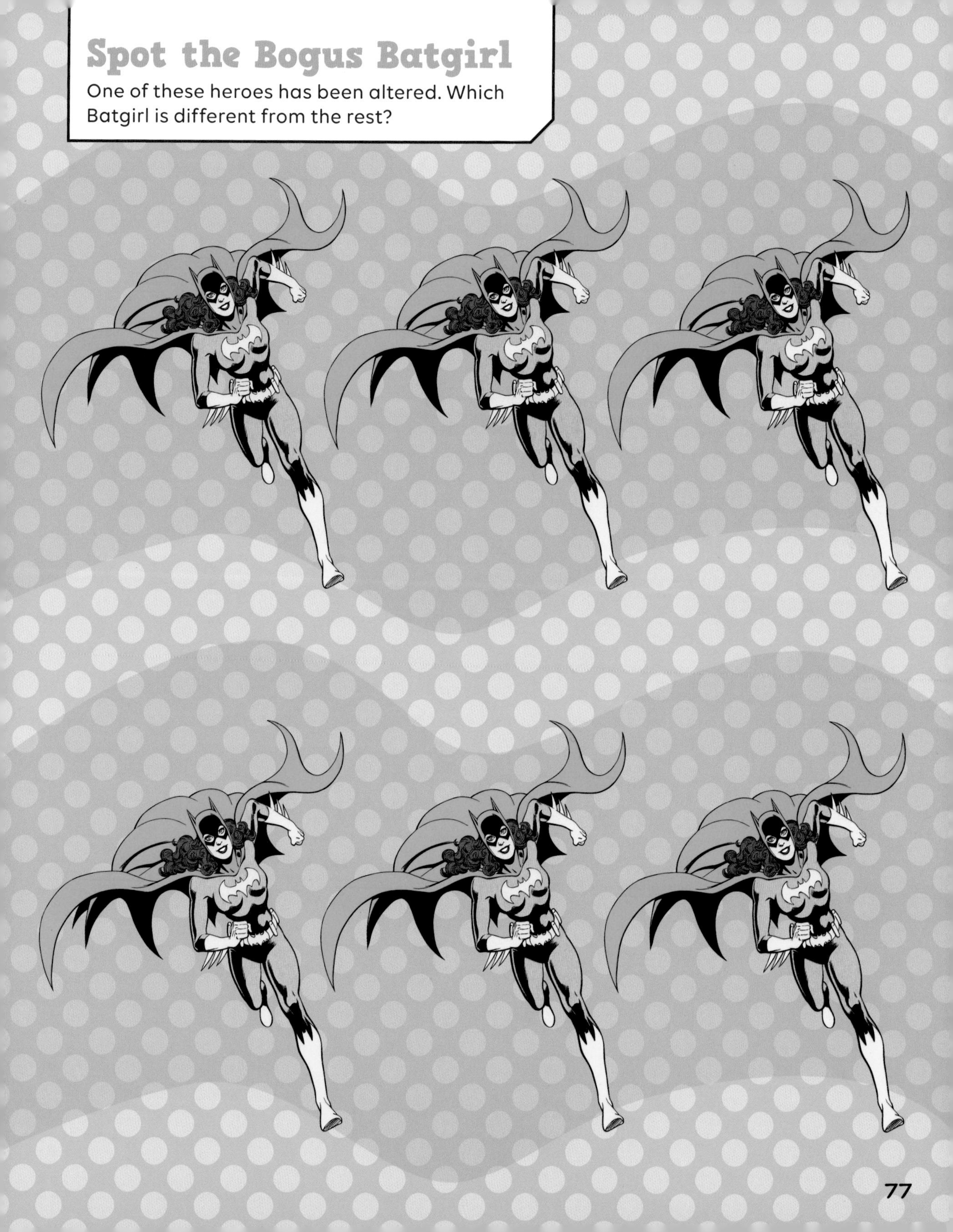

X-Ray Exam

Supergirl is using her X-ray vision to look inside this creature. What does she see?

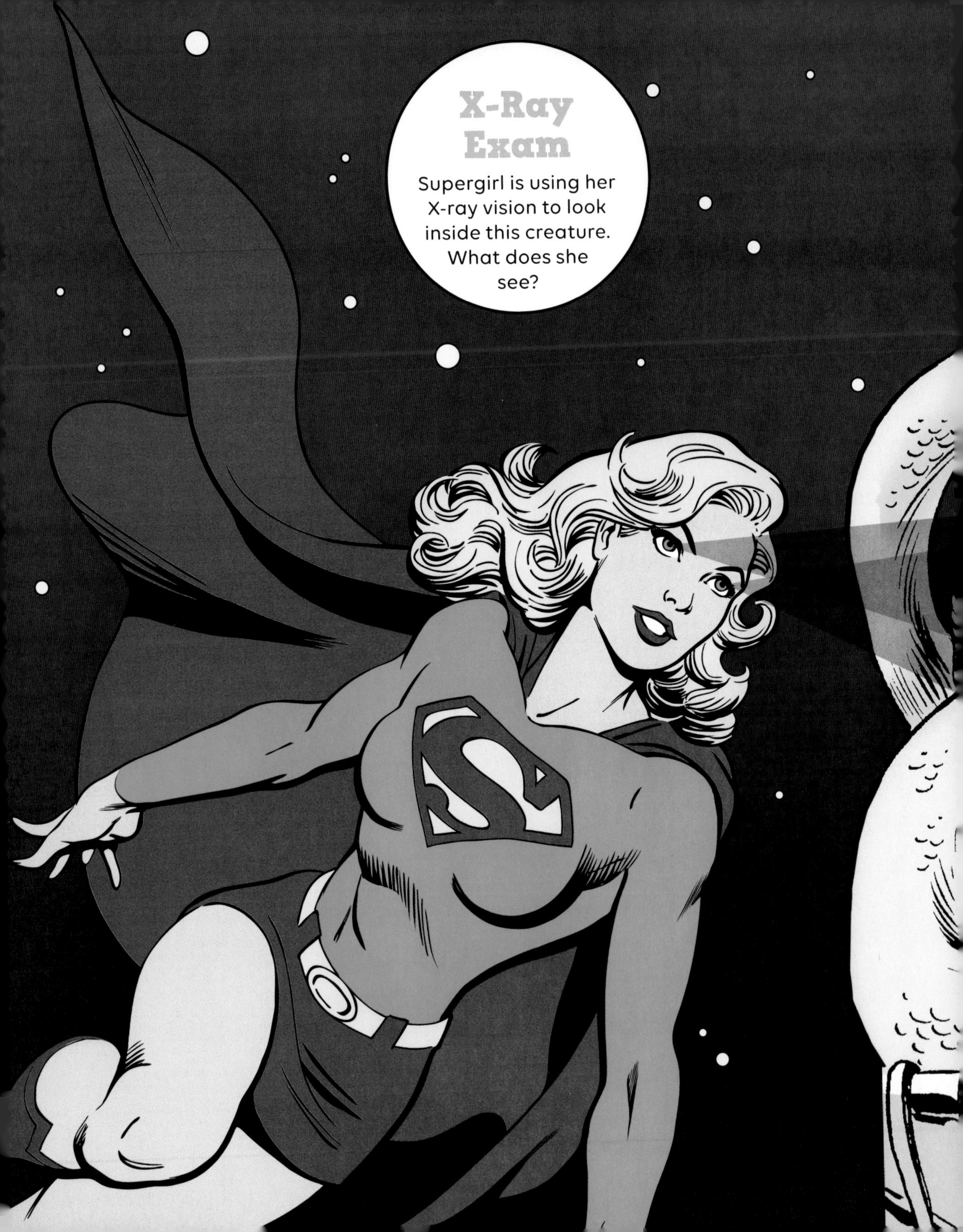

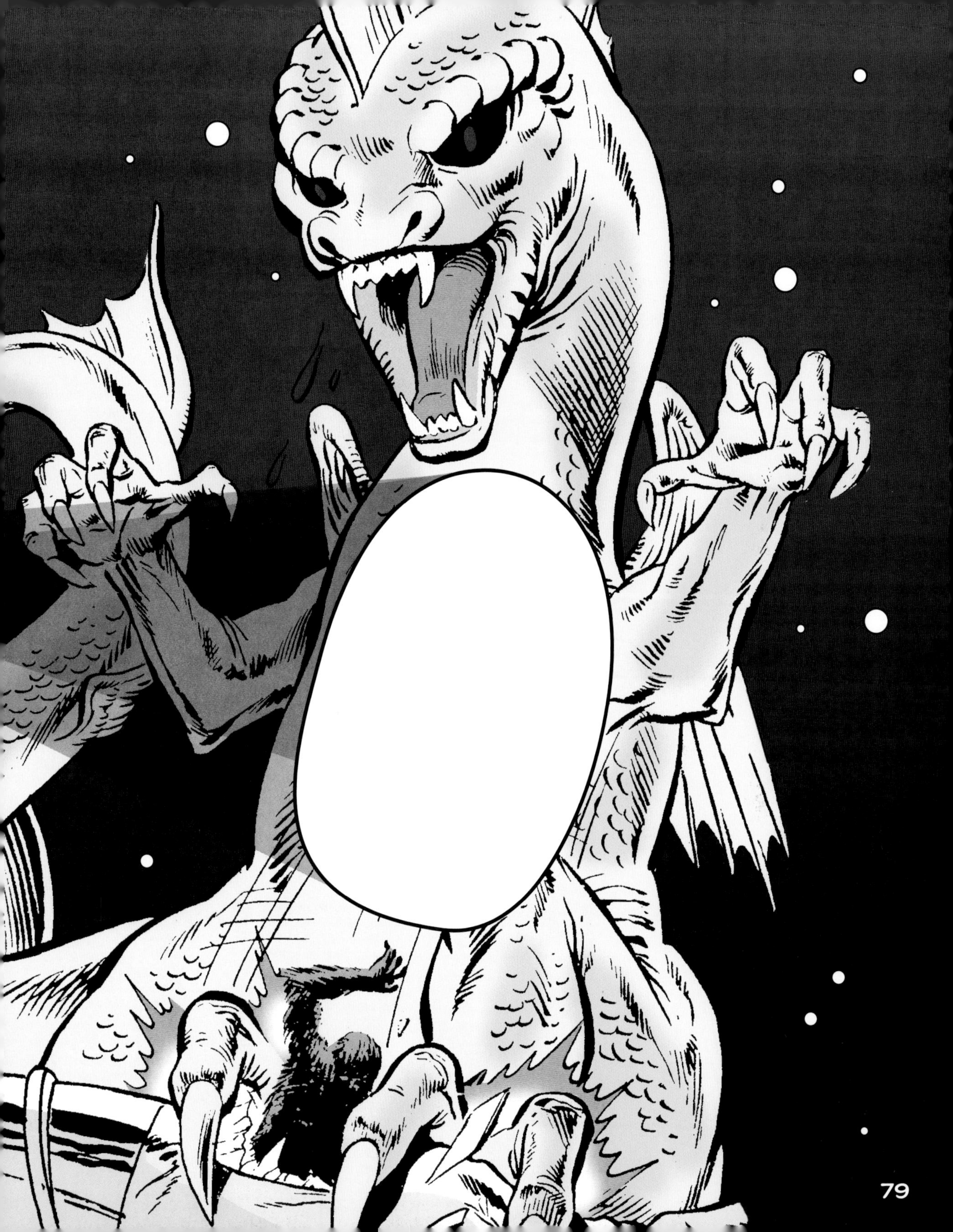

1, 2, 3—Look out for Poison Ivy!

Count each item on the page. Which green item appears the most? Circle each one.

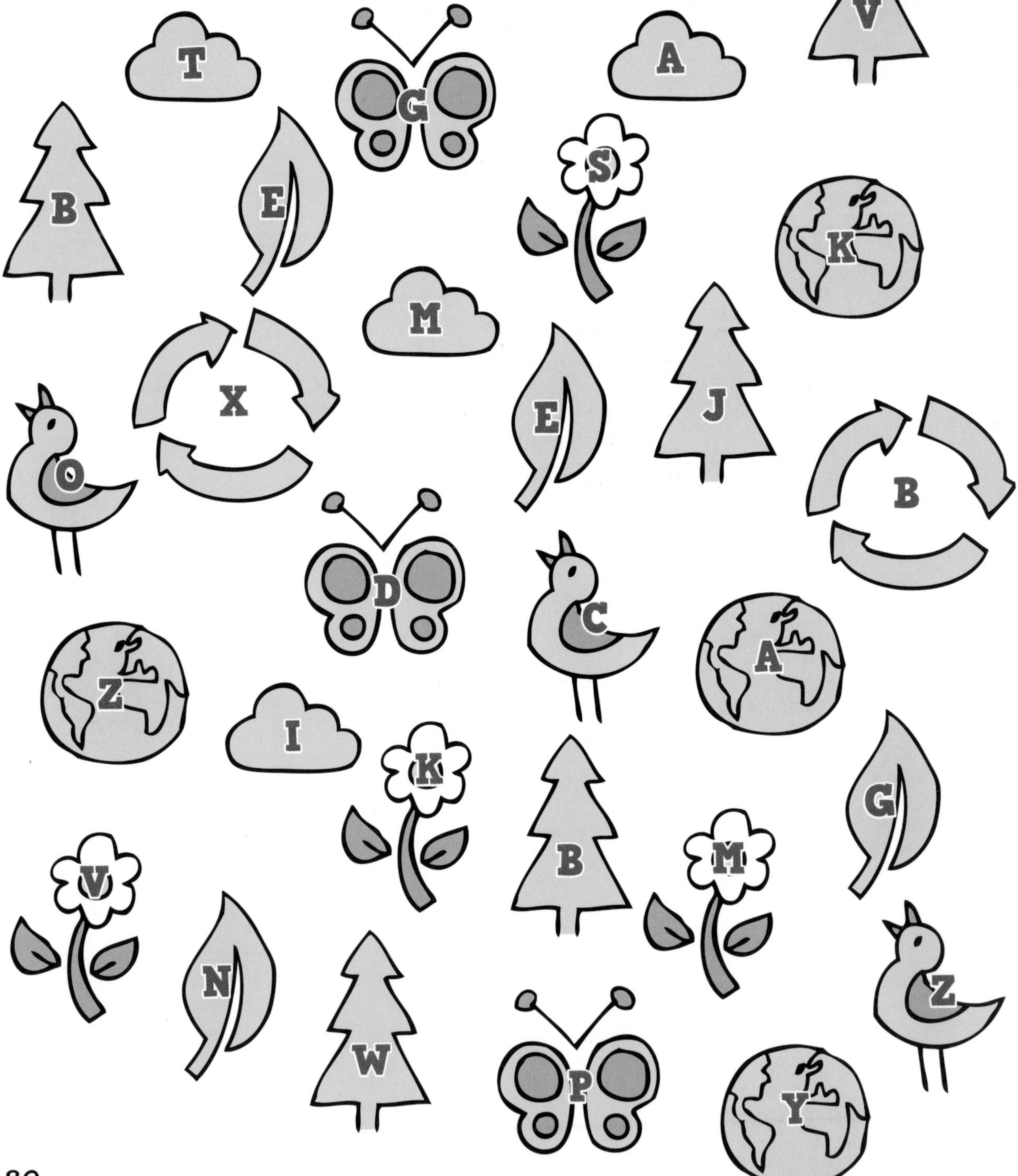
T
G
A
V
B
E
S
K
M
X
E
J
O
B
D
C
A
Z
I
K
G
V
M
B
N
W
P
Z
Y

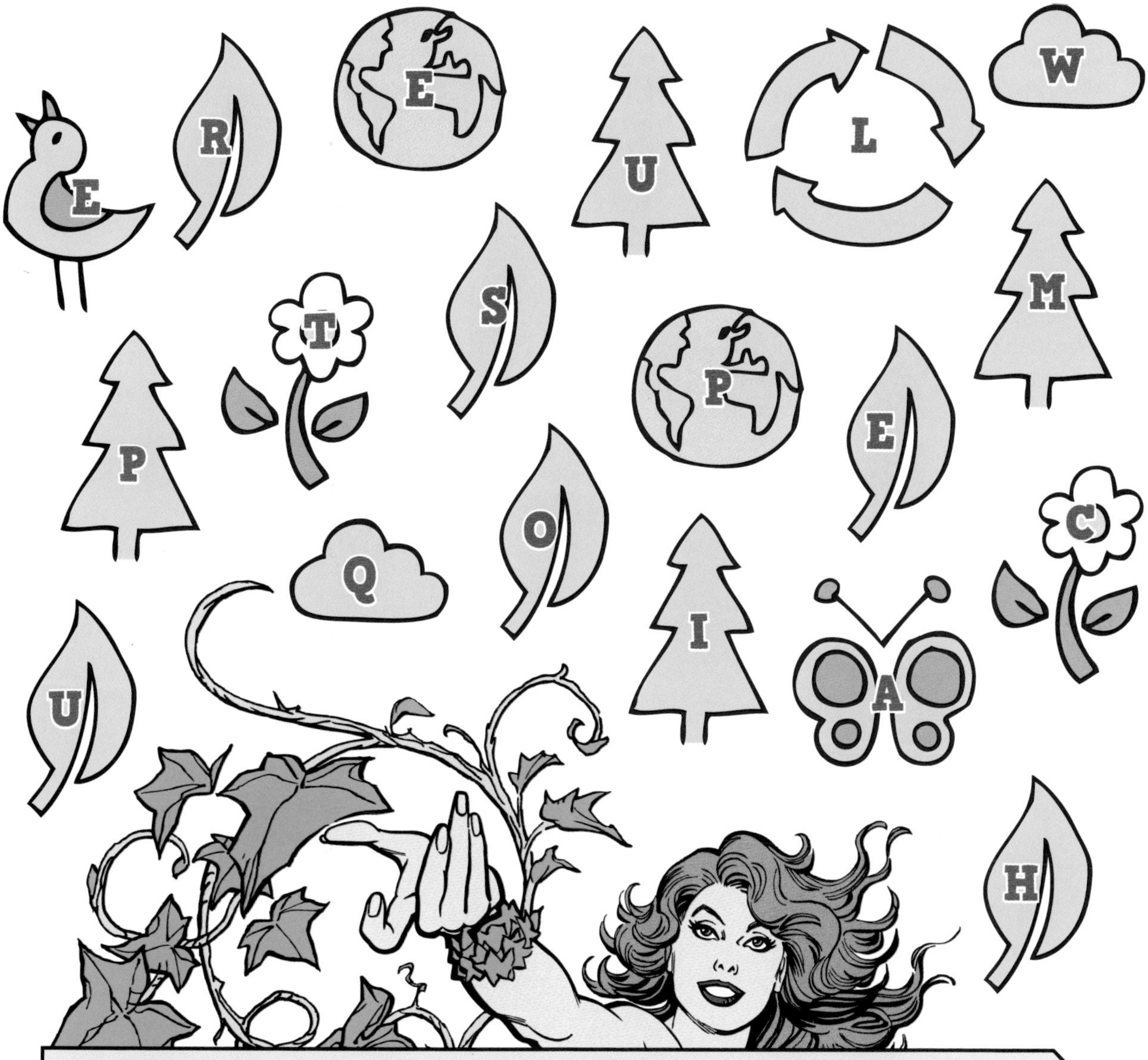
E
R
E
U
L
W
M
S
T
P
E
P
C
O
Q
I
A
U
H

There is a letter on each of the circled items. Write them below. Then unscramble the letters to find where Poison Ivy stashed the antidote to her newest poison.

FOUND LETTERS:

____

UNSCRAMBLED WORD:

____

Spectacular Speller

Supergirl is always busy saving the citizens of Metropolis. She's very clever, and she's got lots of powers. One of them is the power of speed. Are you clever and speedy too? Use the timer on your phone or watch to see how quickly you can come up with 10 words using the letters found in the word M-E-T-R-O-P-O-L-I-S? (If you don't have a timer handy, that's okay.) Ready, set, GO!

M-E-T-R-O-P-O-L-I-S

Time: ____________

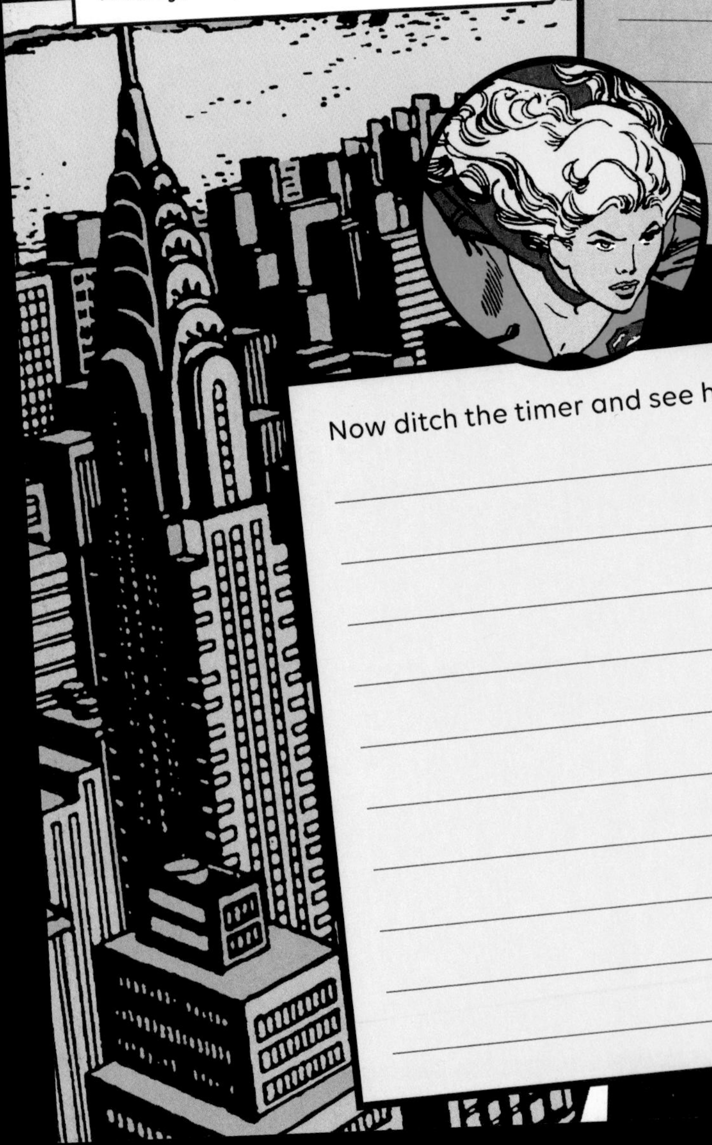

Now ditch the timer and see how many more words you can make.

Supergirl also has the power of invulnerability. That means she is incapable of being harmed by things that hurt most people. Bullets may bounce off her, but Kryptonite can really slow her down. Let's test your speed again. How quickly can you come up with 10 words using only the letters found in

I-N-V-U-L-N-E-R-A-B-I-L-I-T-Y?

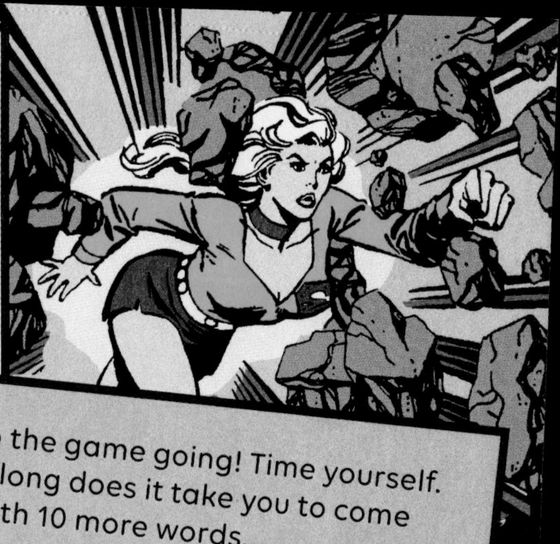

Time:

Keep the game going! Time yourself. How long does it take you to come up with 10 more words.

Time:

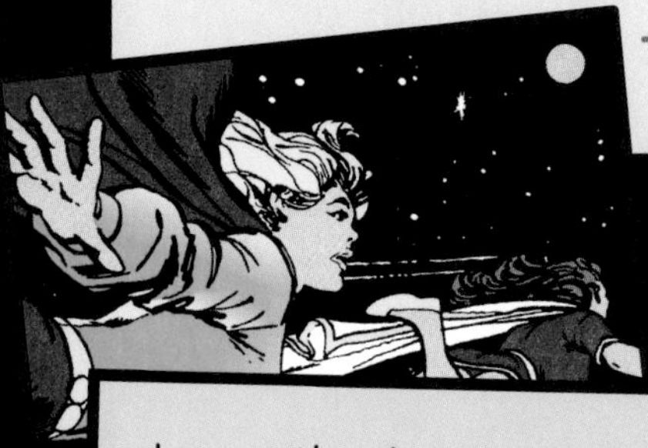

Ignore the timer. How many more words can you make?

Words, Words, Words

Give your brain a power boost by challenging your powers of description.

What are 5 words that describe Wonder Woman?

____

____

____

____

____

What are 5 things Wonder Woman is good at?

____

____

____

____

____

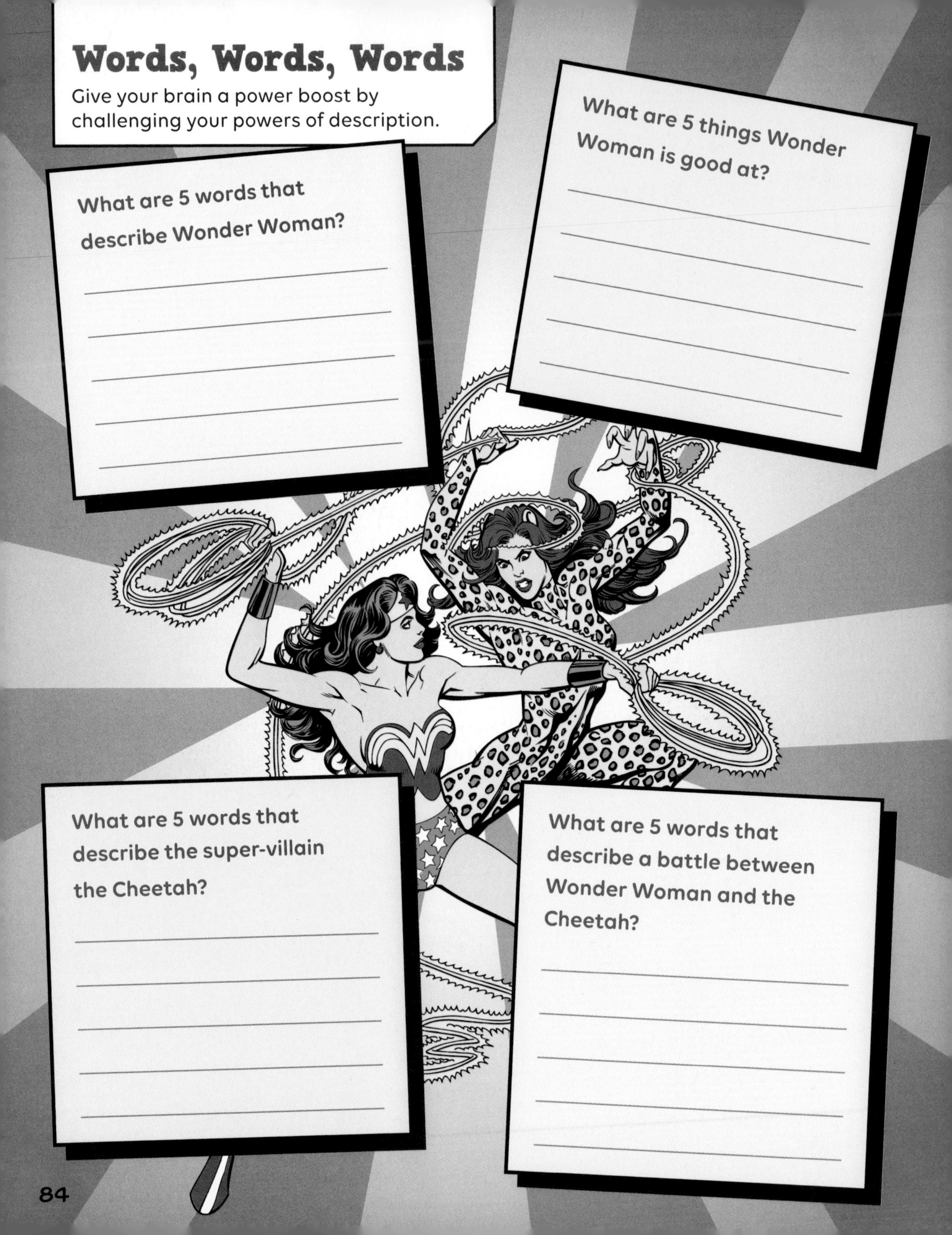

What are 5 words that describe the super-villain the Cheetah?

____

____

____

____

____

What are 5 words that describe a battle between Wonder Woman and the Cheetah?

____

____

____

____

____

One of These Heroes Is Not Like the Others

Something has shifted in one of these pictures. Find the altered hero.

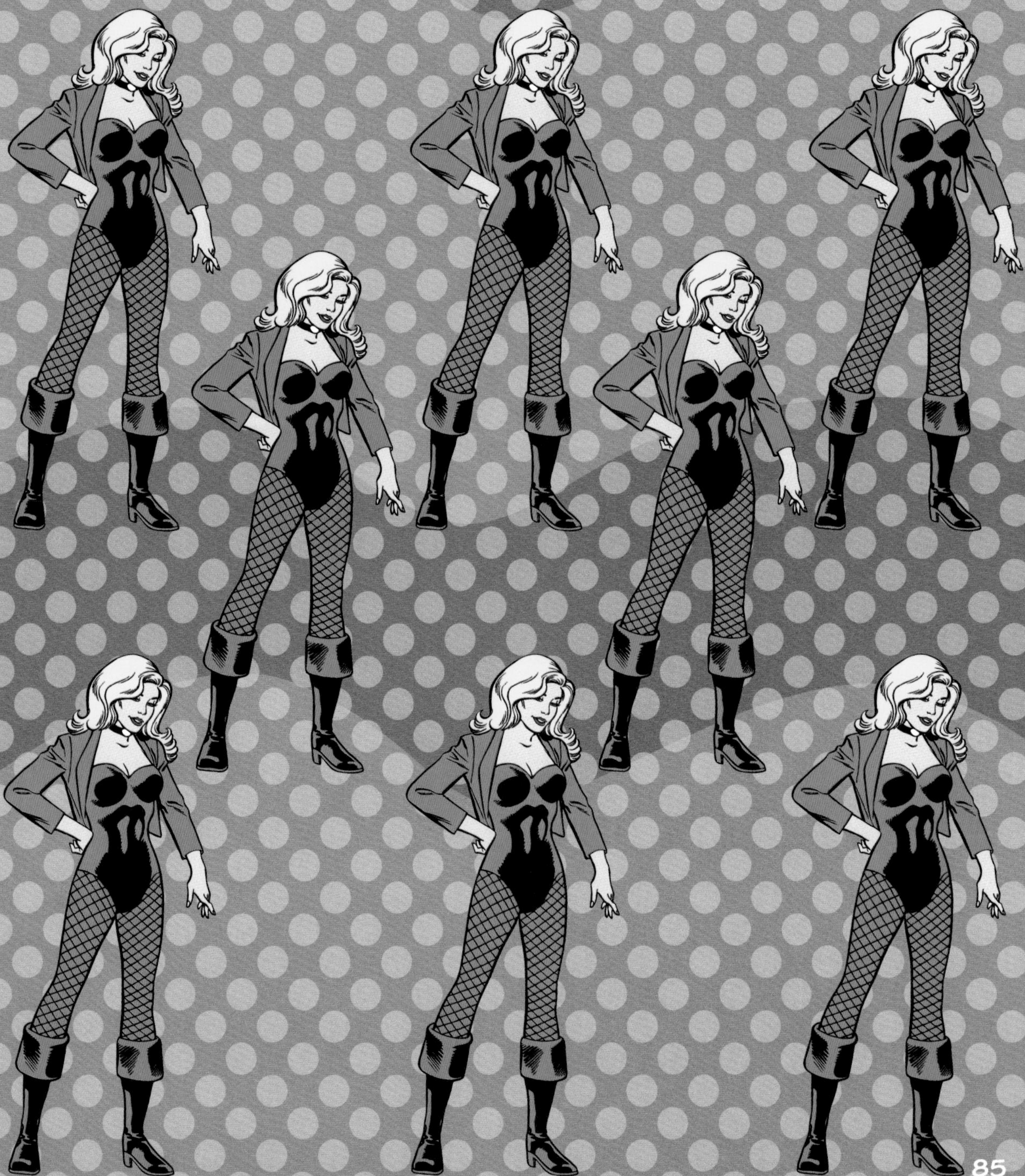

Amazing Amazon Drawing Challenge

Is drawing one of your superpowers? Is it a skill you can practice? Let's find out. Use the grid on the left as your guide and draw Wonder Woman in the grid on the right. Start with the black lines and move on to the color.

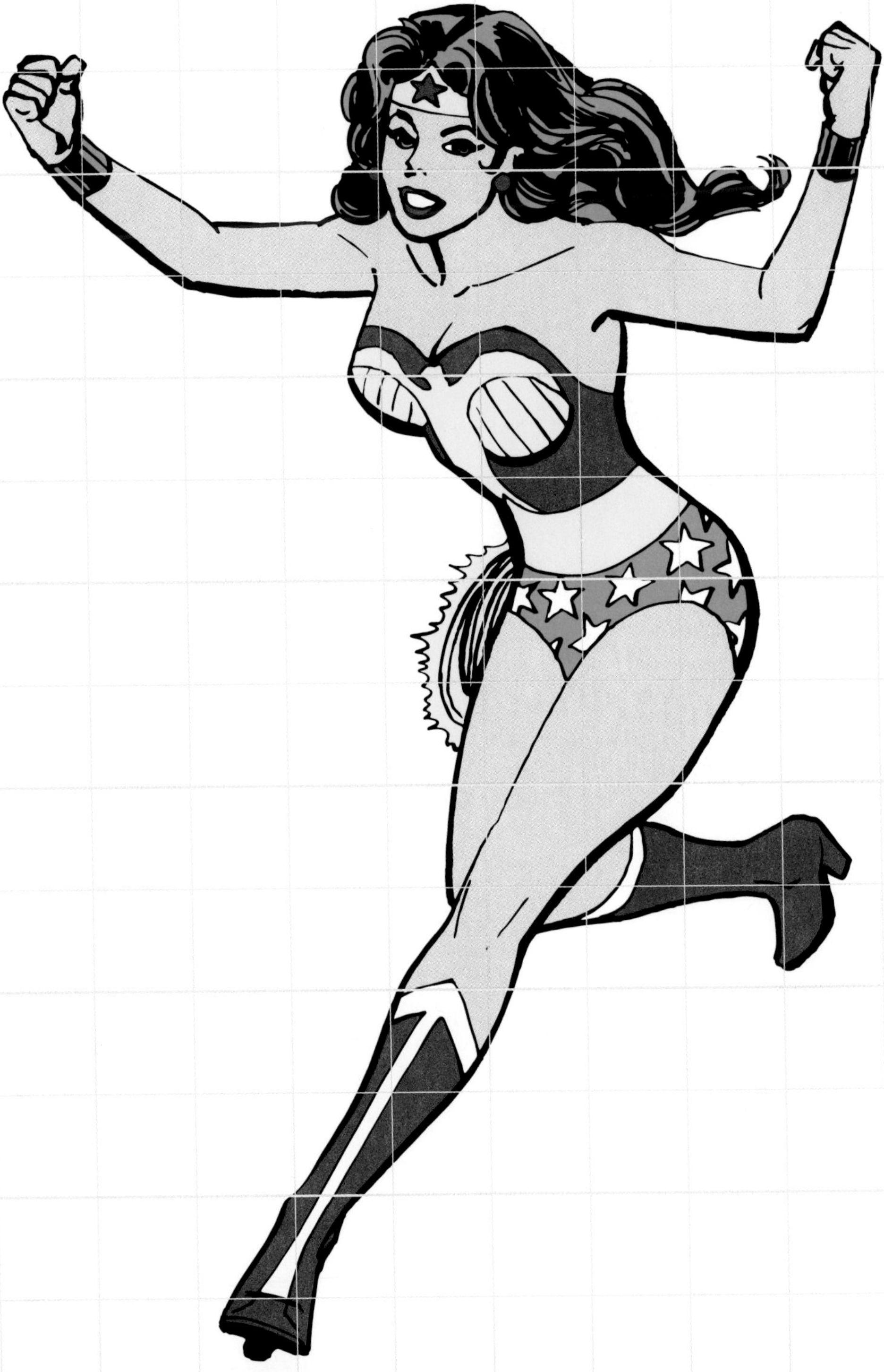

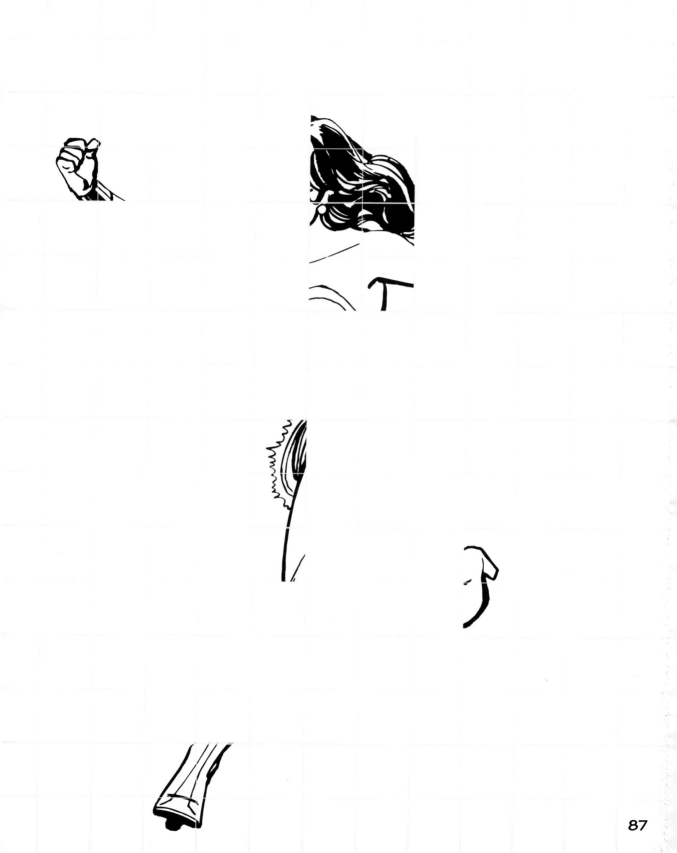

What's New?

This comic cover introduces the new Batgirl. A few other new things have cropped up too. Can you spot 10 things that have changed from the first picture to the second?

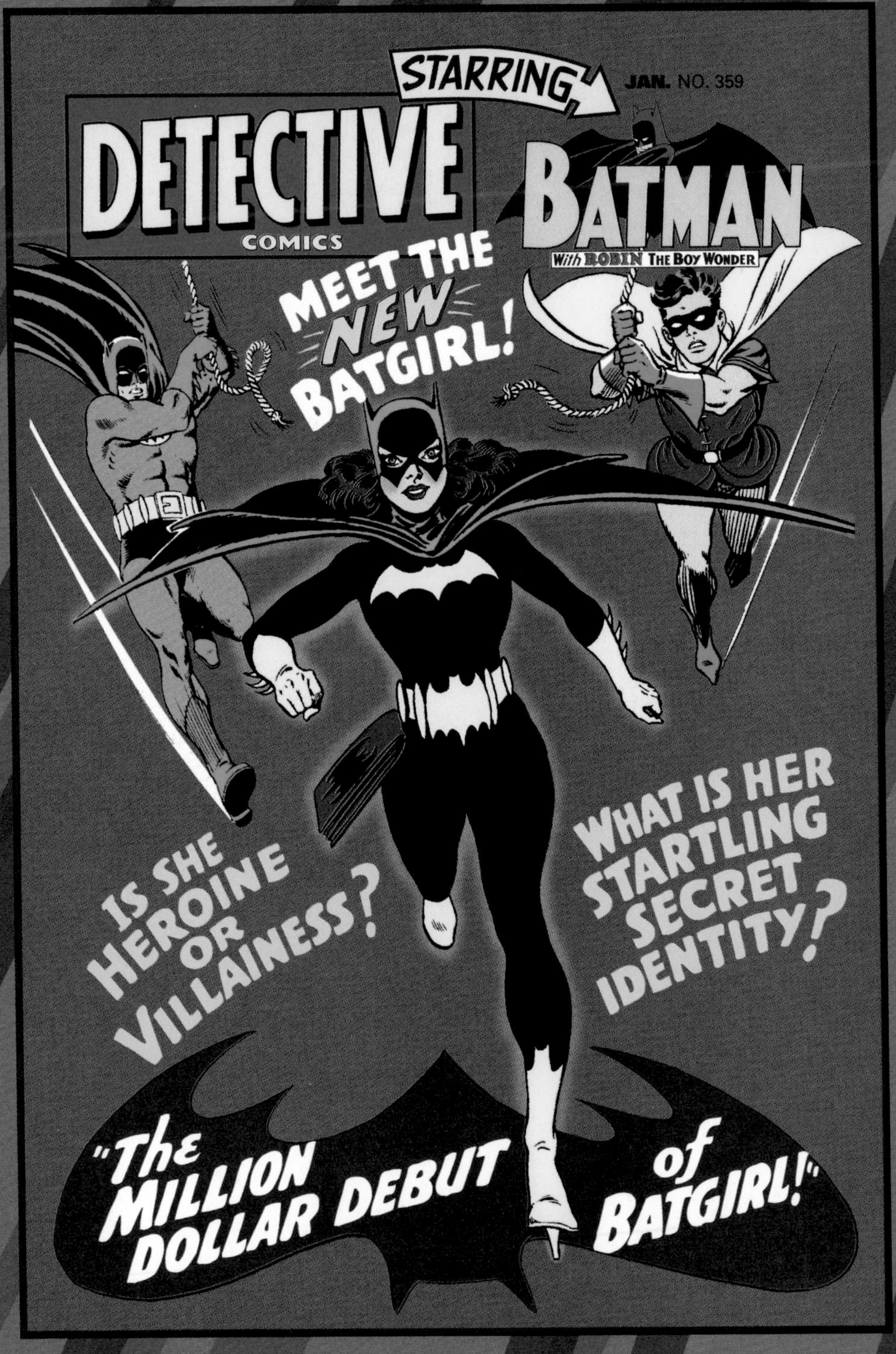
STARRING
JAN. NO. 359
DETECTIVE COMICS
BATMAN
With ROBIN THE BOY WONDER
MEET THE NEW BATGIRL!
IS SHE HEROINE OR VILLAINESS?
WHAT IS HER STARTLING SECRET IDENTITY?
"The MILLION DOLLAR DEBUT of BATGIRL!"

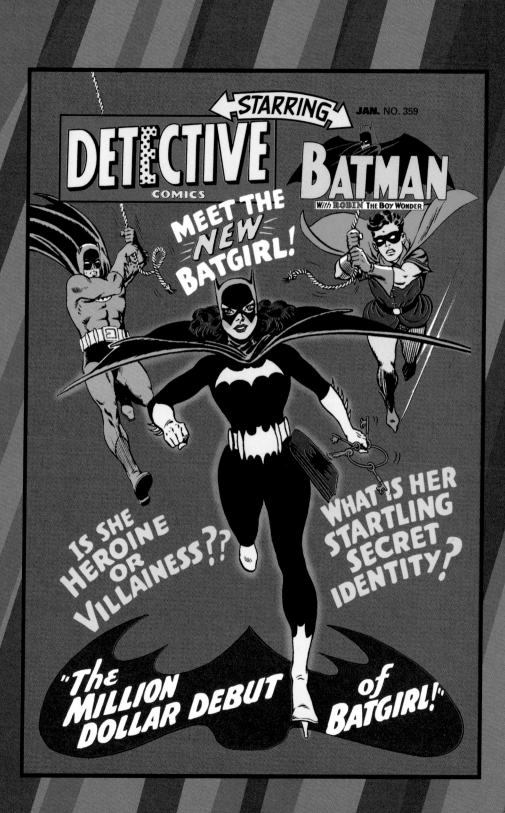

Ha-Ha-Ha-Humdingers!

Use the key below to decode each of the letters and uncover the answers.

KEY

A	B	C	D	E	F	G	H	I	J	K	L	M	N	O

P	Q	R	S	T	U	V	W	X	Y	Z

How does Supergirl use her heightened senses to find the nearest beach?

90

Is Batgirl creative?

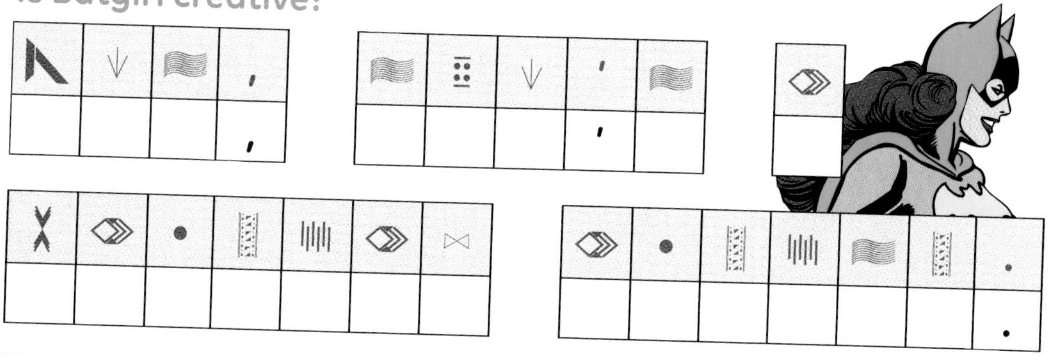

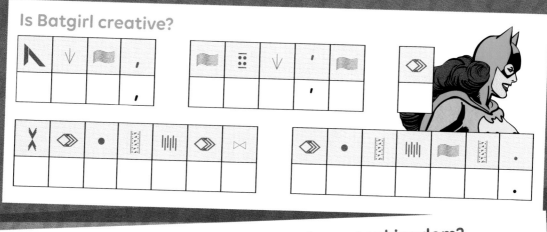

Where did Mera learn to run her underwater kingdom?

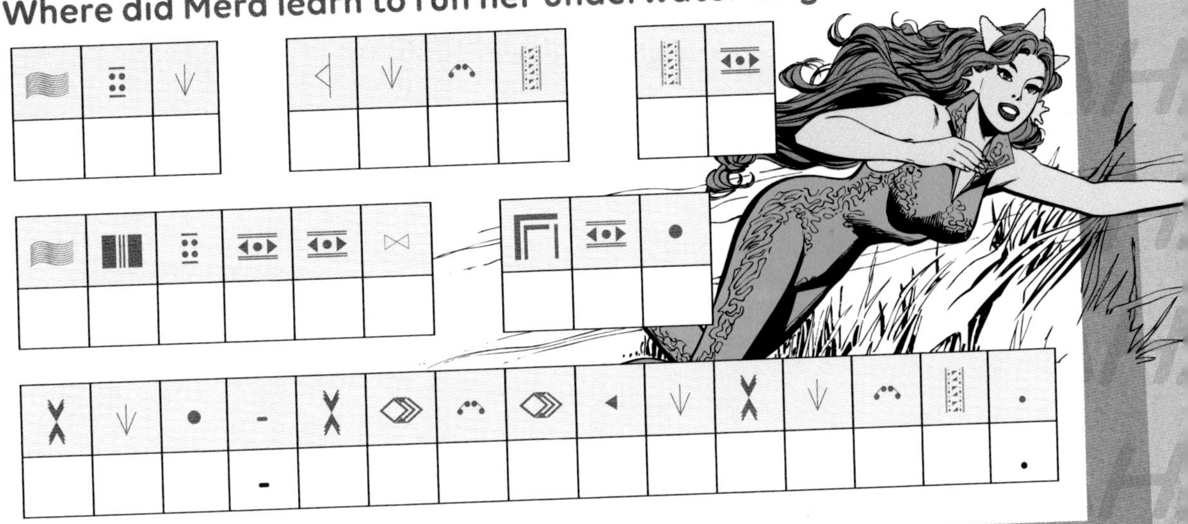

If Wonder Woman cuts tomatoes with her tiara and Katana slices strawberries with her sword, how does Harley Quinn cook?

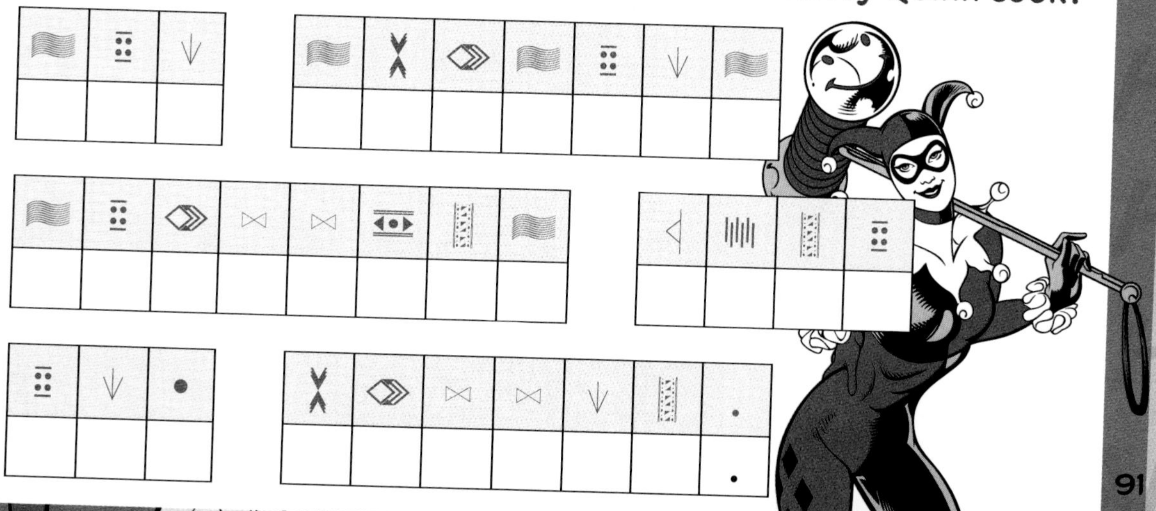

Tell a Wonder Woman Tale

Look at the picture. What do you see? How did Wonder Woman end up in this perilous situation? Write a story about the picture.

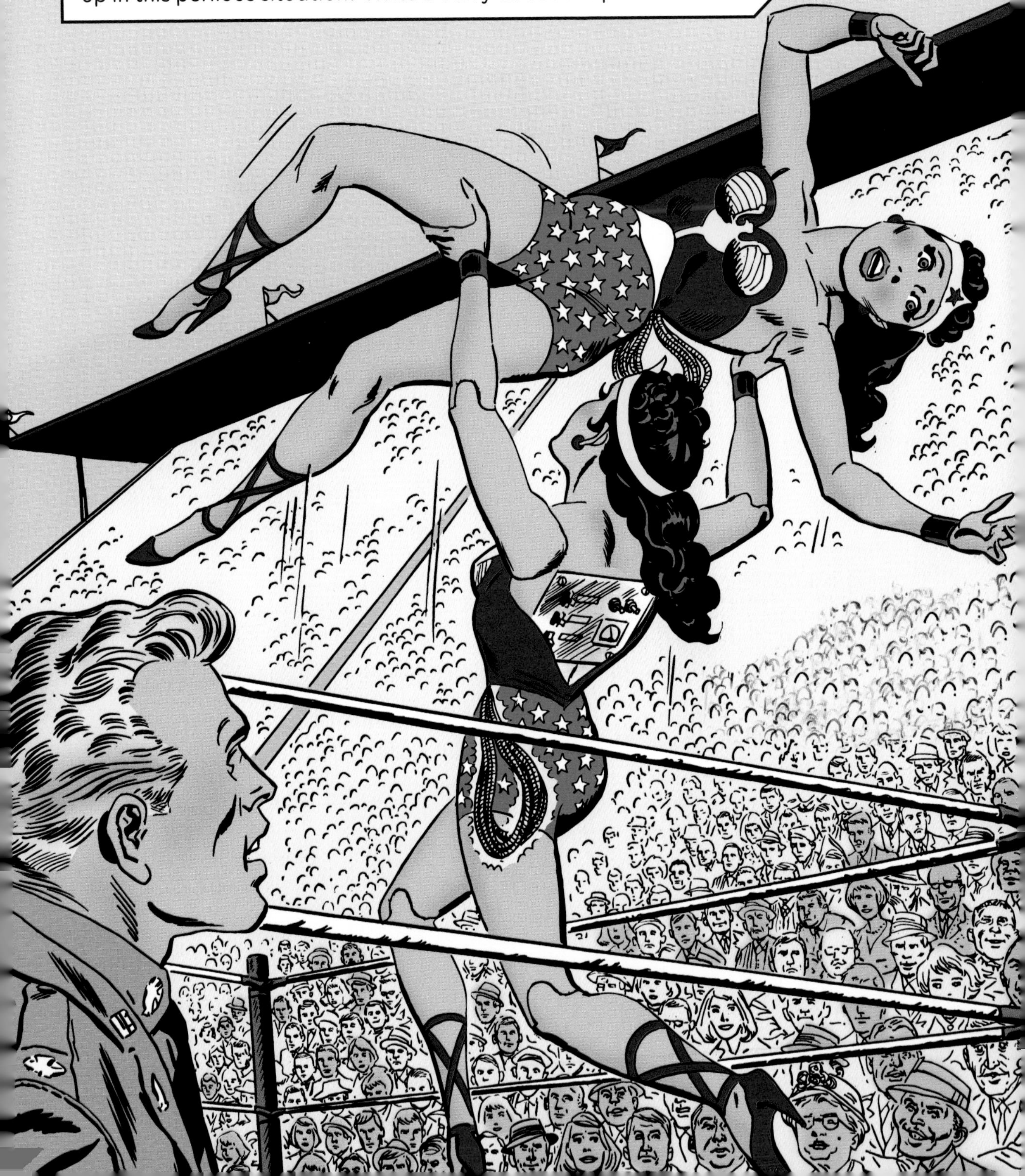

Supergirl Word Search

Like her **cousin** Superman, **Supergirl** is from the planet **Krypton**. She came to **Metropolis** on a **rocket**. Her name is **Kara Zor-El**. She has many superpowers, like super-strength, super-speed, and **invulnerability**. In addition to **X-ray vision** and heat vision, she has **freeze** breath. She keeps the world **safe** from terrible villains like **Brainiac**, **Darkseid**, **Lex Luthor**, and **Poison Ivy**.

Find the bold words in the grid on the right. They appear forward, backward, up, down, or diagonally.

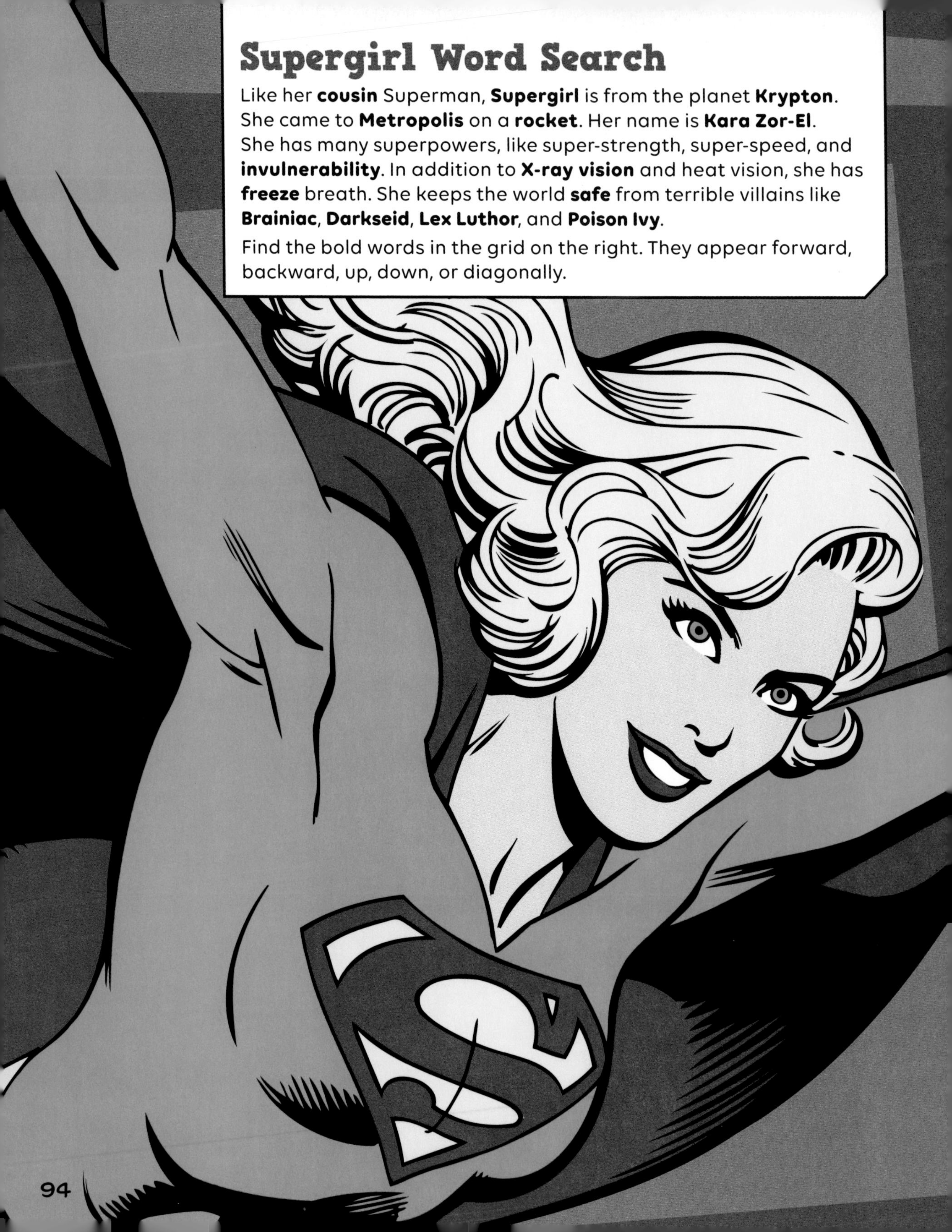

```
I N V U L N E R A B I L I T Y
X E E A T K L E X L U T H O R R
R H A R H O A L E C G P A R X
E E L I A L D I D O N I N P A Y
Y H L C R E E D A R K S E I D
V E T H O R N I E O I Z N E B
E I Z M D O N C N K T Z A E K
S E H E L Z U O O S A A H M E
S R M A E A T U T U E U C H I
I F E N O R S S P P S N I Z J
L I T A L A F U Y E R I F O Y
O A X T E K C O R R R D N E V
P R O A I A A N K G A E R L I
O A I G F L M L R I W R E U N
R K N H E A E E A R O T T L O
T L T A F W H S S L H H S R S
E R X R A Y V I S I O N V A I
M O H V S I T S E I E R O I O
S W E B R A I N I A C S L N P
```

Brain Training

Like the other Amazons she grew up with, Wonder Woman trains to keep in tip-top fighting shape. But she doesn't just train her body. She trains her mind. Are you ready for a brain workout? Use the timer on your phone or watch to see how quickly you can come up with 10 words using the letters found in the words below. (If you don't have a timer handy, that's okay. You'll still get an intellectual boost!)

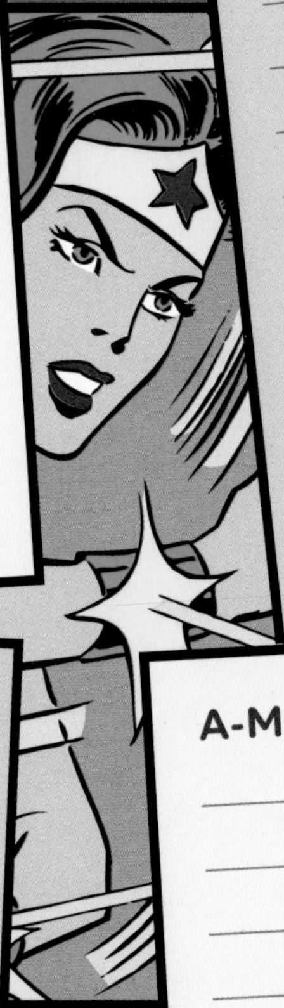

P-A-R-A-D-I-S-E I-S-L-A-N-D

Time: ____________

I-N-V-I-S-I-B-L-E J-E-T

Time: ____________

L-A-S-S-O O-F T-R-U-T-H

Time: ____________

A-M-A-Z-O-N P-R-I-N-C-E-S-S

Time: ____________

Is Your Memory Robot-Ready?

Study this picture for 30 seconds, then turn the page and test your memory.

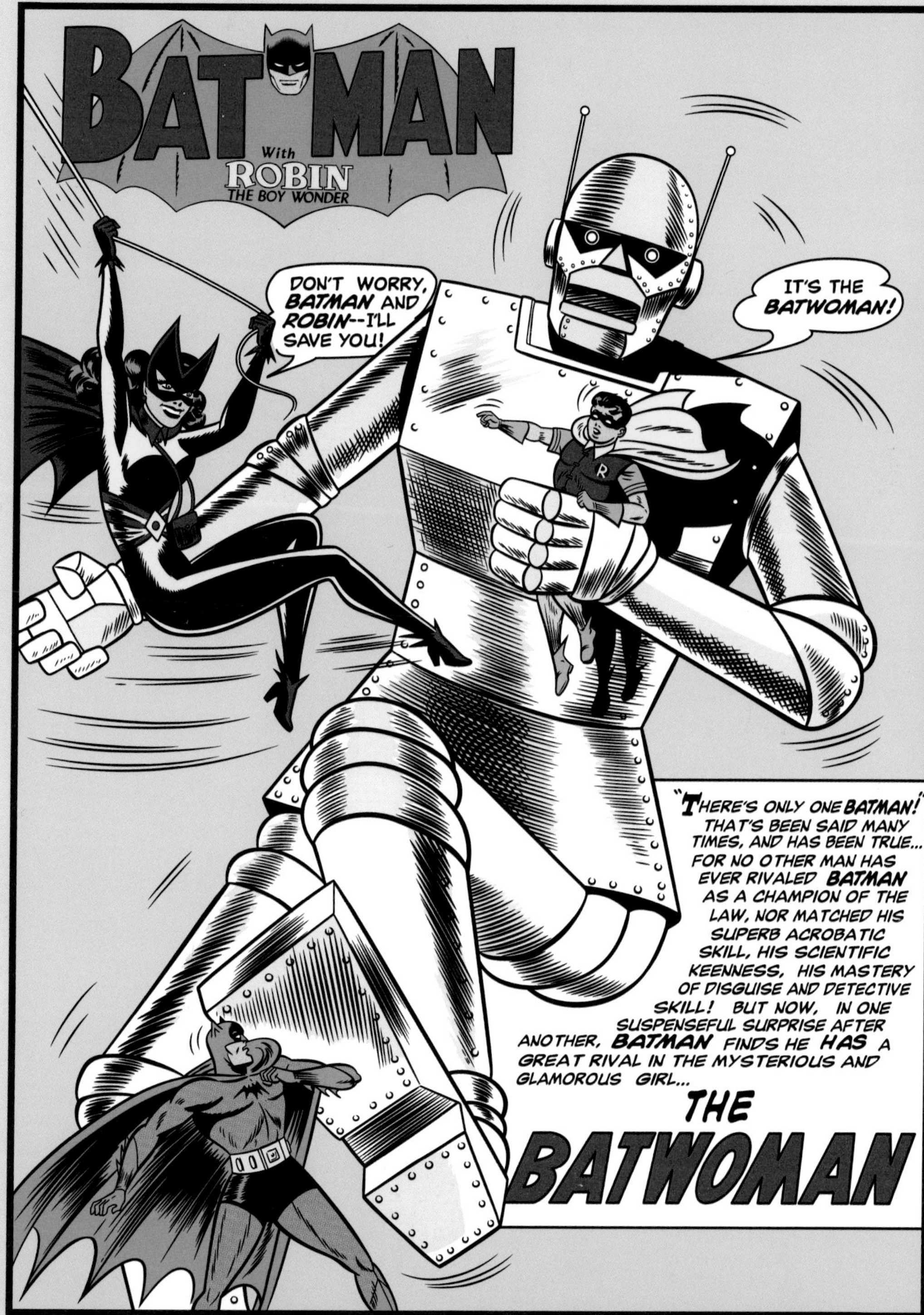
BATMAN
With ROBIN THE BOY WONDER
DON'T WORRY, BATMAN AND ROBIN--I'LL SAVE YOU!
IT'S THE BATWOMAN!
R
"THERE'S ONLY ONE BATMAN!" THAT'S BEEN SAID MANY TIMES, AND HAS BEEN TRUE... FOR NO OTHER MAN HAS EVER RIVALED BATMAN AS A CHAMPION OF THE LAW, NOR MATCHED HIS SUPERB ACROBATIC SKILL, HIS SCIENTIFIC KEENNESS, HIS MASTERY OF DISGUISE AND DETECTIVE SKILL! BUT NOW, IN ONE SUSPENSEFUL SURPRISE AFTER ANOTHER, BATMAN FINDS HE HAS A GREAT RIVAL IN THE MYSTERIOUS AND GLAMOROUS GIRL...
THE BATWOMAN

Is Your Memory in Good Shape?

Answer the questions below based on the picture on page 97.

1. What color are Batwoman's boots?

a. Blue

b. Gray

c. Yellow

d. Red

2. How many fingers does the giant robot have?

a. Two fingers, like a crab claw

b. Four fingers, no thumb

c. Five fingers, like a person

d. No fingers, just a giant hook on each hand

3. What is Batman doing?

a. Swinging to Robin's rescue

b. Avoiding getting stomped

c. Throwing his Batarang at the robot

d. Climbing up the robot's leg

4. What color are the robot's eyes?

a. Glowing red

b. Bright yellow

c. Black and white

d. Green laser beams

5. What is Robin saying?

a. "Batman, help!"

b. "It's the Batwoman!"

c. "Batwoman, grab my hand!"

d. "Stop this evil robot!"

6. Which skill is not mentioned in the list of talents that Batman and Batwoman have?

a. Scientific keenness

b. Superb acrobatic skill

c. Mastery of martial arts

d. Mastery of disguise

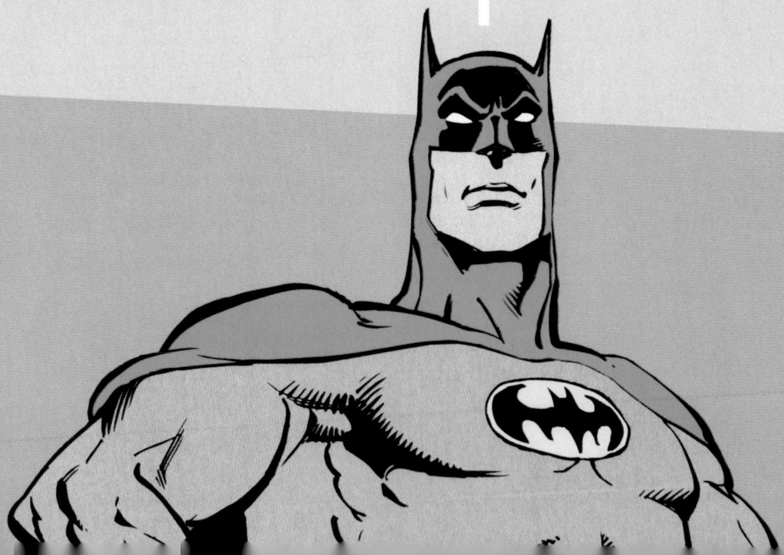

One A-MAZE-ing Amazon!

The Cheetah ran through the maze and escaped. If Wonder Woman picks the right path, she can rush through the maze and catch up to her enemy. Can you help out the Amazing Amazon? Which path should she take?

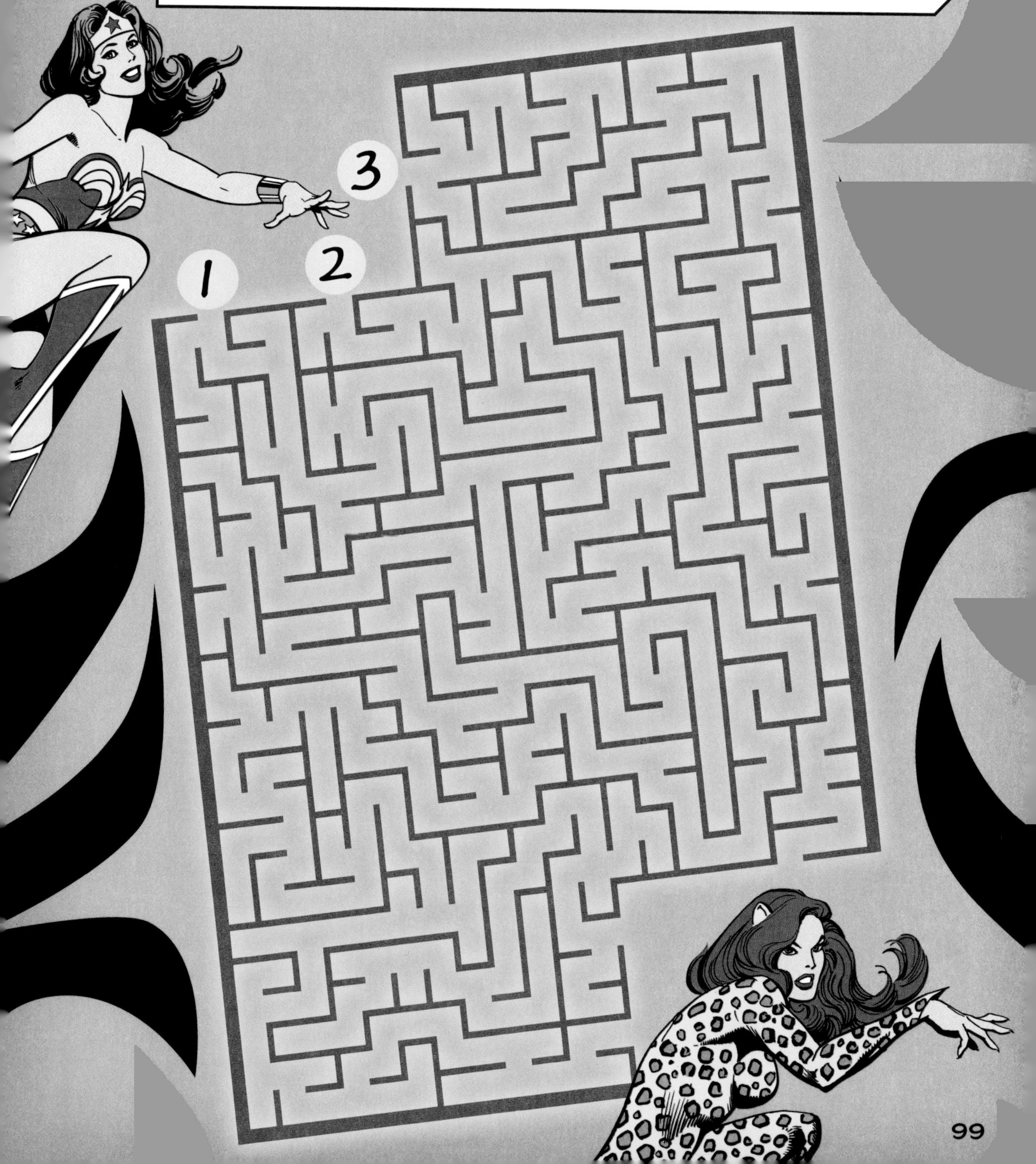
3
2
1

Mera's Underwater Kingdom

Mera and Aquaman live underwater, in harmony with all sea creatures. Can you find all the awesome aquatic animals in the word search below? They appear forward, backward, up, down, or diagonally.

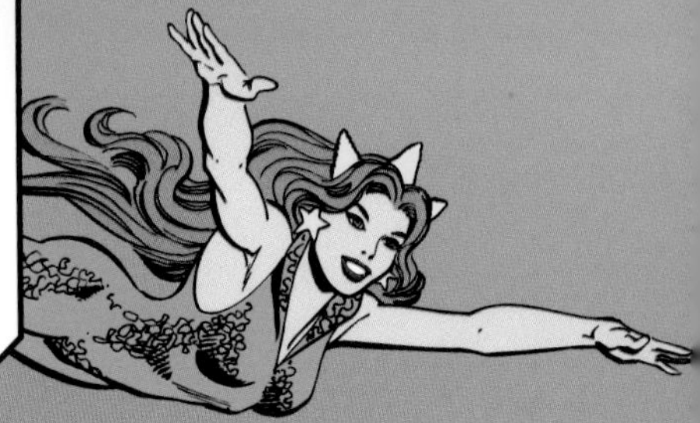

WORD LIST

clown fish
dolphin
eel
flounder
giant squid
halibut
jellyfish
octopus
penguin
porpoise
puffin
sea turtle
seahorse
shark
snapper
stingray
swordfish
tuna
whale

V	C	F	A	M	C	E	I	N	I	H	P	L	O	D
Q	E	L	I	S	U	A	Y	E	R	O	F	R	C	E
A	N	O	O	O	Y	P	A	Y	M	U	J	E	Y	S
E	R	U	M	W	B	U	R	S	I	R	E	Z	U	W
N	U	N	C	E	N	F	G	A	T	N	L	S	N	O
I	O	D	X	V	E	F	N	D	E	E	L	Y	S	R
U	Y	E	S	T	S	I	I	U	L	U	Y	J	E	D
G	A	R	Z	U	U	N	T	S	A	D	F	O	A	F
N	S	R	E	B	P	E	S	N	H	N	I	X	T	I
E	C	A	U	I	O	M	O	A	W	Q	S	K	U	S
P	O	I	S	L	T	I	A	P	K	Y	H	V	R	H
N	T	U	N	A	C	E	U	P	E	R	E	B	T	I
A	S	E	A	H	O	R	S	E	W	H	A	S	L	C
E	S	I	O	P	R	O	P	R	A	R	Q	H	E	R
G	I	A	N	T	S	Q	U	I	D	I	Z	O	S	E

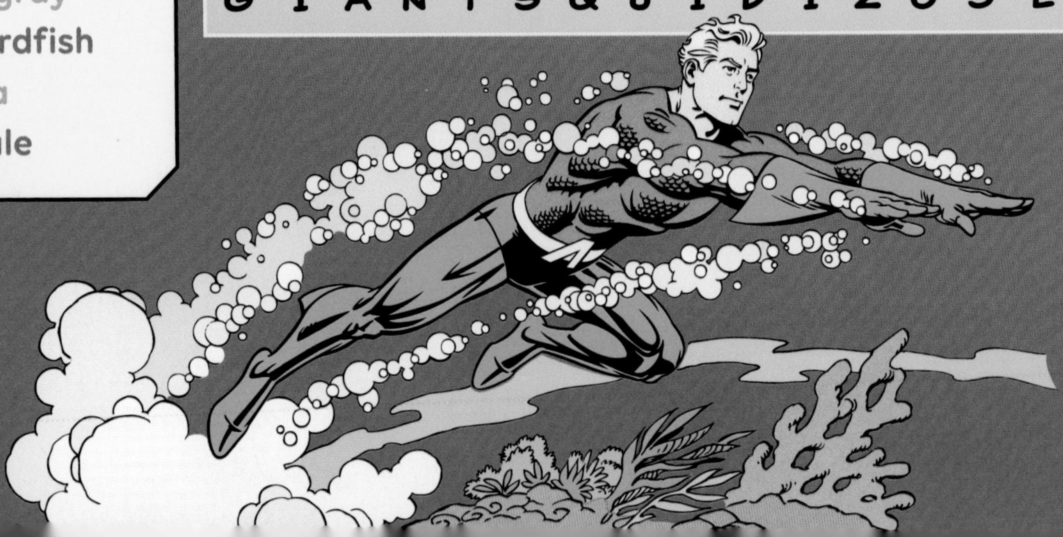

Celebrating Super Heroes!

The balloons aren't floating away, but they are changing. Circle 7 things that are different in the second picture.

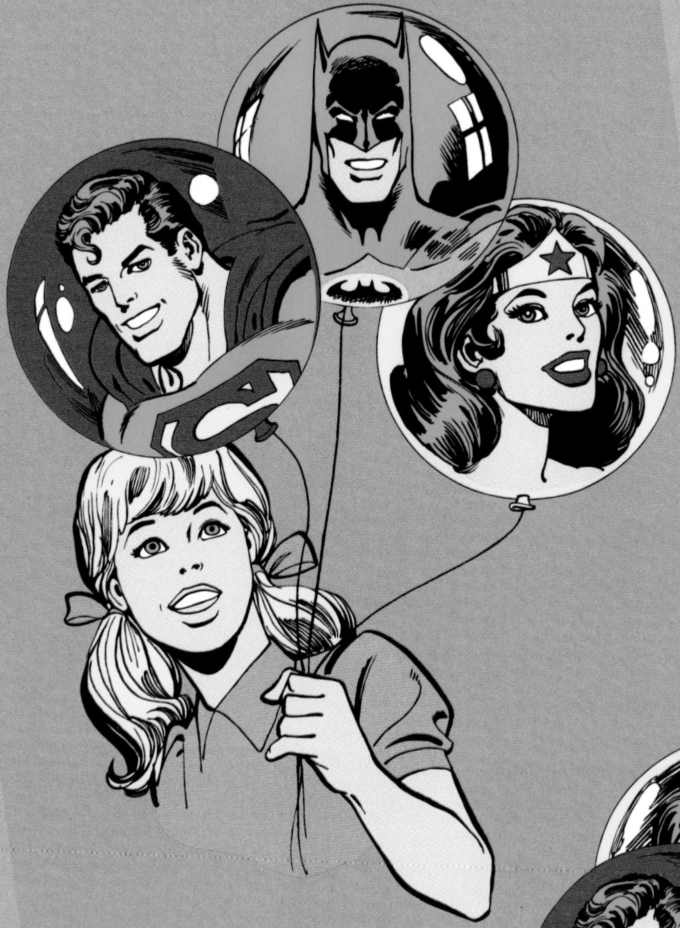

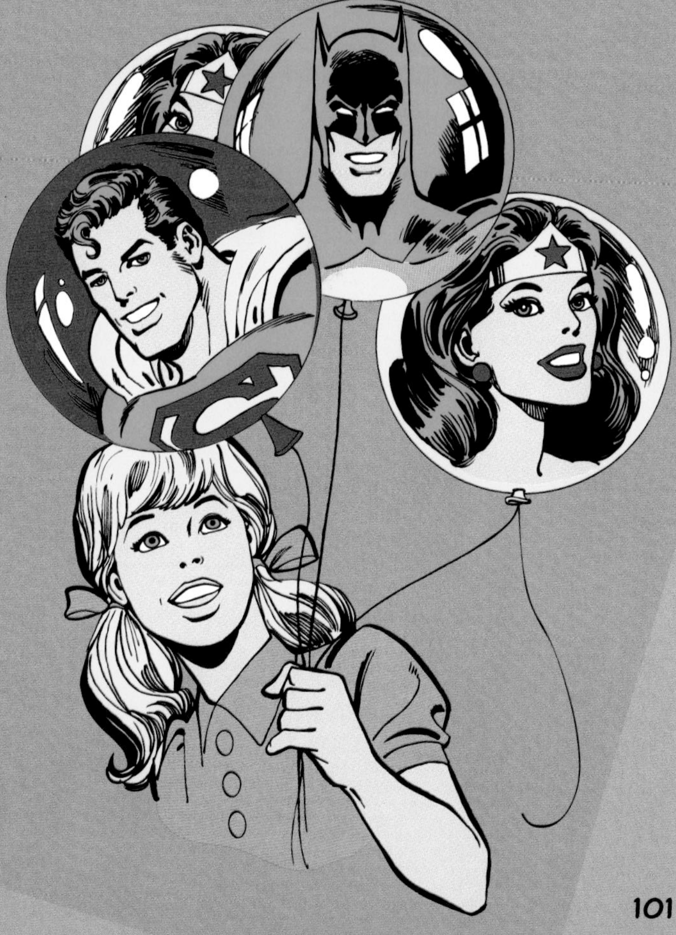

Follow the Pattern

Follow the pattern on the right to get through this pattern maze. You can go right, left, up, or down—but not diagonally. Make sure to steer clear of Poison Ivy and the Cheetah!

THE PATTERN

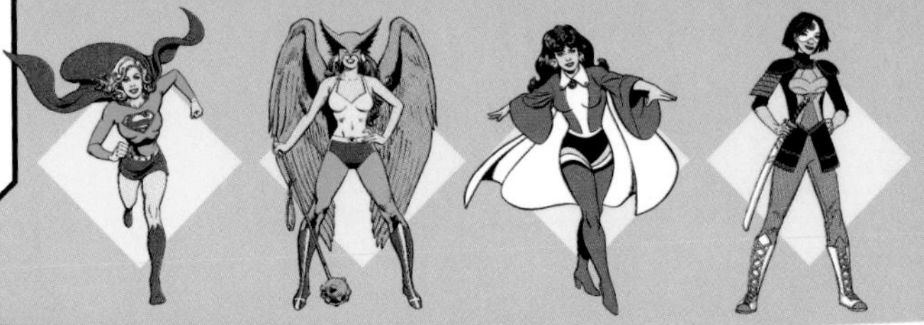

START

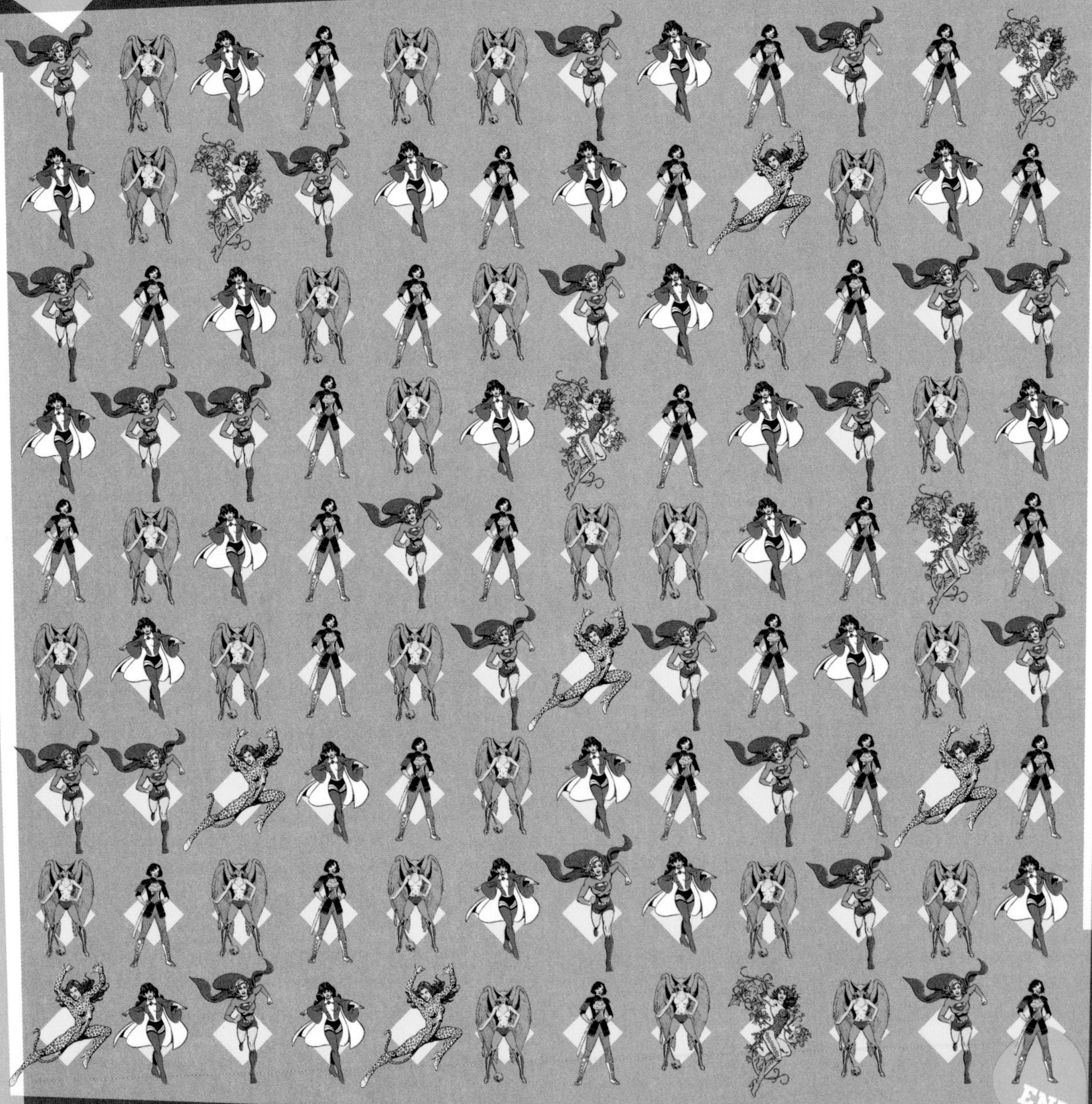

END

Bee Careful!

You'll have to look closely to find the tiny change that makes one of these super hero pictures different from the rest.

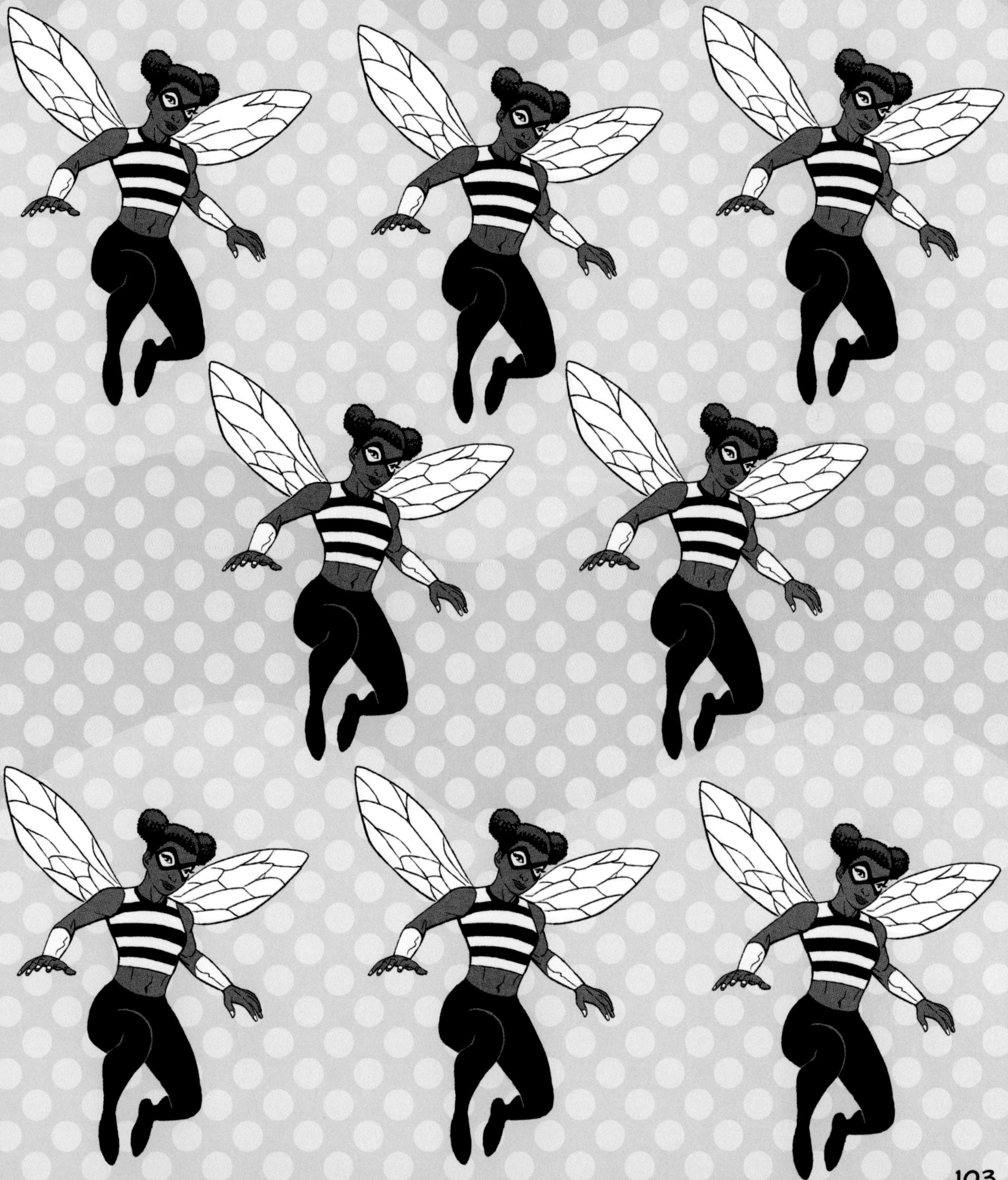

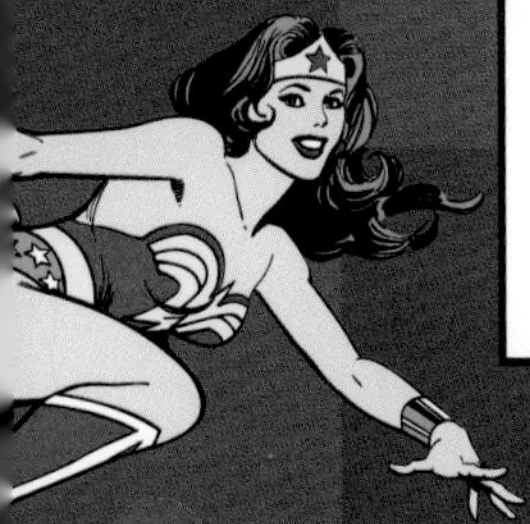

Crime-Fighting Crossword

Use your extensive super hero knowledge to complete this crossword.

ACROSS

3 Wonder Woman uses her powerful leg muscles to ________ fast.

4 Mera lives in the ocean. She can ________ faster than a shark!

7 Starfire comes from another ________ called Tamaran.

9 Superman's good friend ________ Lane is a reporter for the *Daily Planet.*

11 Poison Ivy isn't always a fan of people, but she sure loves ________.

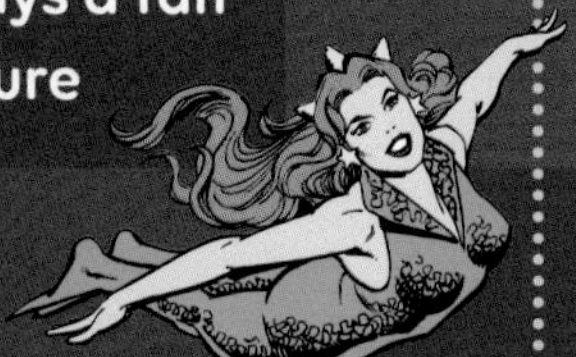

13 Living underwater, Mera can communicate with ________.

14 Harley Quinn wears a two-colored jester cap. One side of Harley's cap is ________.

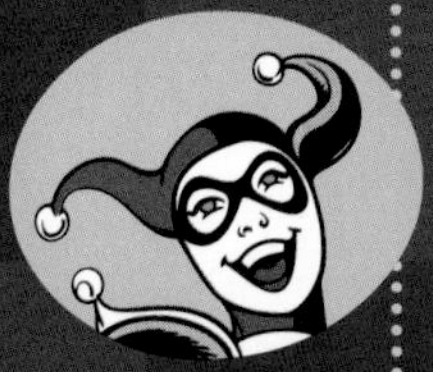

15 The other side of Harley's cap is ________.

17 Catwoman prowls in the night, under the light of the ________.

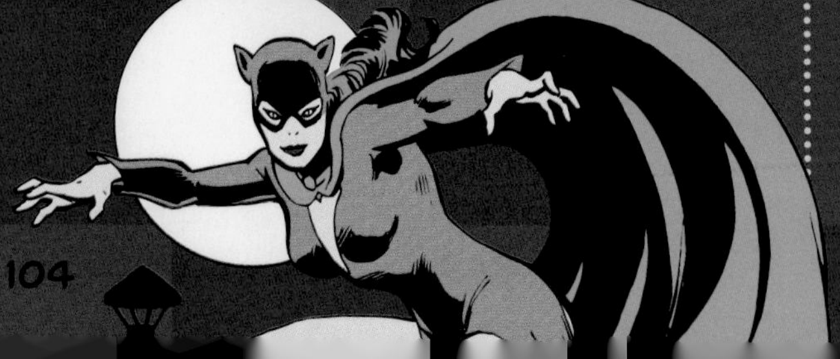

DOWN

1 Wonder Woman uses her powerful leg muscles to ________ high.

2 Bumblebee's bee suit lets her shrink down until she is ________.

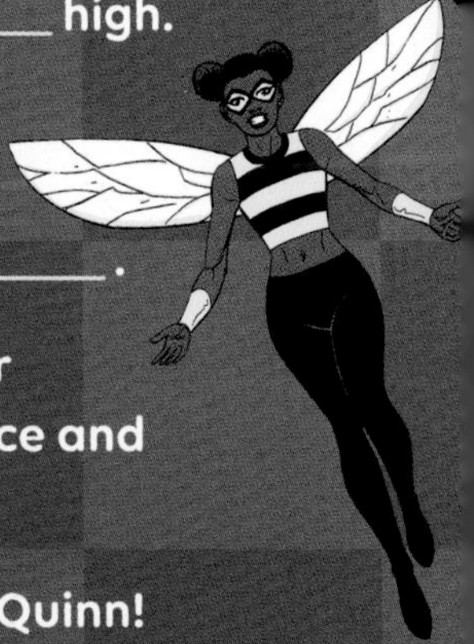

5 Supergirl can use her heat vision to thaw ice and turn it into ________.

6 Be careful of Harley Quinn! She swings a heavy ________.

8 Hawkgirl can fly when she wears her giant ________.

10 Batgirl is a computer whiz. She can defeat any computer ________.

12 Supergirl and Superman get their powers from the ________.

13 Wonder Woman goes after villains whether they are near or ________.

14 Black Canary's Canary Cry is a sound that can ________ glass!

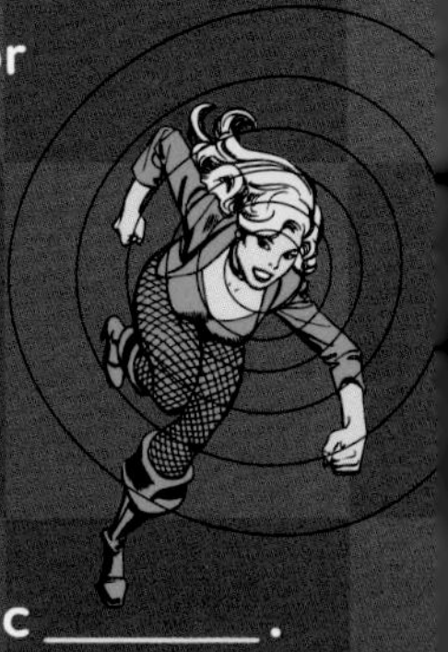

16 Batman and Robin are often called the Dynamic ________.

18 Super heroes protect everyone, no matter how young or how ________!

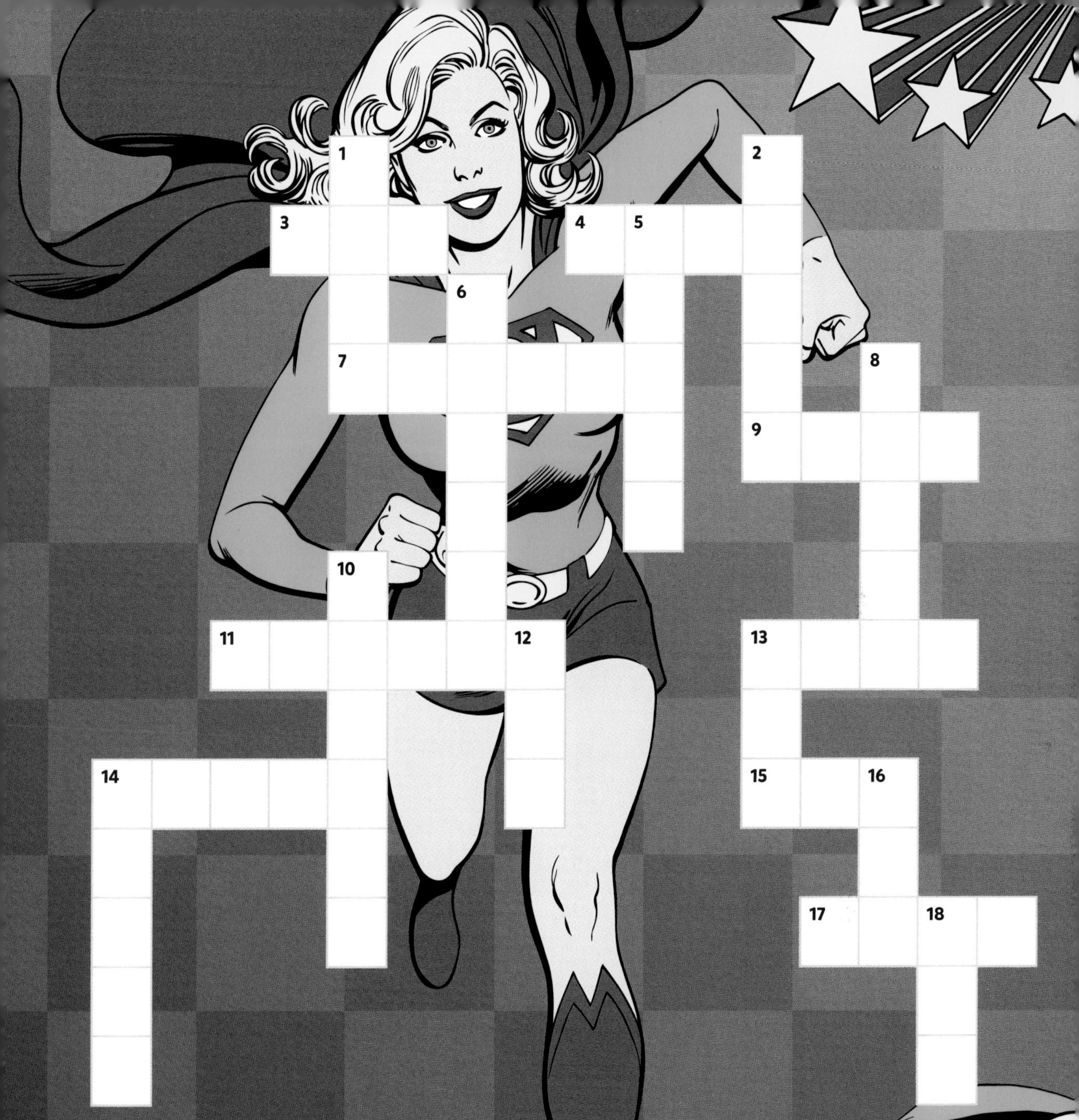
1
2
3
4
5
6
7
8
9
10
11
12
13
14
15
16
17
18

WORD LIST Need a hint? All the words in the crossword are below:

black	fish	mallet	plants	sun
break	hacker	moon	red	swim
duo	jump	old	run	water
far	Lois	planet	small	wings

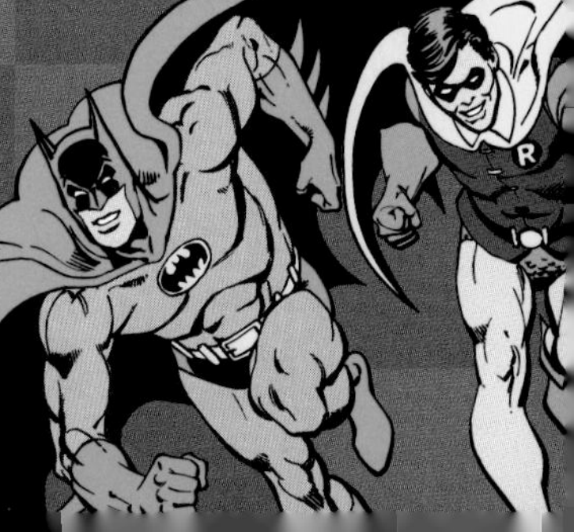

Sword-Slinging Switcheroos

Katana spends a lot of time practicing her martial arts moves. Now you can practice spotting what's moving in these pictures. Circle 7 things that are altered in the second image of Katana.

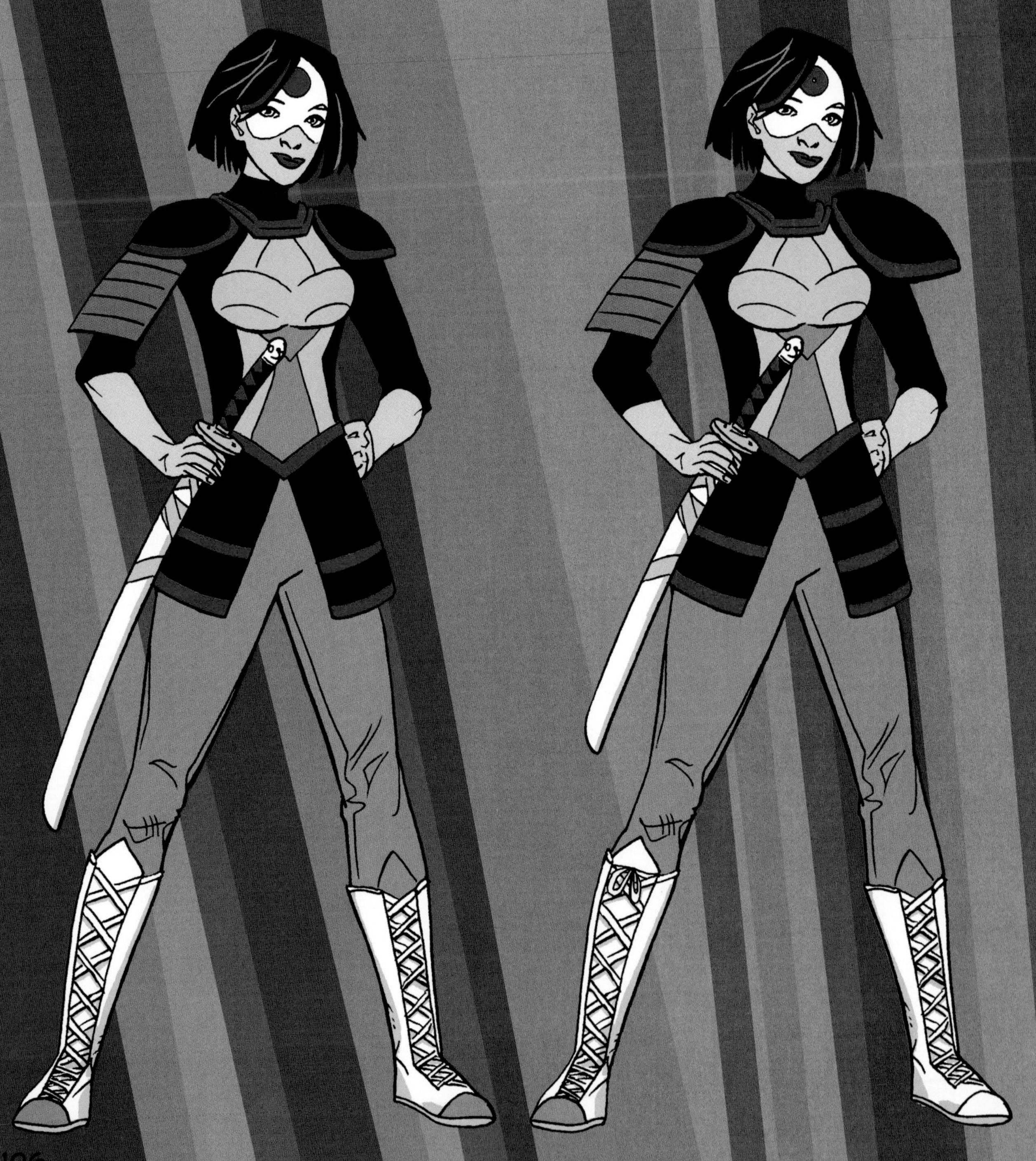

What Rhymes with Race?

Show off your rhyming skills.

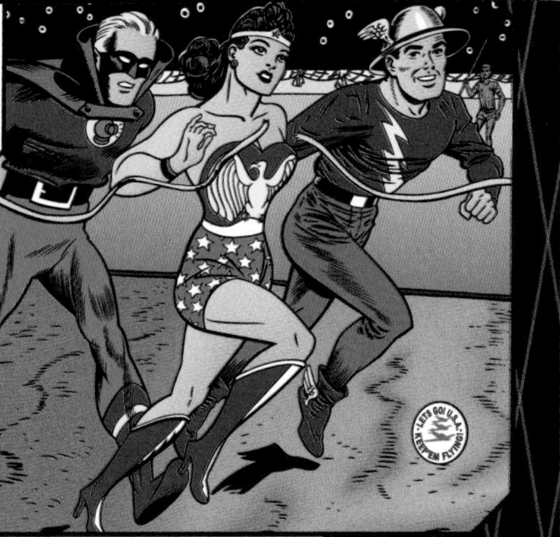

In this R A C E, Wonder Woman won first _ _ _ _ _ .

To get to Earth, Supergirl had to travel through _ _ _ _ _ .

Katana wears a mask that covers part of her _ _ _ _ .

Detectives like Batgirl and Batman follow clues to solve each _ _ _ _ .

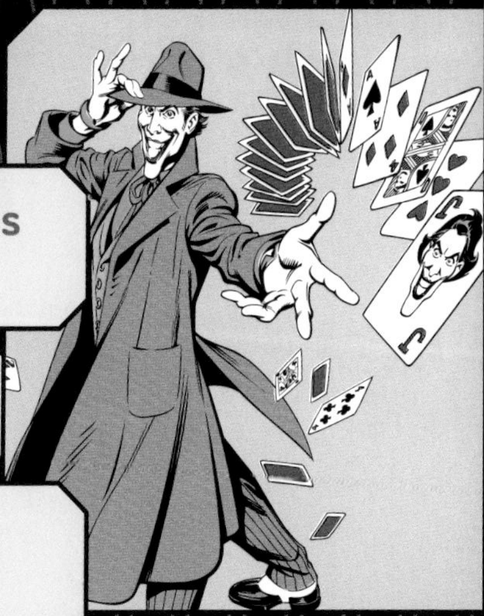

The Joker loves card games. His most special cards are the king, queen, jack, and _ _ _ .

Hawkgirl's weapon is a big, heavy _ _ _ _ .

Supergirl was tracking a robot sent by Lex Luthor, but it vanished without a _ _ _ _ _ .

Poison Ivy loves flowers, but she prefers them to be growing in a garden rather than standing up in a _ _ _ _ .

When the Cheetah ran off into the night, Wonder Woman had to _ _ _ _ _ after her.

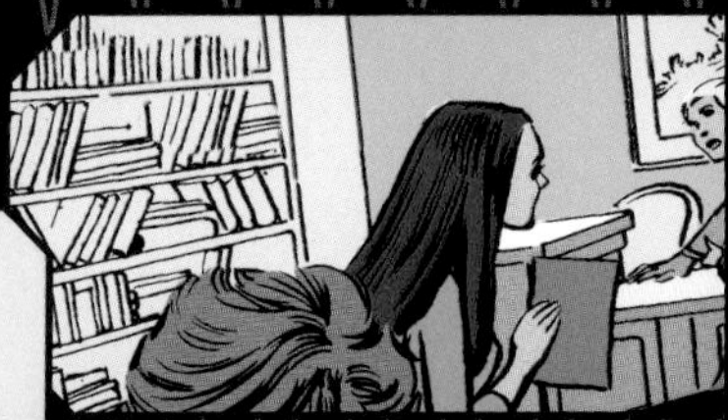

Batgirl loves to read. She keeps her favorite titles on a tall, wooden _ _ _ _ _ _ _ _ .

It's hard to win when you play kickball with The Flash. You can never catch him when he runs from _ _ _ _ to _ _ _ _ .

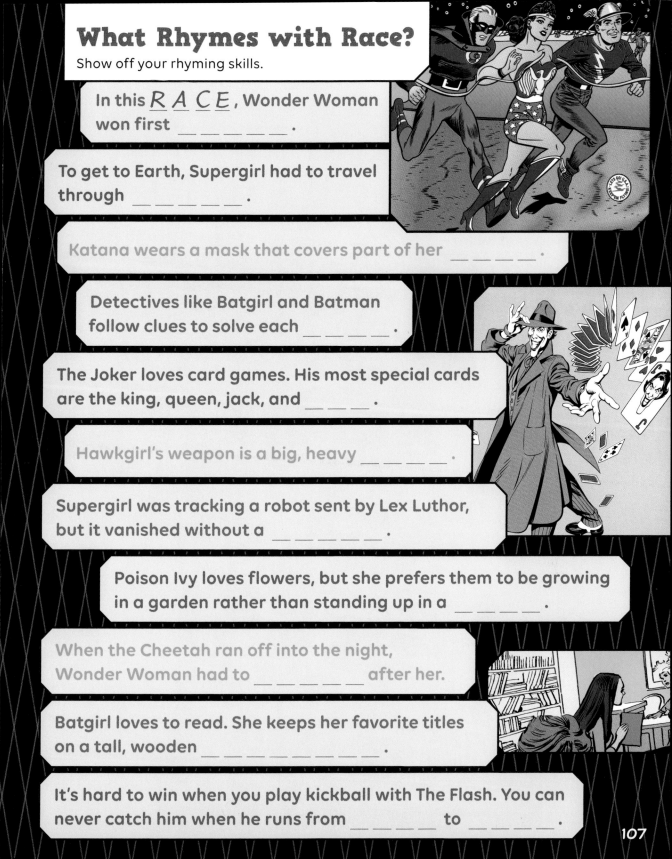

High-Stakes Chess

Something funky is afoot at this game table. Can you circle 8 things that are different in the picture on the right?

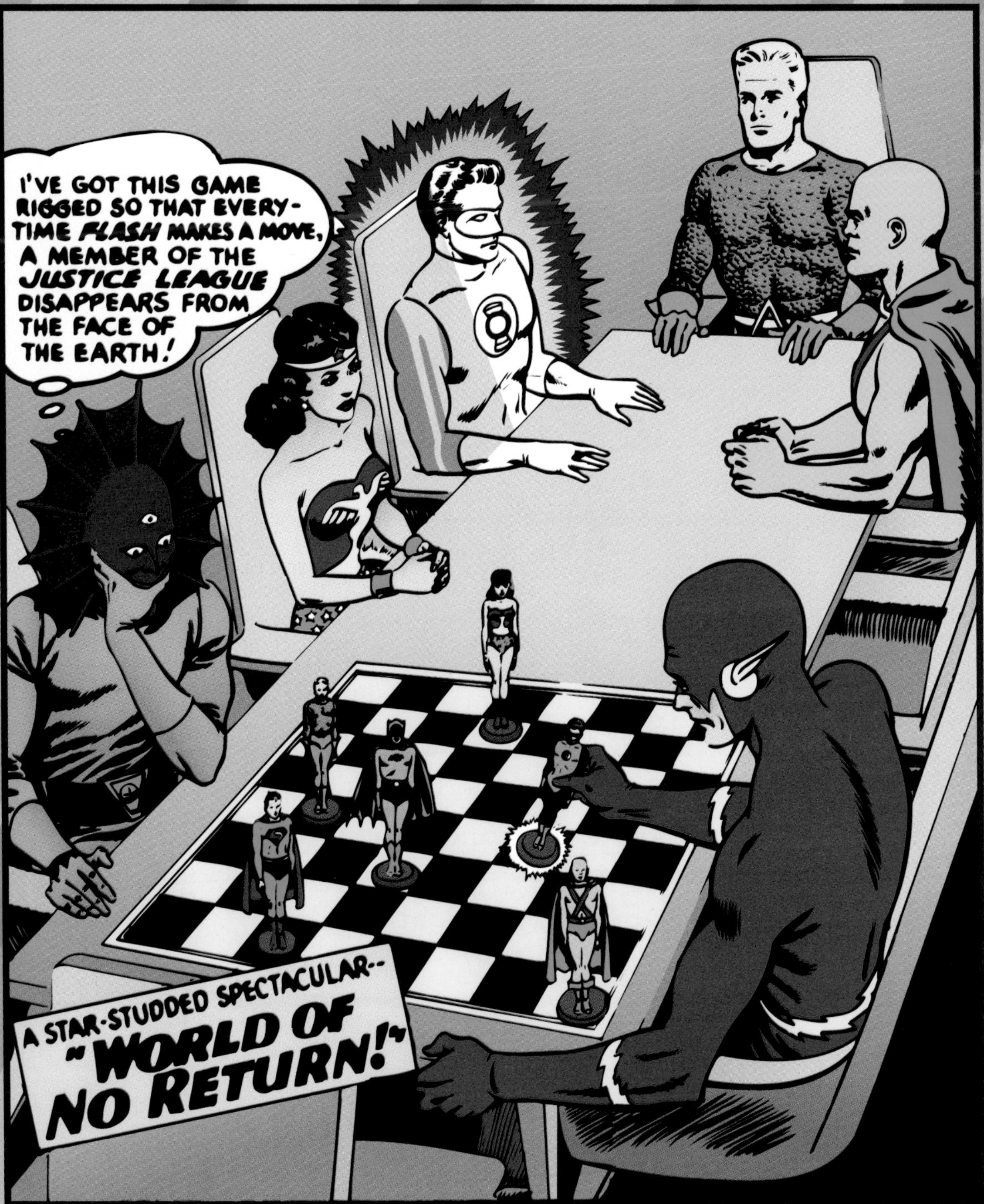

I'VE GOT THIS GAME RIGGED SO THAT EVERY-TIME *FLASH* MAKES A MOVE, A MEMBER OF THE *JUSTICE LEAGUE* DISAPPEARS FROM THE FACE OF THE EARTH!
A STAR-STUDDED SPECTACULAR-- "WORLD OF NO RETURN!"

109

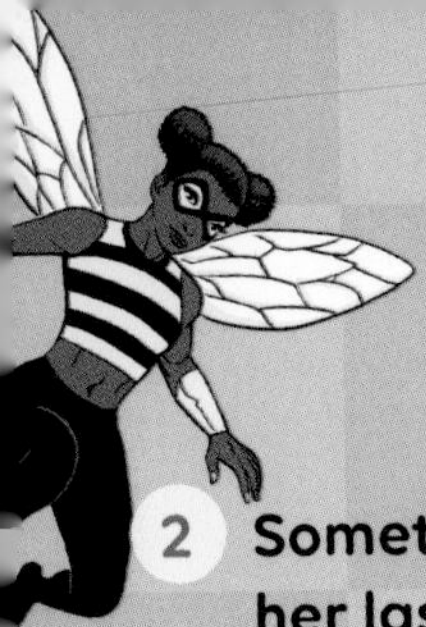

Crossword Conundrums!

Can you fill in all the blanks to complete this crossword?

ACROSS

2 Sometimes Wonder Woman uses her lasso to ________ crooks.

4 Super heroes remind us all how important it can be to do ________ deeds.

6 Wonder Woman works hard to prevent war. She is a warrior for ________.

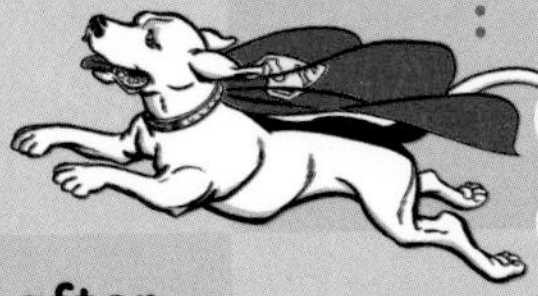

8 Raven ties her cloak around her ________.

9 Batgirl came running after a robbery when she heard the store owner yell, "Stop, ________!"

10 Batgirl often teams up with ________ to fight crime.

13 Raven uses her special powers to take away people's pain and help them ________ after being hurt.

15 Supergirl can use her X-ray ________ to see through walls.

17 Super heroes never want to cause harm. They are here to ________!

18 When Giganta grows to be incredibly tall, watch out for her ________! She might step on you!

20 Katana's weapon is a ________.

21 Together, Mera and ________ rule the Seven Seas!

DOWN

1 When she activates her super hero suit, Bumblebee can ________ down to the size of a buzzy bee.

2 Batgirl and Batman constantly have to remind Catwoman that stealing is a ________.

3 Supergirl came to Earth aboard a ________.

5 Krypto is Superman's pet ________.

6 ________ Ivy uses plants in her wicked schemes.

7 Not *always* naughty, ________ is a complicated character who loves kitties and looks out for her neighbors (but also helps herself to jewelry that belongs to others).

11 Batgirl is usually busiest battling criminals at ________.

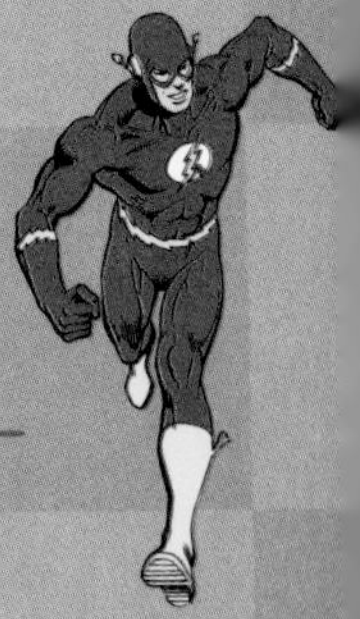

12 The ________ is the Fastest Man Alive.

13 With her super senses, Wonder Woman can ________ even the quietest of sounds.

14 When wrapped in Wonder Woman's Lasso of Truth, it is impossible to tell ________.

16 Captain Cold has a special weapon that shoots ________.

19 Using her trusty motorcycle helps Batgirl get to crime scenes before it is too late. She's always on ________.

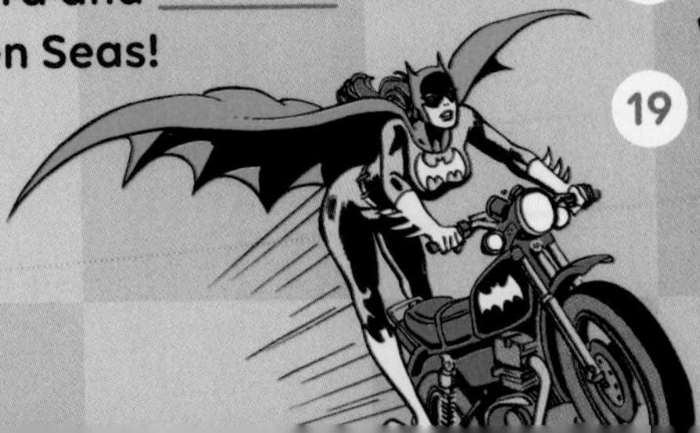

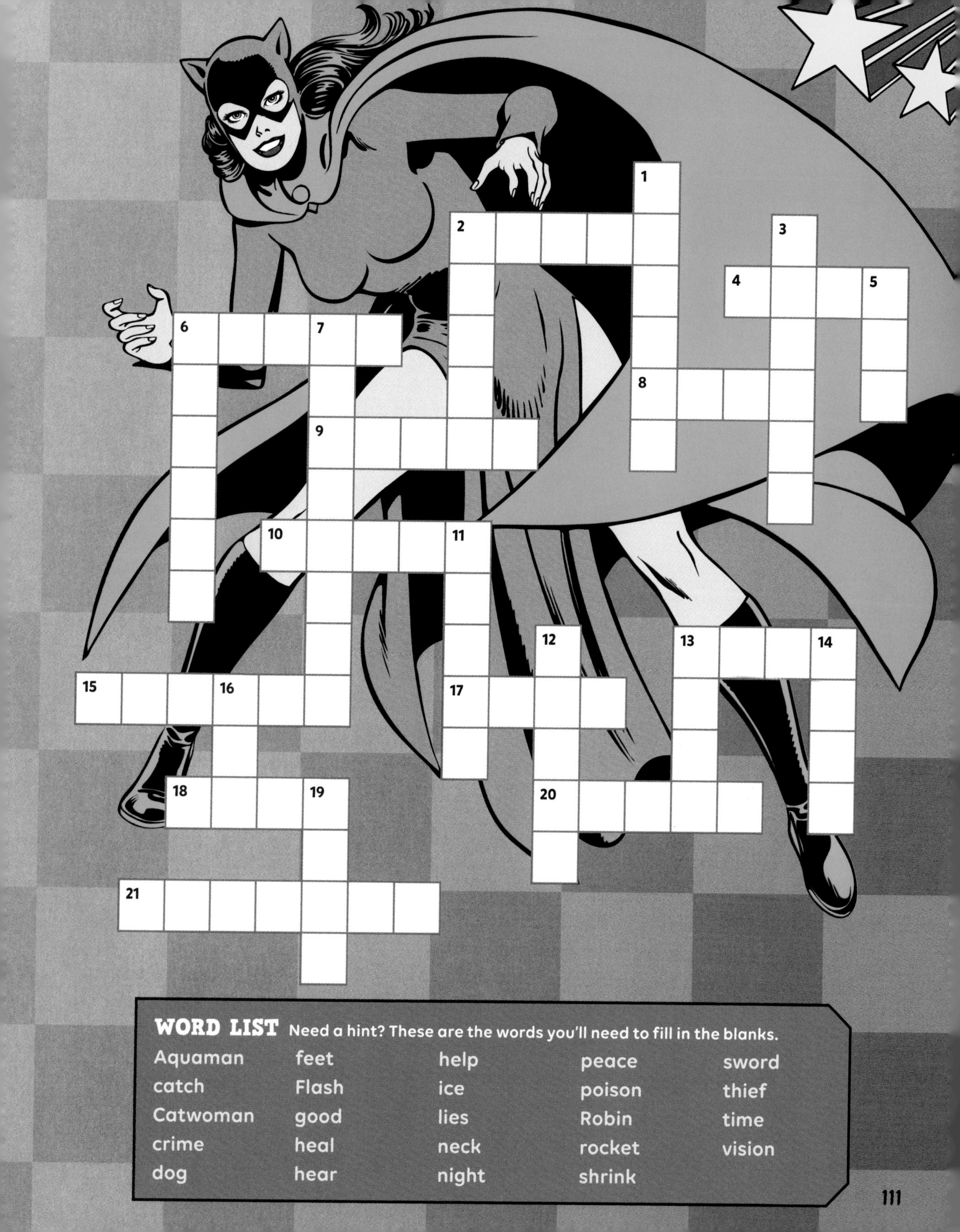
1 2 3 4 5 6 7 8 9 10 11 12 13 14 15 16 17 18 19 20 21

WORD LIST Need a hint? These are the words you'll need to fill in the blanks.

Aquaman	feet	help	peace	sword
catch	Flash	ice	poison	thief
Catwoman	good	lies	Robin	time
crime	heal	neck	rocket	vision
dog	hear	night	shrink	

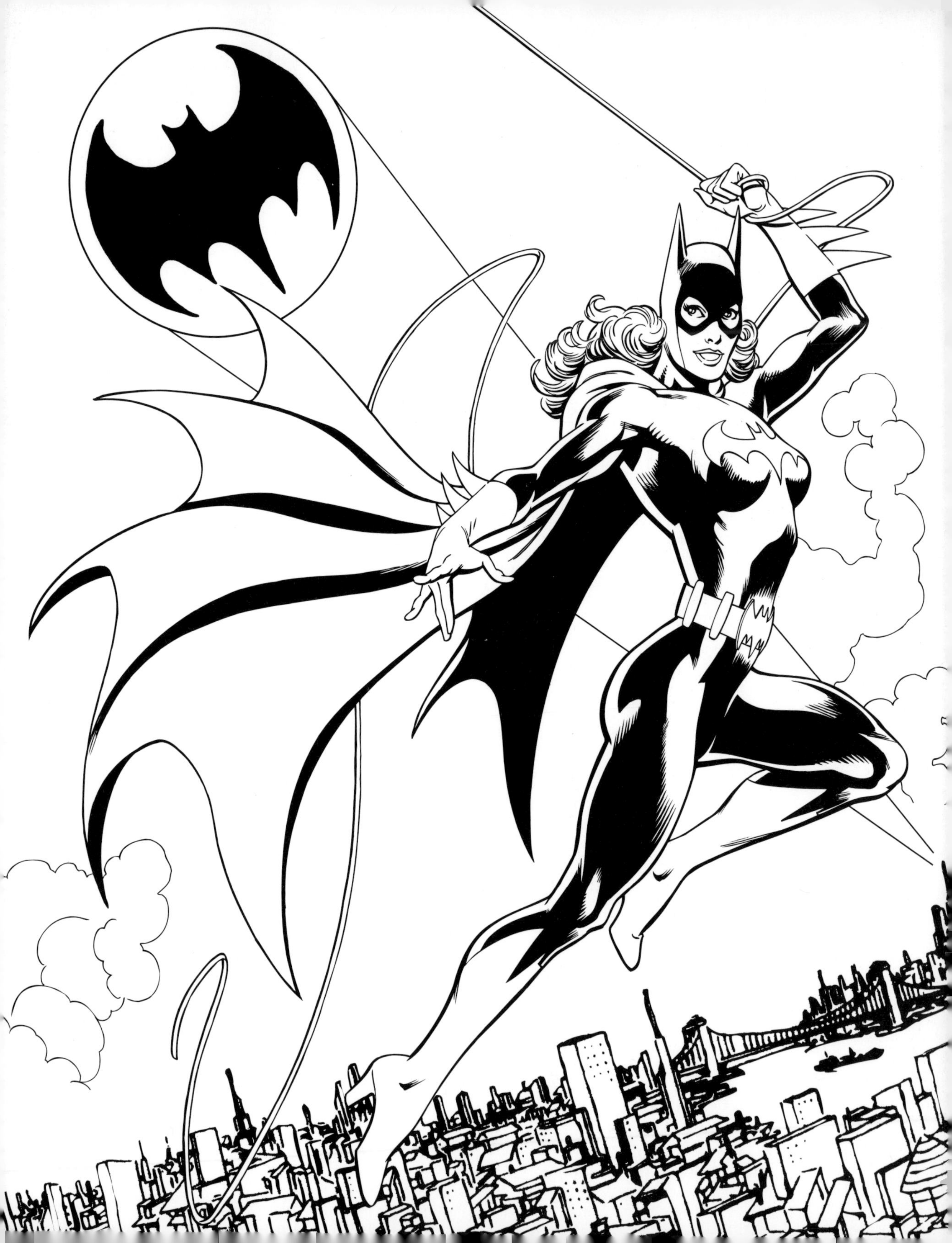

Wonder Woman Word Search

Wonder Woman has many incredible superpowers. She is also a strong, kind, smart woman. Here are 12 words that describe this amazing super hero.

bold	confident	fearless	invincible
brainy	courageous	generous	kind
caring	daring	gutsy	strong

Can you find them all? They can go up, down, forward, backward, or diagonally.

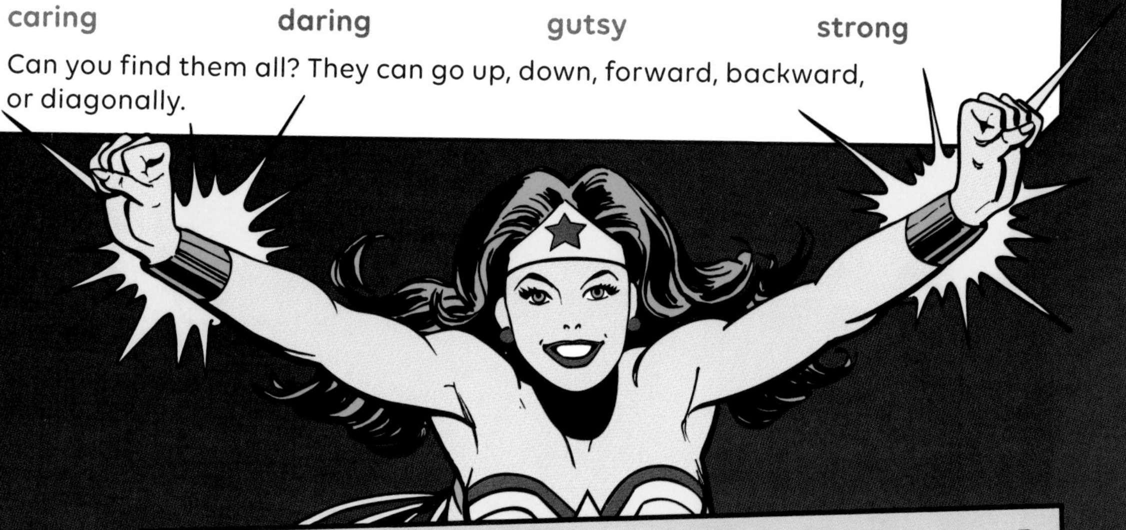

A	E	L	B	I	C	N	I	V	N	I	Q	S	H	I
Q	R	I	F	R	U	Y	X	G	Y	F	Y	W	O	J
U	O	P	M	E	E	S	J	N	U	F	T	A	Y	U
J	I	U	E	W	T	E	I	O	Y	G	J	S	N	R
I	C	D	O	S	L	A	O	R	S	E	T	U	E	T
S	A	E	D	I	R	P	X	T	A	U	R	O	H	Y
T	R	T	C	B	O	L	D	S	G	I	V	E	F	P
Y	I	K	U	D	T	K	A	K	Y	L	U	G	E	U
I	N	E	Y	F	E	A	R	L	E	S	S	A	B	K
U	G	P	L	I	G	H	I	U	S	I	A	R	I	A
R	W	F	O	R	E	Q	N	J	C	D	E	U	P	D
S	H	K	A	Z	F	D	G	E	N	E	R	O	U	S
G	A	O	P	I	T	N	H	R	V	O	Y	C	V	X
U	I	C	O	N	F	I	D	E	N	T	L	E	I	W
T	U	R	Q	Y	E	K	E	U	O	D	Q	U	A	Y

New and Improved?

Wonder Women is trying out a new look. But her clothes aren't the only things changing. Can you find 8 differences in the second version of the picture?

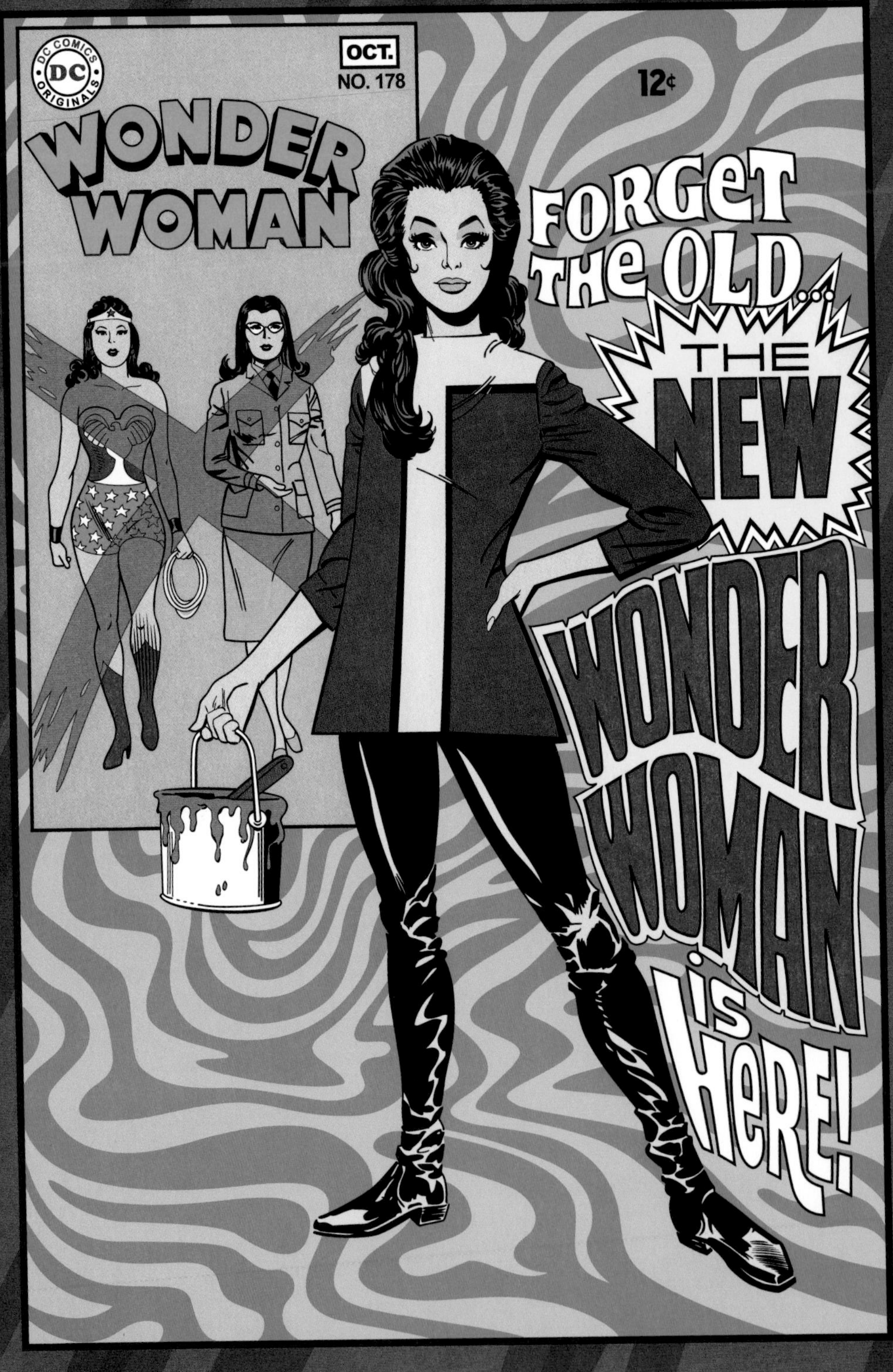

DC COMICS ORIGINALS DC
OCT.
NO. 178
WONDER WOMAN
12¢
FORGET THE OLD...
THE NEW
WONDER WOMAN IS HERE!

Writing Warm-Up

Harness your creative might and show off your descriptive powers!

What are 5 words that describe Batgirl?

Name 5 things that Batgirl does really well.

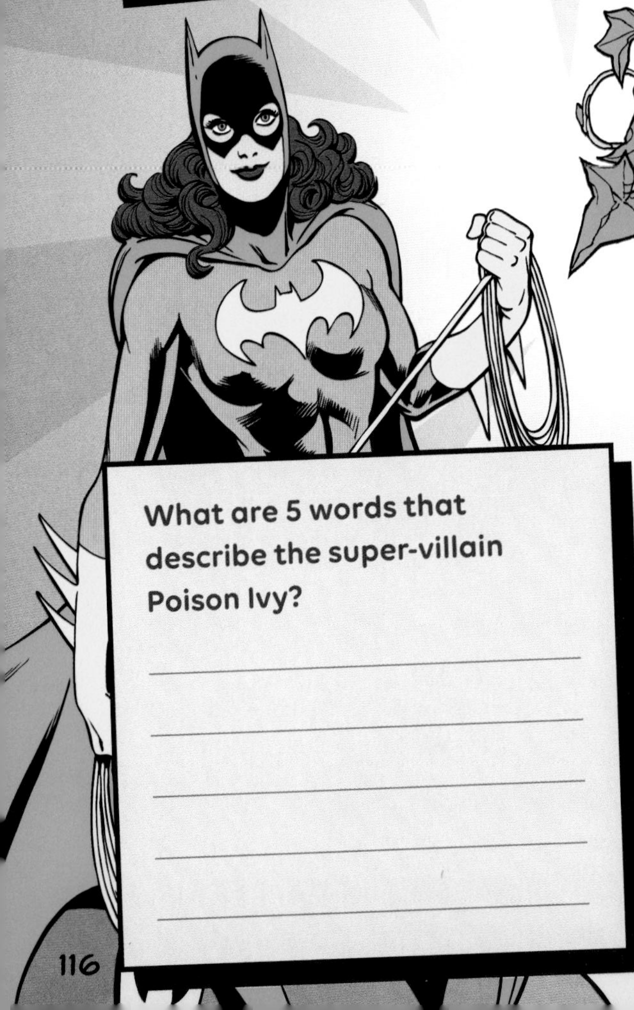

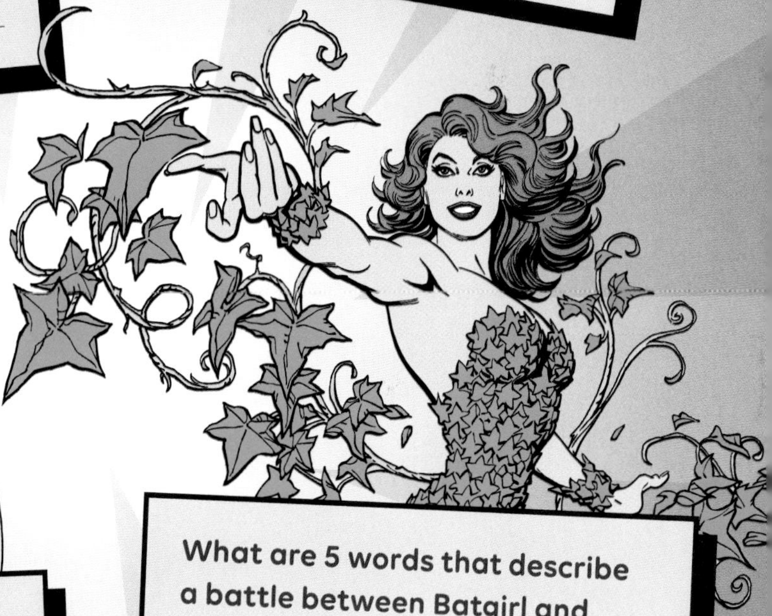

What are 5 words that describe the super-villain Poison Ivy?

What are 5 words that describe a battle between Batgirl and Poison Ivy?

Trace the Pattern

Follow the pattern on the right to get through this pattern maze. You can go right, left, up, or down—but not diagonally. Look out for Harley Quinn and the Joker!

THE PATTERN

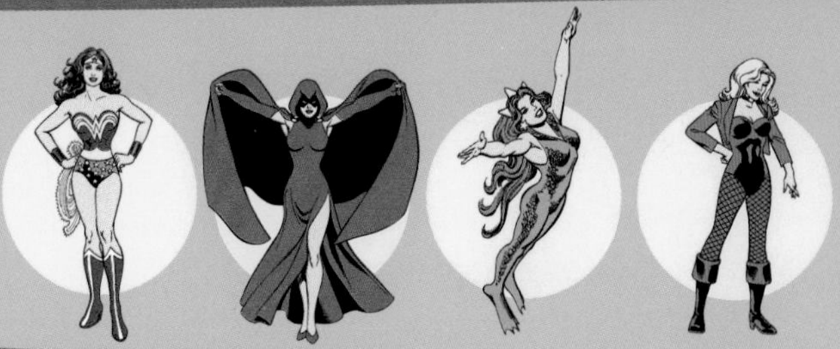

START

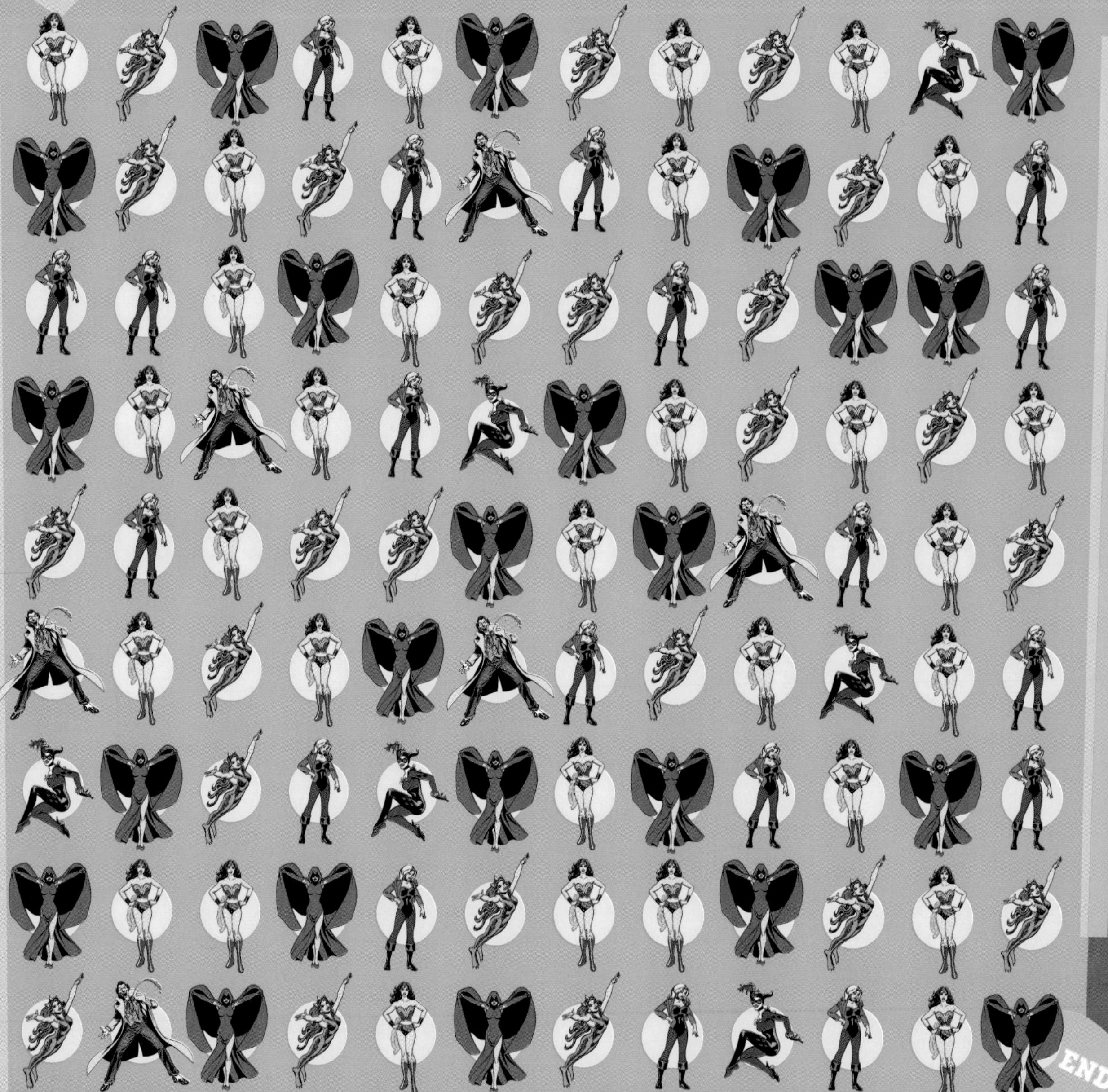

END

Seek and Find

How strong is your sense of sight?

SCAN THIS PICTURE AND SEE IF YOU CAN FIND:

1 VEIL

2 KANGAROOS

3 SWORDS

1 BOOK

4 LASSOS

6 BLUE STARS

1 RED LIGHTNING BOLT

1 BATTLE-AX

1 PLAID SUIT

8 YELLOW BOOTS

1 PAIR OF GLASSES

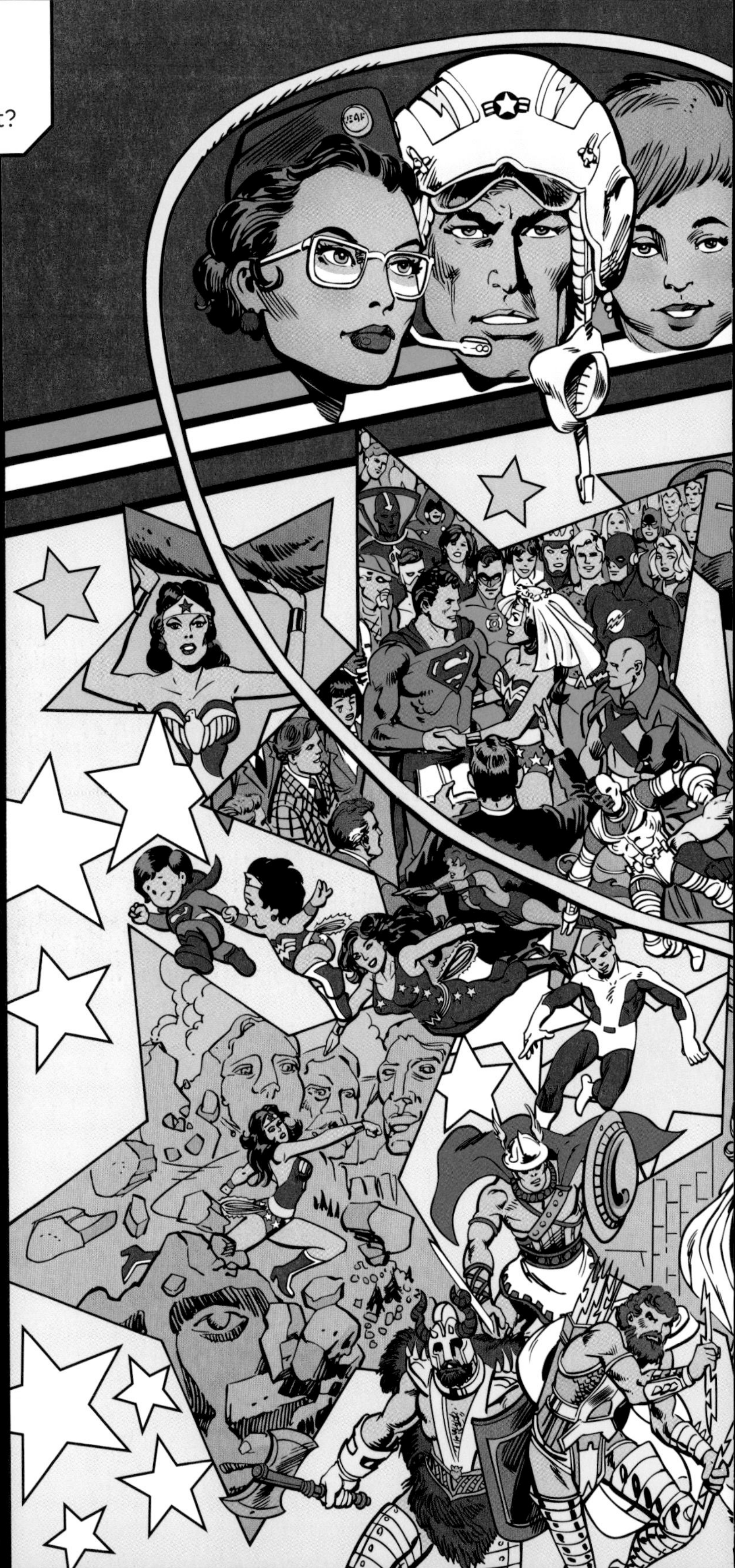

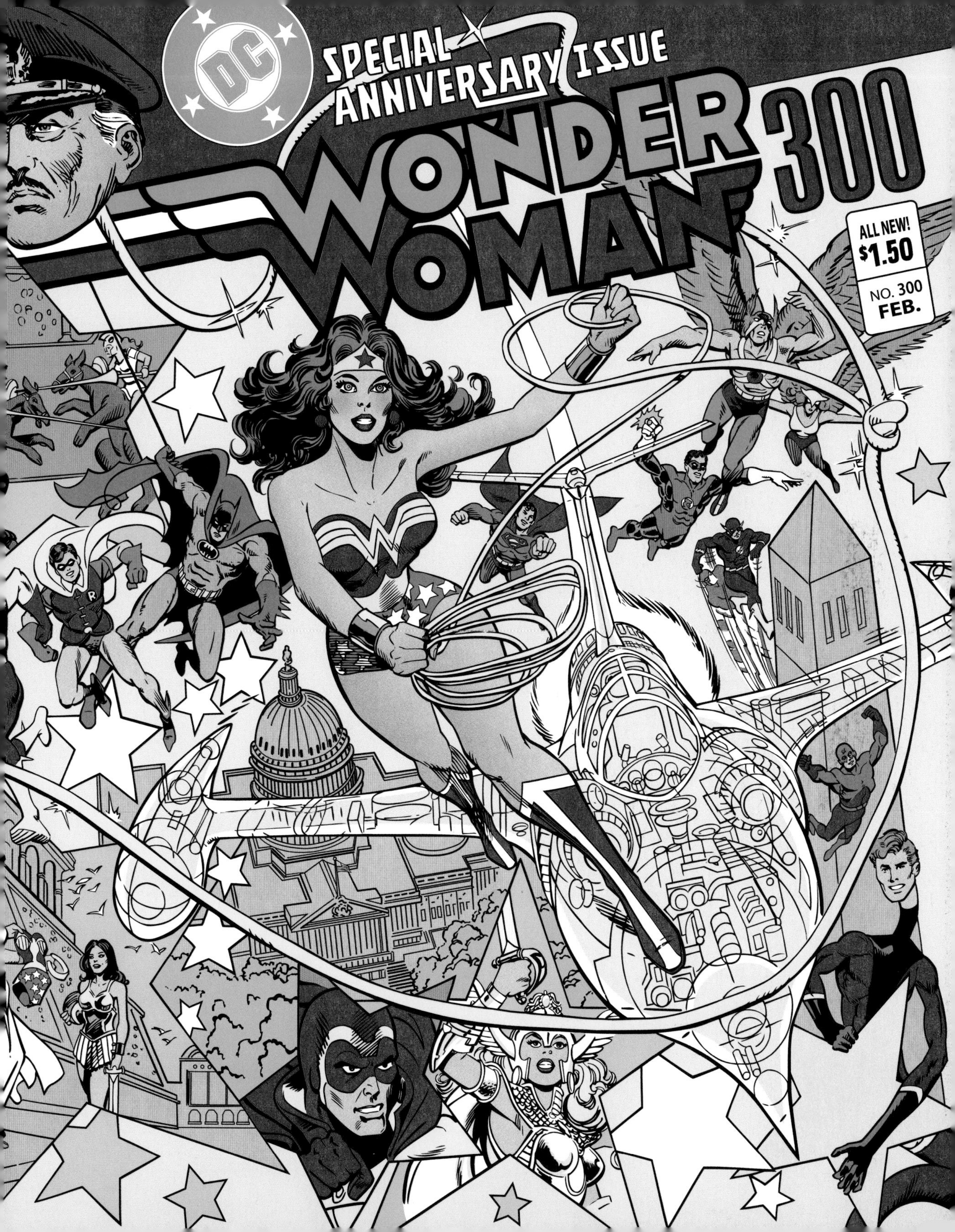

DC
SPECIAL ANNIVERSARY ISSUE
WONDER WOMAN
300
ALL NEW!
$1.50
NO. 300
FEB.

Letter Smash!

Each of the words below contains three extra letters. Channel your inner martial artist and karate chop out the three unnecessary letters to reveal the names of super heroes and super-villains.

TSUPIERGZIRL

CRYHEGETAH

MOELRAI

IKALTANGA

WRAIVTEN

AJOKSERS

BOARTGFIRL

CROALBIN

STUIPERMBAN

DHARFLEYQUTINN

ABUMOBLEBREE

COATSWORMAN

The Name Game

In this type of acrostic, the first letter of each line spells out a word or message. Use some of your favorite super heroes' names to make acrostics.

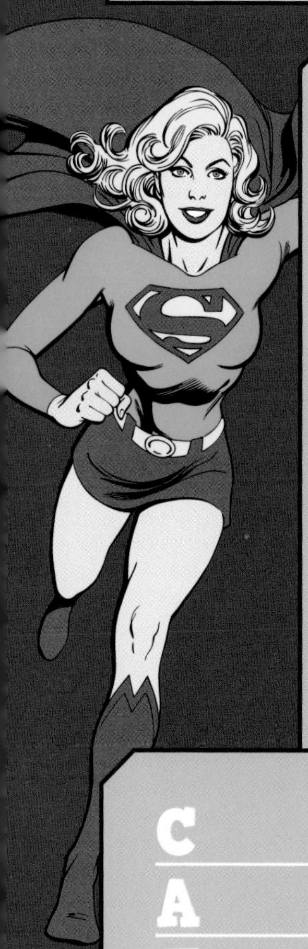

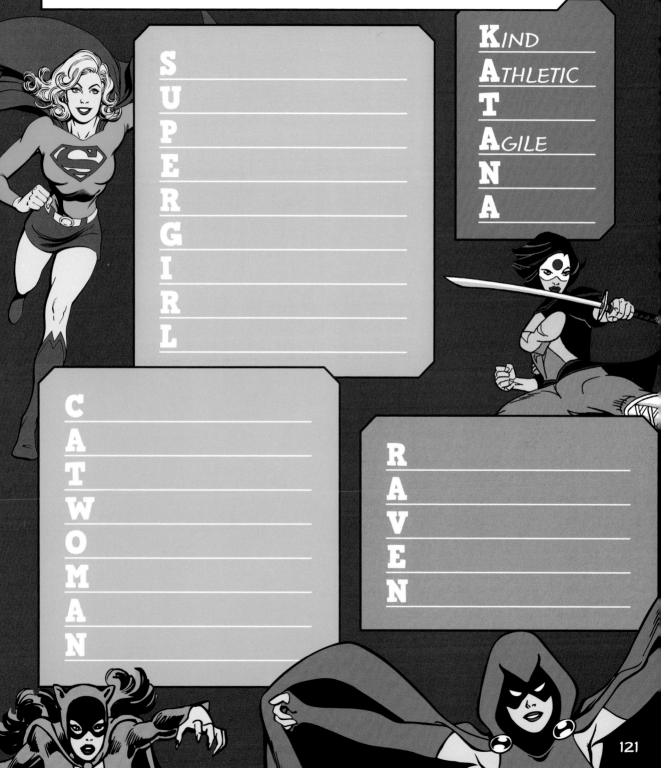

S ____________________
U ____________________
P ____________________
E ____________________
R ____________________
G ____________________
I ____________________
R ____________________
L ____________________

KIND
ATHLETIC
T ____________________
AGILE
N ____________________
A ____________________

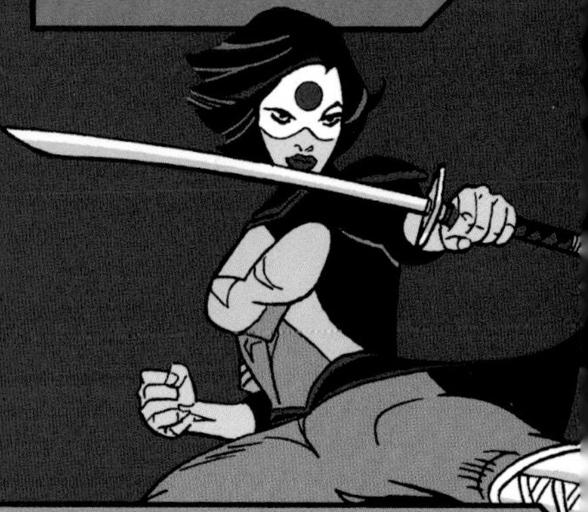

C ____________________
A ____________________
T ____________________
W ____________________
O ____________________
M ____________________
A ____________________
N ____________________

R ____________________
A ____________________
V ____________________
E ____________________
N ____________________

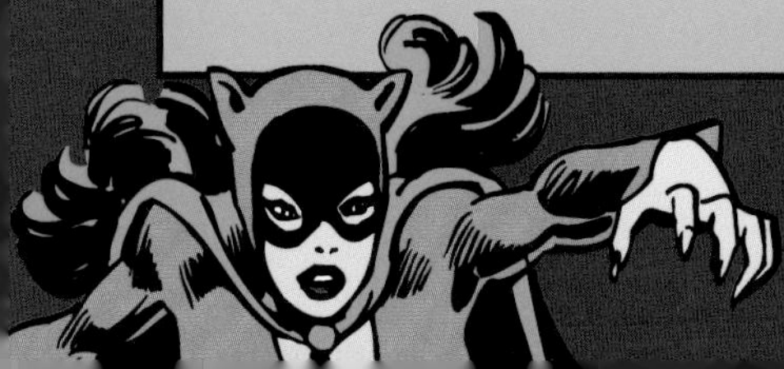

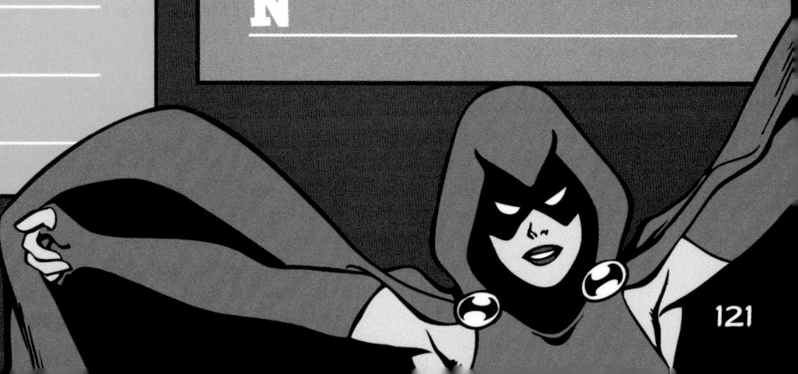

Puzzling Pathways!

Draw a line that connects each pair of identical pictures. You can draw lines horizontally and vertically, but not diagonally. Make sure no lines cross. When you are done, every box in the grid will have either a line or a picture in it.

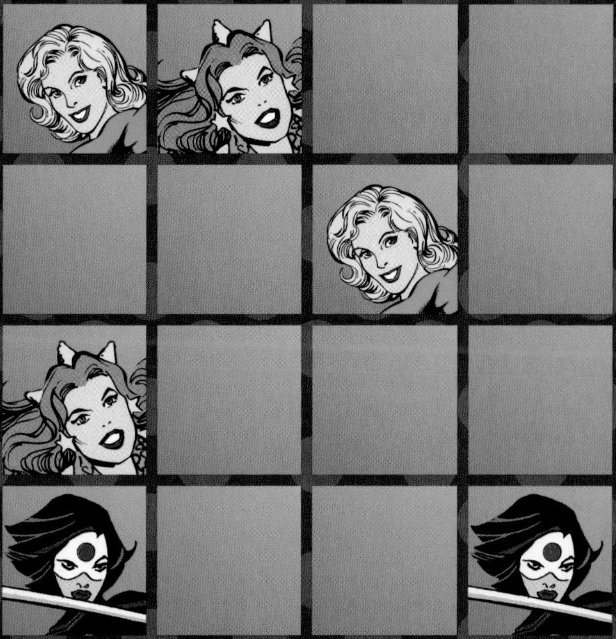

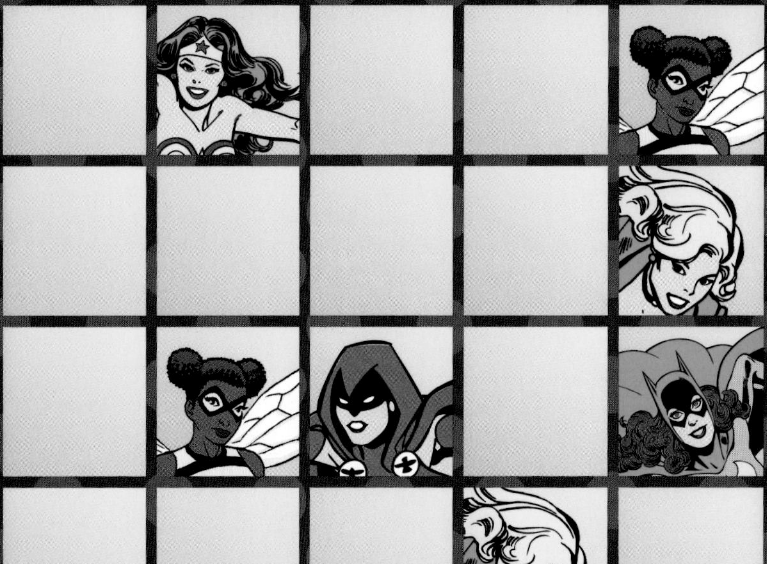

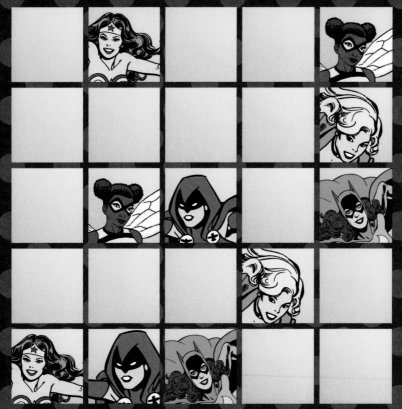

Mind the Magic

Zatanna is more than just a stage magician. Her magic is real! Can you find all the magic words in the grid below? They can go up, down, forward, backward, or diagonally.

WORD LIST

abracadabra
bewitching
charm
enchantment
hocus pocus
illusions
mystical
sorcery
spells
trance
trick
wizard

```
W I E R Y S N O I S U L L I T
G F T A L U A J F C L I A H R
O E D L O H S W I Z A R D F I
U M E Z Q I N K L E Y K E N C
L P A U S E P M C I X W N Y K
S R G B D S O R C E R Y C S A
U T Y E R H J A E A F V H M T
C O K W O A Z H C P Q I A I C
O E P I S D C C M O D P N H U
P U Y T O T R A N C E G T Y O
S L U C R W I J D V B E M L R
U Q G H F I N T U A D X E I S
C A S I E O Y U X N B P N H J
O K R N A T R I G O B R T U E
H I Y G M Y S T I C A L A Q H
```

Unmask the Imposter!

Something has shifted in one of these pictures. Find the altered hero.

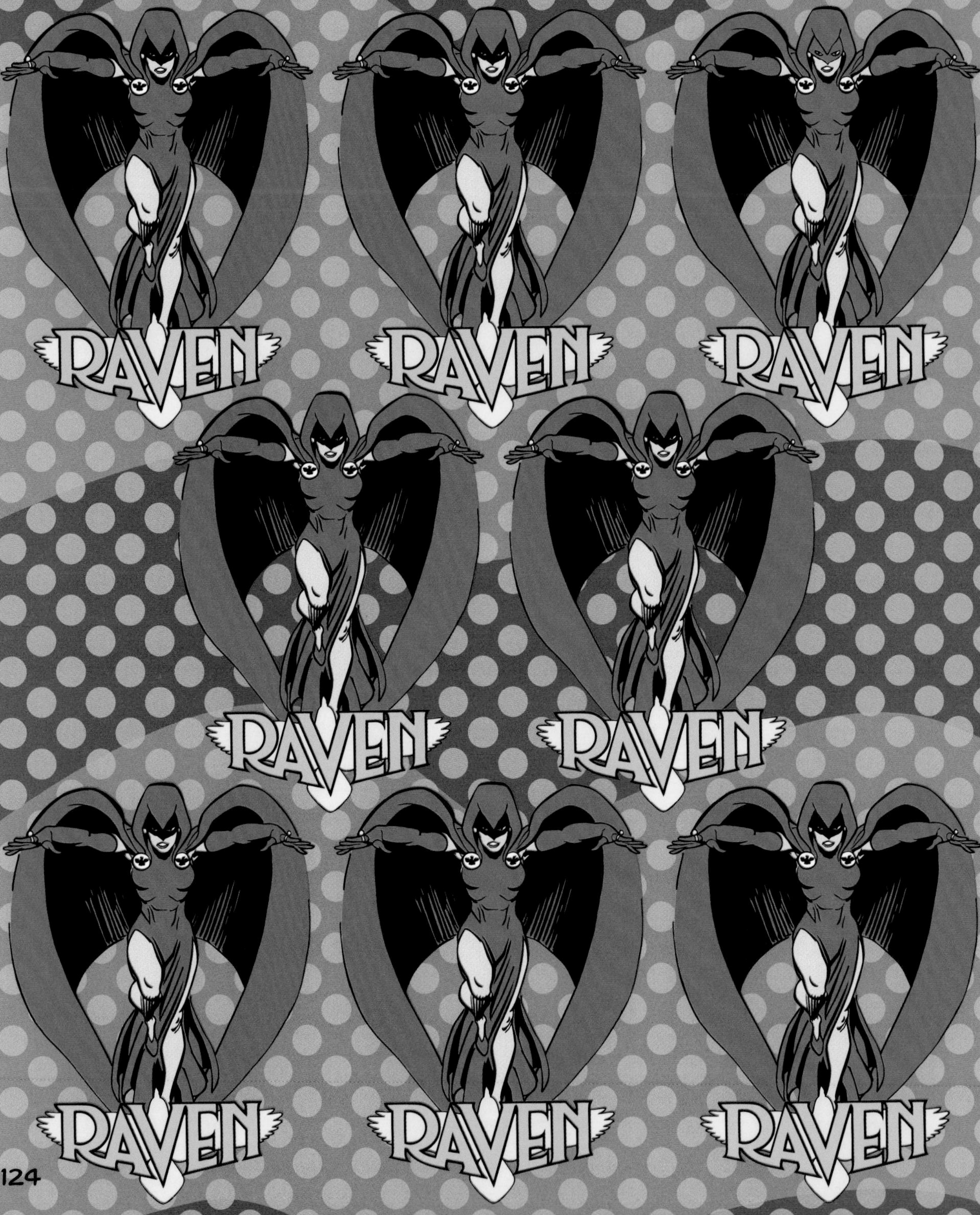
RAVEN
RAVEN
RAVEN
RAVEN
RAVEN
RAVEN
RAVEN
RAVEN

Spot the Missing Letters?

This alphabet is incomplete! Figure out which letters do not appear on this page at all. Rearrange the missing letters to reveal one special super hero's name. Then find all the letters that appear three times each. Rearrange them to reveal one of this super hero's powers.

P G W C X D O
O B L P
I M K U F J M
K H T H B S
B C L Y F O Y Z
T Y H Q G
I B L I
T F G

MISSING LETTERS:
_____

SUPER HERO NAME:
_____

LETTERS THAT APPEAR THREE TIMES EACH:
_____

ONE OF THE HERO'S SUPERPOWERS:
_____

Identify the Villain

Wonder Woman has tracked a troublemaker to the circus. Follow the clues to figure out which ne'er-do-well is planning to disrupt the big top.

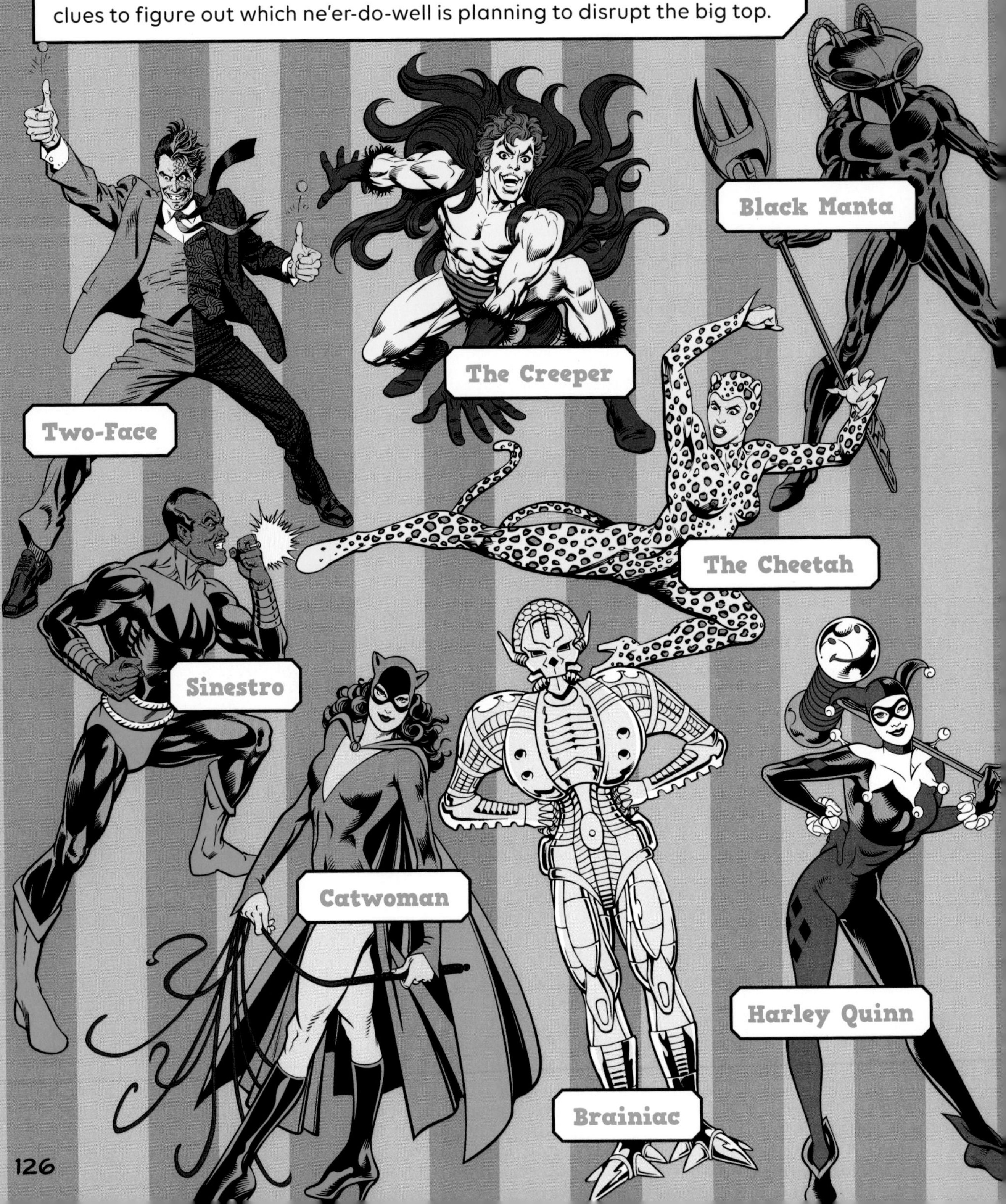
Black Manta
The Creeper
Two-Face
The Cheetah
Sinestro
Catwoman
Harley Quinn
Brainiac

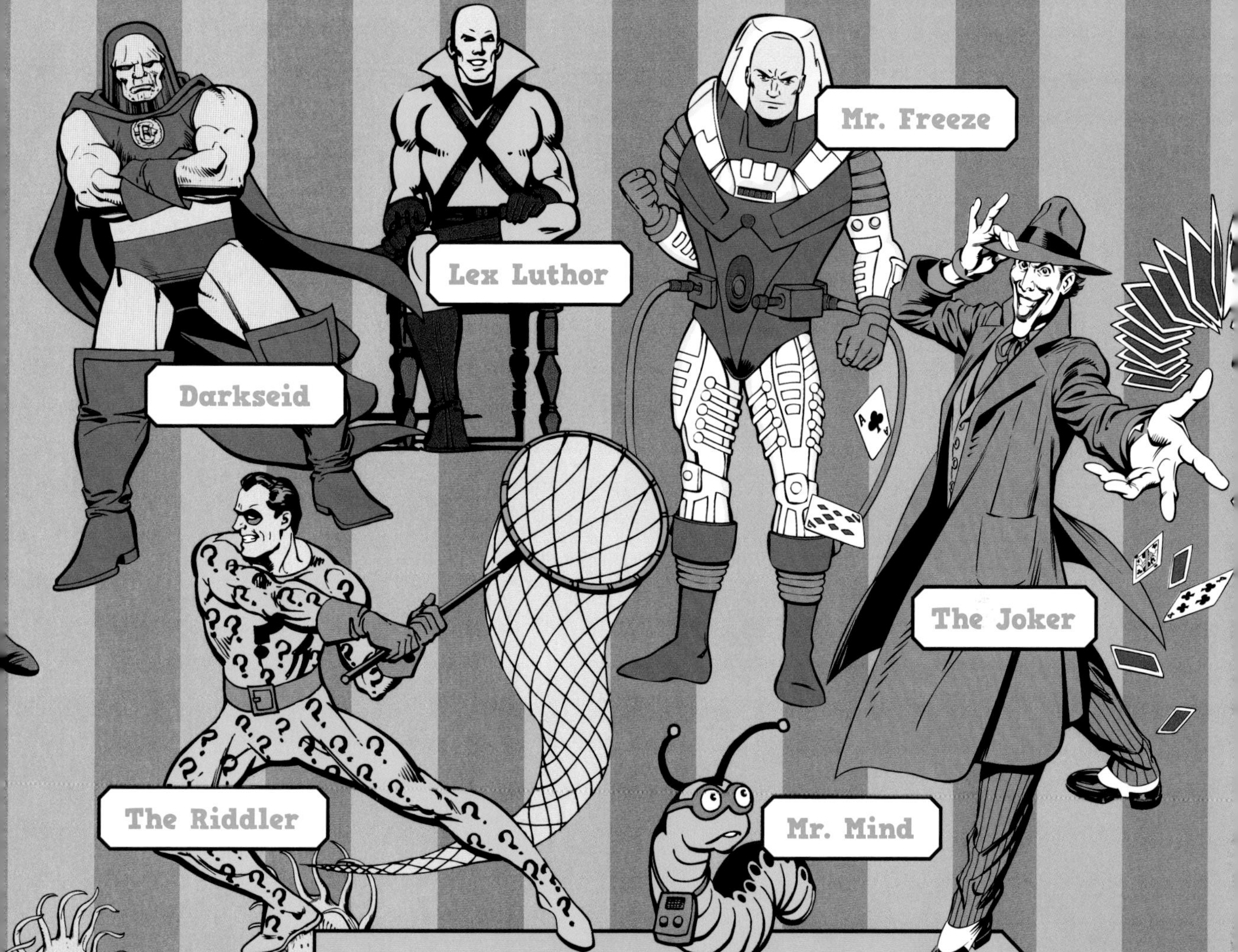
Darkseid
Lex Luthor
Mr. Freeze
The Joker
The Riddler
Mr. Mind

This villain has arms.

This villain is not wearing a cape.

This villain is not sitting down.

This villain's head is covered in some way.

This villain is not wearing blue boots.

This villain does not have a tail.

This villain is not throwing anything.

This villain is smiling. Who is it?

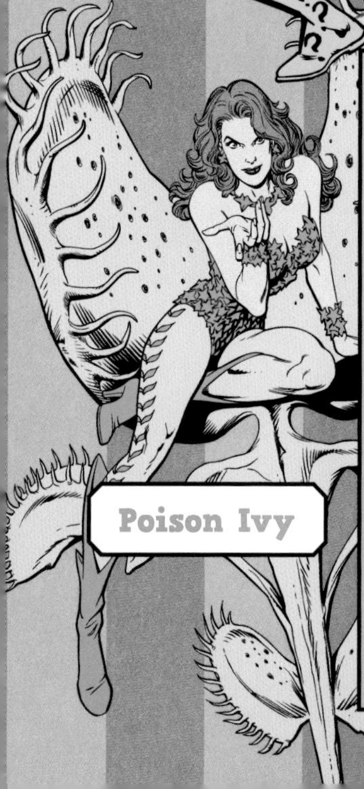
Poison Ivy

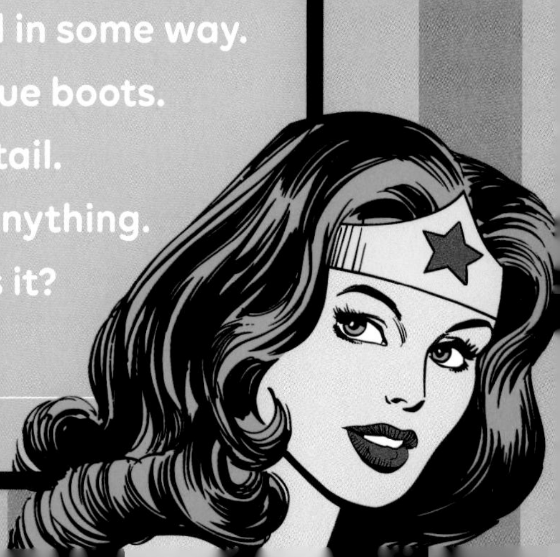

What's Up with Batgirl?

Look at the picture and use your imagination. How did Batgirl end up here? And what on Earth is going on?

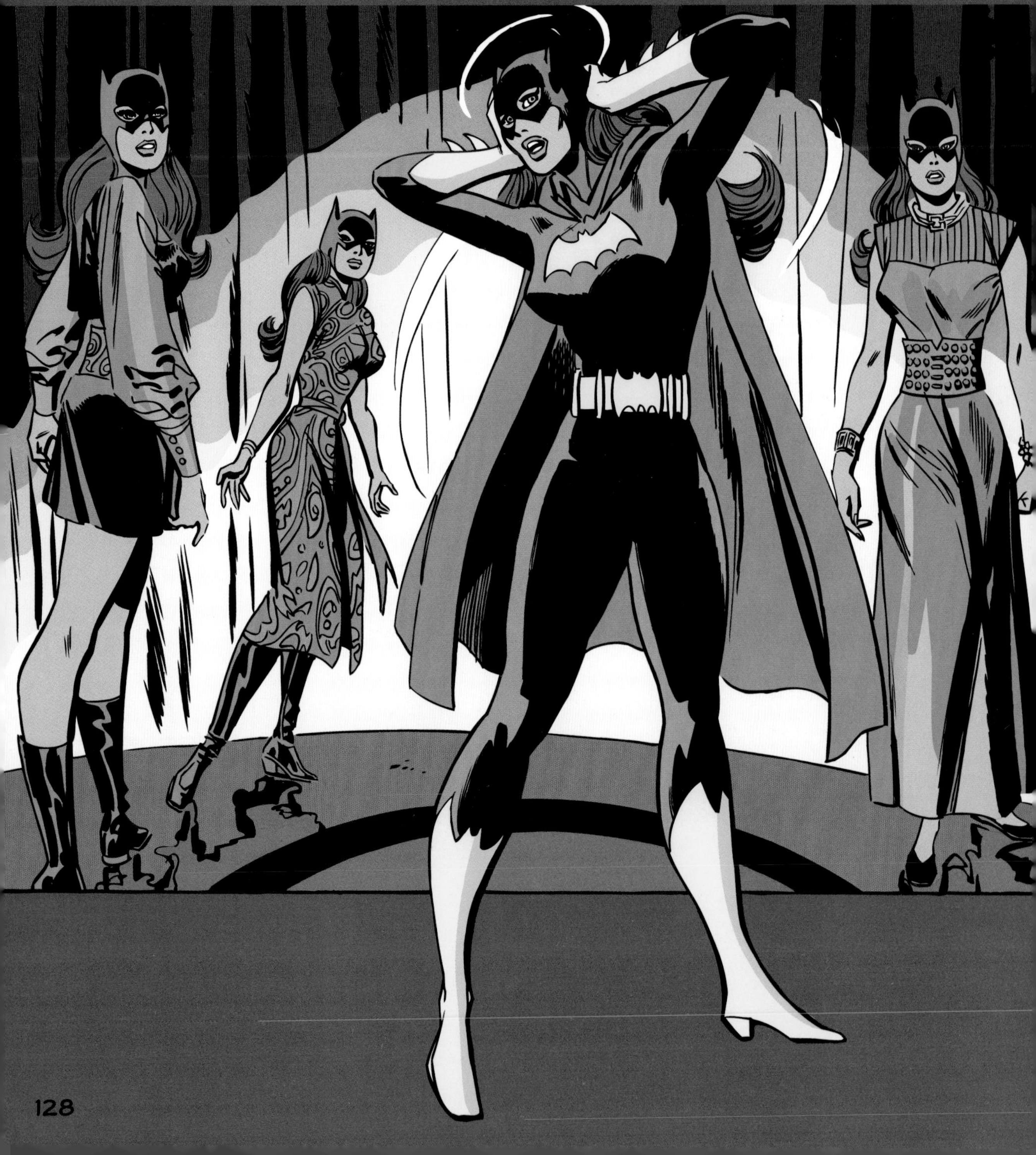

BATGIRL

Acrostic Builder

To make these acrostics, add a word or phrase to each line that describes the super hero or mischievous villain. The big white letters do not have to be the first letters of the words you add.

TRI**C**KY
FIG**H**TS WONDER WOMAN
SN**E**AKY
E
T
A
H

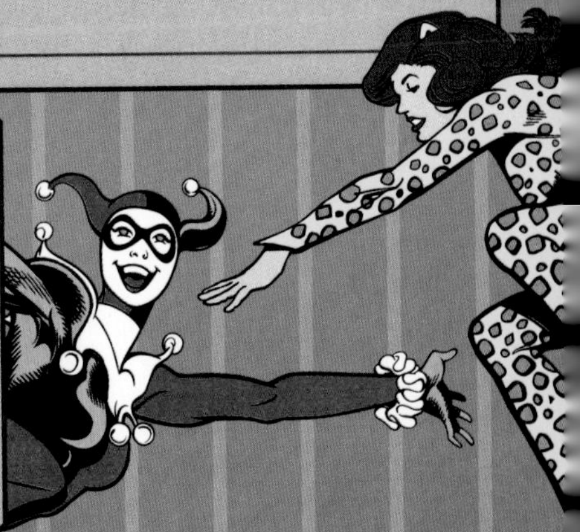

H
A
R
L
E
Y

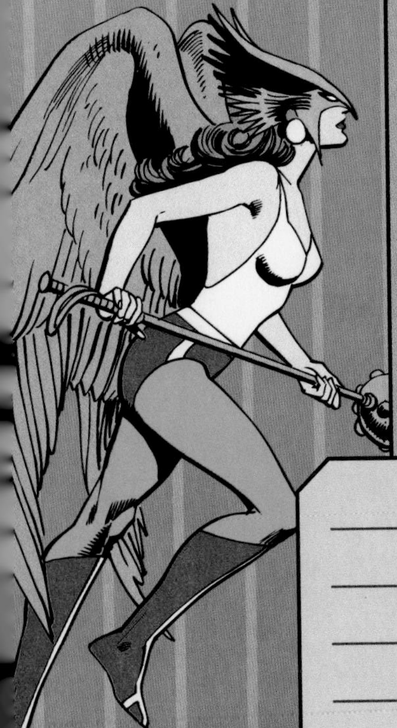

H
A
W
K
G
I
R
L

B
A
T
M
A
N

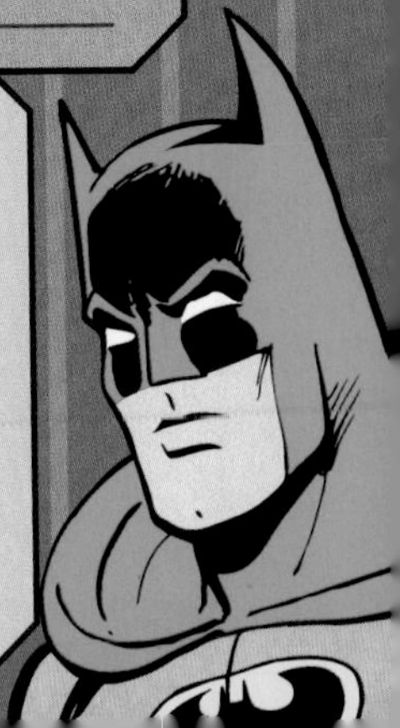

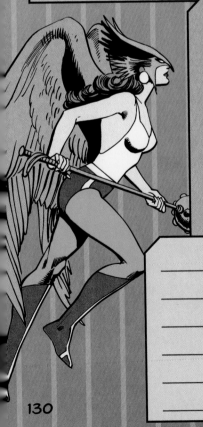

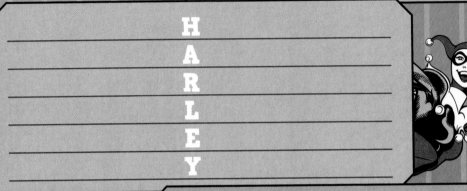

How Sharp Is Your Memory?

Study this comic cover for 30 seconds. Then turn the page and see how many questions you can answer correctly.

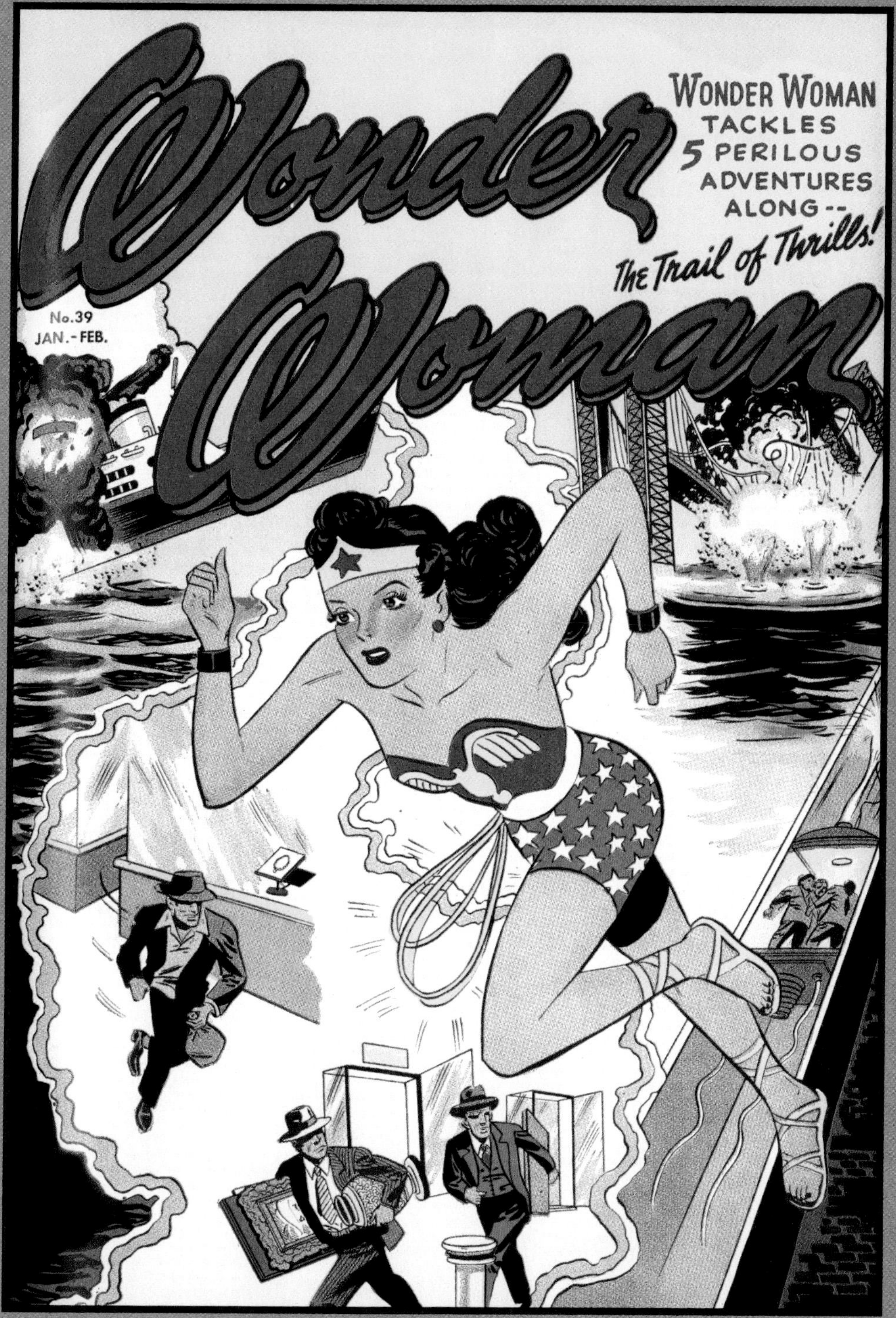

Wonder Woman
WONDER WOMAN TACKLES 5 PERILOUS ADVENTURES ALONG --
The Trail of Thrills!
No.39
JAN.-FEB.

Are You a Quick Study?

Answer the questions below based on the picture on page 131.

1. How many people are on the cover?

a. One

b. Two

c. Seven

d. Ten

2. What is Wonder Woman holding in her hand?

a. A fan

b. Her lasso

c. A tennis racket

d. Nothing

3. Which disaster is NOT happening in the picture?

a. A falling elevator

b. A runaway train

c. An explosion on a ship

d. A collapsing bridge

4. What is Wonder Woman wearing on her feet?

a. Red boots

b. Gold sandals

c. Black sandals

d. Winged slippers

5. Are the robbers wearing hats?

a. No.

b. Only one robber is wearing a hat.

c. Two robbers are wearing baseball caps.

d. All three robbers are wearing hats.

6. Inside the comic, Wonder Woman will tackle five perilous adventures along what?

a. The Trail of Threats!

b. The Trail of Teens!

c. The Trail of Thrills!

d. The Trail of Terrors!

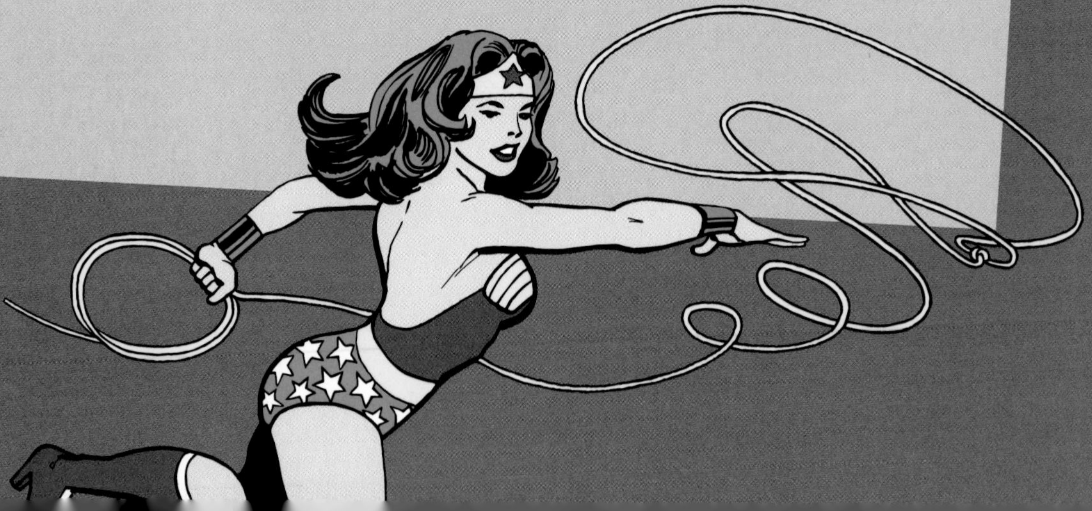

A True Detective

During the day, Batgirl is Barbara **Gordon**, daughter of the **police** commissioner. She works in a **library**, helps people in the community, and hones her **research** skills. She's a computer **genius**, but she isn't afraid to ditch the desk and hop right into the **action**. A talented **fighter** and **dedicated** martial artist, she has taken on countless **criminals** and super-villains. She often fights crime alongside Batman and **Robin**. She races through **Gotham** City on her **Batcycle**, wearing a **Utility Belt** filled with the latest gadgets and Batarangs, always ready to **protect** people and **prevent** disasters. Three cheers for Batgirl! Now, can you find all the bold words in the grid? They can go up, down, forward, backward, or diagonally.

U	G	E	Z	O	H	S	U	B	E	D	K	Y	T	I
B	M	O	N	A	S	L	A	N	I	M	I	R	C	N
O	P	R	T	X	D	E	D	I	C	A	T	E	D	K
L	O	E	T	H	L	I	M	U	J	G	O	S	A	F
N	L	D	I	L	A	S	F	H	A	E	Y	E	K	U
F	I	R	A	U	E	M	E	N	L	N	E	A	S	A
I	C	B	S	X	V	B	Q	C	Y	I	Y	R	O	I
G	E	W	O	Y	O	A	Y	R	R	U	R	C	E	S
H	S	G	I	R	A	C	T	T	Y	S	A	H	T	G
T	E	Y	A	P	T	C	A	F	I	I	R	U	E	Q
E	O	R	Q	A	E	F	I	C	D	L	B	A	U	Y
R	G	Z	B	T	A	E	T	J	T	S	I	F	O	C
A	O	H	O	J	U	H	U	O	B	I	L	T	F	R
U	I	R	N	O	D	R	O	G	A	C	O	E	U	H
Q	P	I	X	E	O	S	P	R	E	V	E	N	T	U

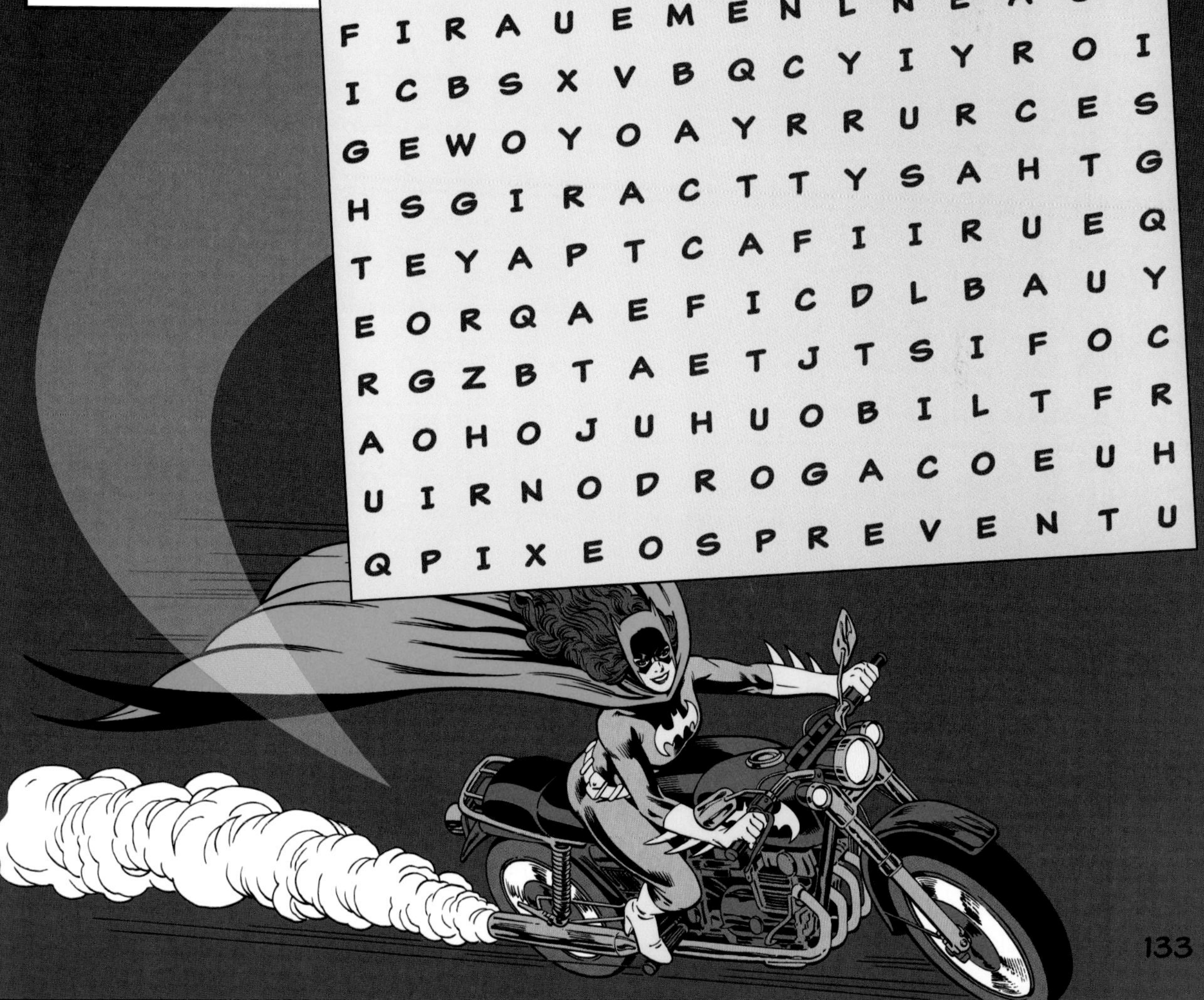

answer key

p. 4 **Which Wonder Woman?**

The decoration on Wonder Woman's top is connected to her belt.

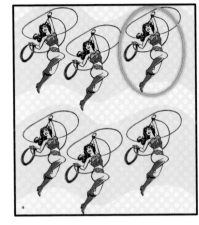

p. 5 **Bumblebee's Word Ladder**

BEES
SEES
SE**T**S
NETS
N**U**TS
OUTS
O**A**TS
OAT**H**
BATH
BAT**S**

p. 6 **Master the Pattern**

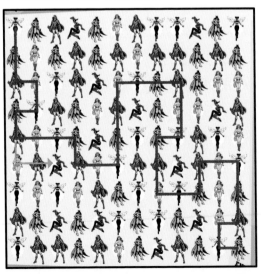

p. 7 **Time to Rhyme**

1. book
2. look
3. shook
4. crook
5. yearbook
6. cook

p. 8–9 **Upon Further Reflection . . .**

GREAT HERA! --MY OWN REFLECTIONS ARE COMING OUT OF THE MIRRORS TO BATTLE ME!
"MENACE OF THE MIRROR WONDER WOMEN!"

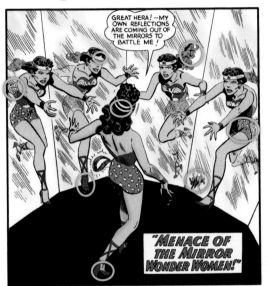

p. 10 **Perplexing Paths!**

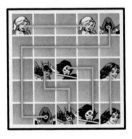

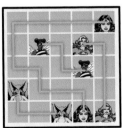

p. 14 **How Do You Say "Word Search" in Tamaranean?**

F H R F A E N D E J Z I M A E
E E H I M A E S E N M M S W E
O R C S M A E S K F A E N G S
B G N R A P S T E S N U D I H
E R E U I X C A Q N D I I W S
S G R E E C U R H I A P S O F
L J F I L G Y A R E R P W O P
E E F I S P A B D A I I A G E
J F R E N G L I S H N E H J P
E G U I H N L C A R A P I E A
E S S P O R I Z Z E I R L U R
O K S P A N I S H J R O I I F
S W I A A G U C H I N D I A D
O T A S P N E P A J O P N I H
M A N D I P O R T U G U E S E

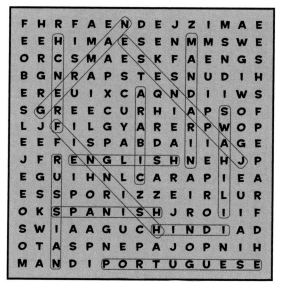

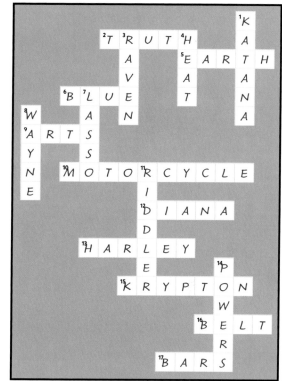

p. 16–17 **After Him!**

Raven catches up with Black Adam.

p. 18–19 **Crossword Showdown!**

1 KATANA
2 TRUTH
3 RAVEN
4 HEAT
5 EARTH
6 BLUE
7 LASSO
8 WAYNE
9 ARTS
10 MOTORCYCLE
11 RIDDLER
12 DIANA
13 HARLEY
14 POWER
15 KRYPTON
16 BELT
17 BARS

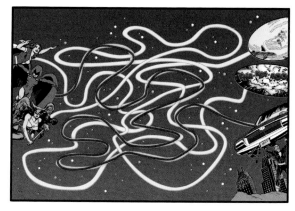

p. 20–21 **Decode the Jokes!**

She's never stressed in her nest.

Purr-adise Island

A cloak who croaks

Because he was barking up the wrong bee.

p. 22 **Symbol Strategy**

Puzzle 1

x
= 21
= 5
= 3
= 7

Puzzle 2

= 5
= 4
= 16

Puzzle 3

= 3
= 6
= 2

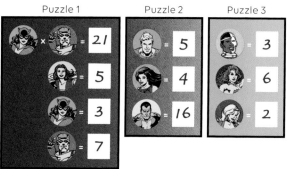

answer key

p. 24 **How Does Your Memory Stack Up?**

1. **b.** Two
2. **c.** Purple
3. **a.** One
4. **d.** None
5. **d.** Smoke from the wreck
6. **a.** He is surprised.
7. **d.** Metallo
8. **a.** Yellow
9. **b.** Is she friend or foe?
10. **c.** 10 cents

p. 25 **Climb the Word Ladder**

SAFE
CAFE
CAVE
CAP**E**
CA**P**S
CATS
MAT**S**
MATH
B**A**TH
BOTH

p. 26–27 **Meet Mera!**

Q U P S Y O R R E A Y O T S F
A E I A Q U A M A N C L A W E
F Y U V I X S A D S W R U I H
I S D N O R K G Q U E E N M A
P E I A D Z I P I Z F D E O T
R V W G M E R A E U T N I K N
Z E U F S X R M L H E P J S A
R N I O S B O W D I A M R E M
E S C D I T C E A S D J Z U K
A E W N T A P G U T N A Q K C
L A T O N Y J R H E E C O I A
E S A Q A U D S I M Z R T Y L
D I V E L M I E W P E V S M B
U W F G T F P X D E A G O O D
E Q S R A Y L I V R C I E X S

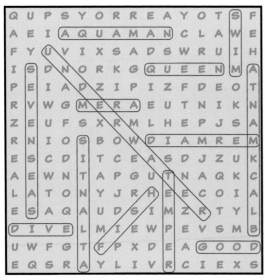

p. 32–33 **The Real Catwoman**

ROGUES' GALLERY
UNDERCOVER POLICE AGENTS
A·B·C
A·B·C
D·E·F
D·E·F
G·H·I
G·H·I

p. 35 **Supergirl to the Rescue!**

Supergirl should take path B.

A
B
C

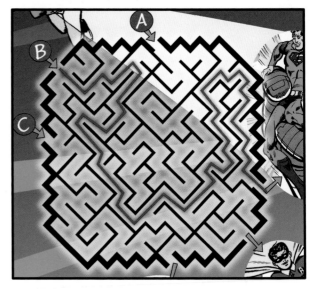

p. 38 Connect the Matches!

p. 39 Which Letters Are Missing?

MISSING LETTERS: E J K O R
SUPER-VILLAIN NAME: Joker

p. 40–41 Funny Fill-Ins

Yes, she puts the bat in combat.
In an arc-hive
No, she was just borrow-wing it.
The Lassoap of Truth

p. 42 One Wondrous Change

One of Wonder Girl's stars disappeared.

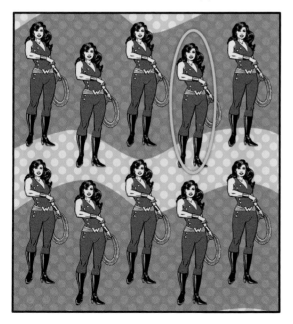

p. 43 Add 'Em Up!

Puzzle 1   Puzzle 2

p. 44 Watch Out for Dead Ends!

p. 46 Do You Have a Photographic Memory?

1. **d.** A crocodile
2. **d.** Seven
3. **b.** A shark
4. **a.** 10 cents
5. **b.** Wonder Woman
6. **c.** Orange
7. **b.** Airplane
8. **c.** "Wonder Woman's Scrapbook!"

answer key

p. 47 **Change a Letter, Build a Word**

REAL
HEA**L**
HEA**T**
HEAR
FEA**R**
FEA**T**
F**L**AT
FLA**P**
CLAP

p. 50 **One Letter at a Time!**

GOOD
FOOD
FO**L**D
COLD
COL**T**
BOLT
B**E**LT
BEL**L**
B**A**LL
TALL
TA**I**L

p. 52 **How Many?**

Puzzle 1 Puzzle 2 Puzzle 3

20
10
7
3
4
6
1
20
11
10

p. 53 **Spot the Standout**

One of Supergirl's cuffs has turned black.

p. 56–57 **Conquer this Crossword!**

1 CUFF
2 STRONG
3 GOTHAM
4 MAGIC
5 FAST
5 FRIEND
6 TEAM
7 CHEETAH
7 COMICS
8 BATMOBILE
9 AMAZONS
10 TIARA
11 SKY
12 FLY
13 PLANE

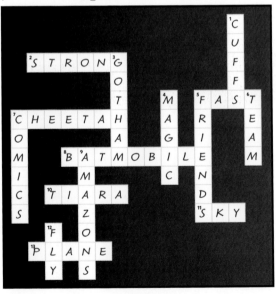

p. 58–59 **Count the Clues and You'll Know Who!**

There are **9** keys.

The Cheetah appears **9** times.

p. 60–61 **Arrows Ahoy!**

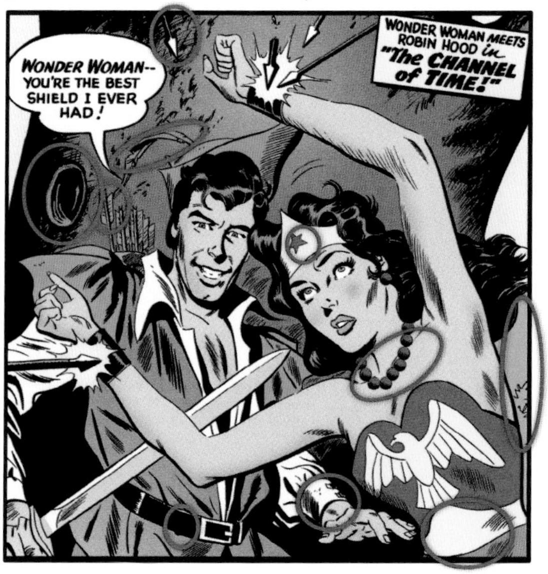
WONDER WOMAN-- YOU'RE THE BEST SHIELD I EVER HAD!
WONDER WOMAN MEETS ROBIN HOOD in "The CHANNEL of TIME!"

p. 62–63 **Which Way Should She Go?**

Wonder Woman should follow the purple arrow.

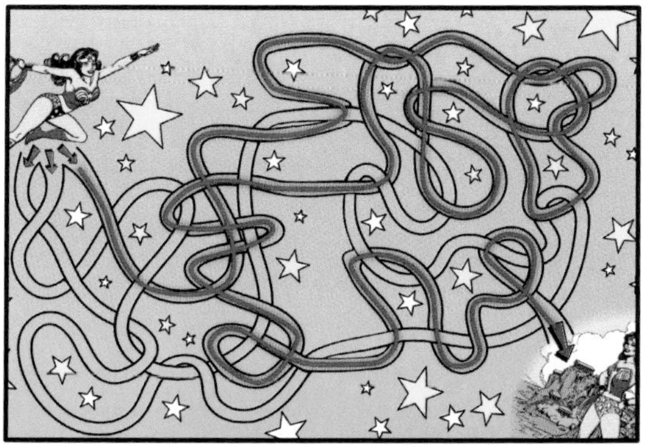

p. 64 **Pick the Lucky Path**

Batgirl gets through the maze.

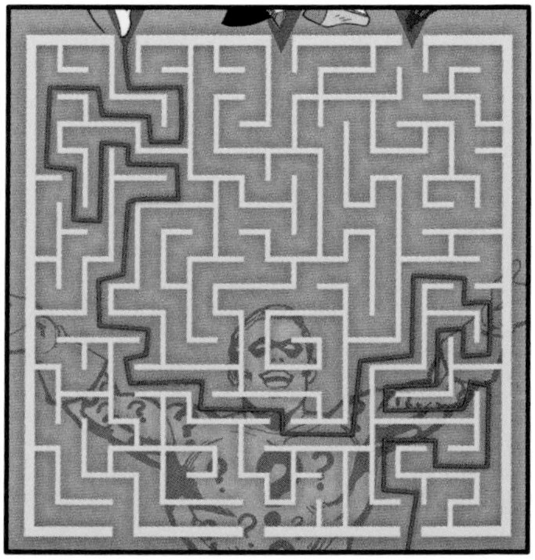

p. 66–67 **Identify the Mystery Hero**

The mystery hero is Wonder Woman.
She is holding the Lasso of Truth.

p. 68–69 **Comedy Code**

Romaine calm and lettuce handle the situation.

Because she doesn't know how to whistle

Swordfish

A high-flying hero with hex-ray vision

p. 70–71 **A Capitol Crime**

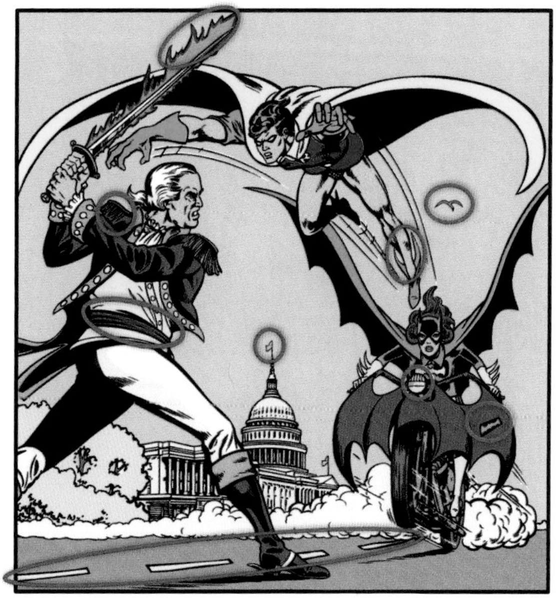

p. 73 **Paw-Some Kitten Maze**

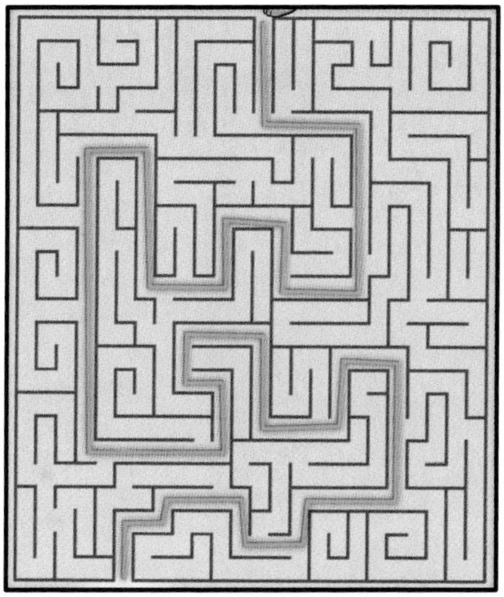

answer key

p. 74–75 **Crossword Challenge**

1 JAIL
1 JOKER
2 COMPUTER
3 NEWSPAPER
4 SUPERMAN
5 ARES
6 VOICE
7 PENGUIN
8 POLICE
9 INVISIBLE
10 SUIT
11 BUZZ
11 BIRD
12 BOOKS
13 KEY
14 MASK
15 CAPE
16 SIZES

p. 76 **Ready to Rhyme?**

choir	tire
vampire	hire
admire	liar
spire	fryer
high-wire	dryer
umpire	buyer
sapphire	higher

p. 77 **Spot the Bogus Batgirl**

Batgirl's cape is different.

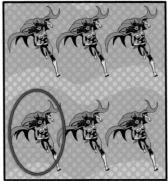

p. 80–81 **1, 2, 3—Look out for Poison Ivy!**

FOUND LETTERS: E, E, E, G, H, N, O, R, S, U

UNSCRAMBLED WORD: GREENHOUSE

p. 85 **One of These Heroes Is Not Like The Others**

Black Canary's choker is missing.

p. 88–89 **What's New?**

STARRING
JAN. NO. 359
DETECTIVE COMICS
BATMAN
MEET THE NEW BATGIRL!
IS SHE HEROINE OR VILLAINESS??
WHAT IS HER STARTLING SECRET IDENTITY?
"The MILLION DOLLAR DEBUT of BATGIRL!"

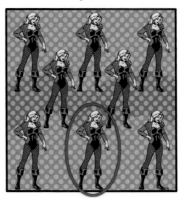

p. 90–91 Ha-Ha-Ha-Humdingers!

She smells seashells by the seashore.

Yes, she's a martial artist.

She went to school for mer-management.

She smashes shallots with her mallet.

p. 94–95 Supergirl Word Search

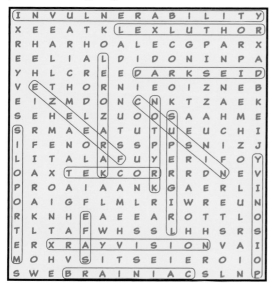

p. 98 Is Your Memory in Good Shape?

1. **d.** Red
2. **c.** Five fingers, like a person
3. **b.** Avoiding getting stomped
4. **c.** Black and white
5. **b.** "It's the Batwoman!"
6. **c.** Mastery of martial arts

p. 99 One A-MAZE-ing Amazon!

Wonder Woman should take path 2.

p. 100 Mera's Underwater Kingdom

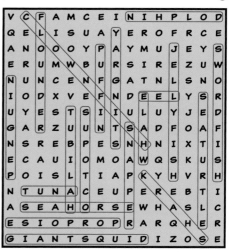

p. 101 Celebrating Super Heroes!

p. 102 Follow the Pattern

answer key

p. 103 **Bee Careful!**

One of Bumblebee's wings is different.

p. 104–105 **Crime-Fighting Crossword**

1 JUMP
2 SMALL
3 RUN
4 SWIM
5 WATER
6 MALLET
7 PLANET
8 WINGS
9 LOIS
10 HACKER
11 PLANTS
12 SUN
13 FISH
13 FAR
14 BLACK
14 BREAK
15 RED
16 DUO
17 MOON
18 OLD

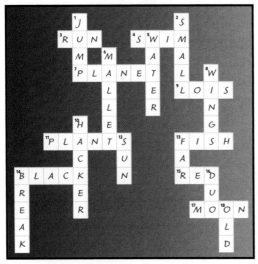

p. 106 **Sword-Slinging Switcheroos**

p. 107 **What Rhymes with Race?**

RACE	CASE	VASE
PLACE	ACE	CHASE
SPACE	MACE	BOOKCASE
FACE	TRACE	BASE/BASE

p. 108–109 **High-Stakes Chess**

I'VE GOT THIS GAME RIGGED SO THAT EVERY-TIME FLASH MAKES A MOVE, A MEMBER OF THE JUSTICE LEAGUE DISAPPEARS FROM THE FACE OF THE EARTH!
A STAR-STUDDED SPECTACULAR- "WORLD OF NO RETURN!"

p. 110–111 **Crossword Conundrums!**

1 SHRINK
2 CATCH
2 CRIME
3 ROCKET
4 GOOD
5 DOG
6 PEACE
6 POISON
7 CATWOMAN
8 NECK
9 THIEF
10 ROBIN
11 NIGHT
12 FLASH
13 HEAL
13 HEAR
14 LIES
15 VISION
16 ICE
17 HELP
18 FEET
19 TIME
20 SWORD
21 AQUAMAN

p. 113 **Wonder Woman Word Search**

A	E	L	B	I	C	N	I	V	N	I	Q	S	H	I
Q	R	I	F	R	U	Y	X	G	Y	F	Y	W	O	J
U	O	P	M	E	E	S	J	N	U	F	T	A	Y	U
J	I	U	E	W	T	E	I	O	Y	G	J	S	N	R
I	C	D	O	S	L	A	O	R	S	E	T	U	E	T
S	A	E	D	I	R	P	X	T	A	U	R	O	H	Y
T	R	T	C	B	O	L	D	S	G	I	V	E	F	P
Y	I	K	U	D	T	K	A	K	Y	L	U	G	E	U
I	N	E	Y	F	E	A	R	L	E	S	S	A	B	K
U	G	P	L	I	G	H	I	U	S	I	A	R	I	A
R	W	F	O	R	E	Q	N	J	C	D	E	U	P	D
S	H	K	A	Z	F	D	G	E	N	E	R	O	U	S
G	A	O	P	I	T	N	H	R	V	O	Y	C	V	X
U	I	C	O	N	F	I	D	E	N	T	L	E	I	W
T	U	R	Q	Y	E	K	E	U	O	D	Q	U	A	Y

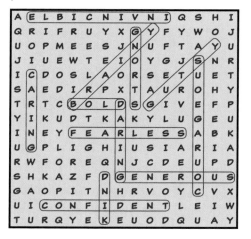

p. 117 **Trace the Pattern**

p. 114–115 **New and Improved?**

WONDER WOMAN
OCT. NO. 178
12¢
FORGET THE OLD...
THE NEW
WONDER WOMAN
is HERE

p. 118–119 **Seek and Find**

Seek and Find
How super is your sense of sight?
SCAN THIS PICTURE AND SEE IF YOU CAN FIND:
1 VEIL
2 KANGAROOS
3 SWORDS
1 BOOK
4 LASSOS
6 BLUE STARS
1 RED LIGHTNING BOLT
1 BATTLE-AX
1 PLAID SUIT
8 YELLOW BOOTS
1 PAIR OF GLASSES
SPECIAL ANNIVERSARY ISSUE
WONDER WOMAN 300
ALL NEW! $1.50
NO. 300 FEB.

answer key

p. 120 **Letter Smash!**

TSUPIERGZIRL = SUPERGIRL
MOEARAI = MERA
AJOKSERS = JOKER
CRYHEGETAH = CHEETAH
IKAATANGA = KATANA
BOARTGRIRL = BATGIRL
WRAIVTEN = RAVEN
CROAABIN = ROBIN
STUIPERMBAN = SUPERMAN
DHARFLEYQUTINN = HARLEY QUINN
ABUMOBLEBREE = BUMBLEBEE
COATSWORMAN = CATWOMAN

p. 122 **Puzzling Pathways!**

p. 123 **Mind the Magic**

W I E R Y S N O I S U L L I T
G F T A L U A J F C L I A H R
O E D L O H S W I Z A R D F I
U M E Z Q I N K L E Y K E N C
L P A U S E P M C I X W N Y K
S R G B D S O R C E R Y C S A
U T Y E R H J A E A F V H M T
C O K W O A Z H C P Q I A I C
O E P I S D C C M O D P N H U
P U Y T O T R A N C E G T Y O
S L U C R W I J D V B E M L R
U Q G H F I N T U A D X E I S
C A S I E O Y U X N B P N H J
O K R N A T R I G O B R T U E
H I Y G M Y S T I C A L A Q H

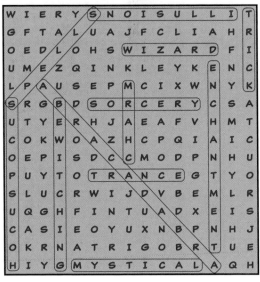

p. 124 **Unmask the Imposter!**

Raven's mask has turned blue.

RAVEN
RAVEN
RAVEN
RAVEN
RAVEN
RAVEN
RAVEN
RAVEN
124

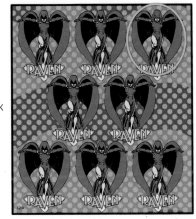

p. 125 **Spot the Missing Letters?**

MISSING LETTERS: A, E, N, R, V
SUPER HERO NAME: RAVEN
LETTERS THAT APPEAR THREE TIMES EACH: F, G, H, I, L, T
ONE OF THE HERO'S SUPERPOWERS: FLIGHT

p. 126–127 **Identify the Villain**

The villain is Harley Quinn.

p. 132 **Are You a Quick Study?**

1. **c.** Seven
2. **d.** Nothing
3. **b.** A runaway train
4. **b.** Gold sandals
5. **d.** All three robbers are wearing hats.
6. **c.** The Trail of Thrills!

p. 133 **A True Detective**

U G E Z O H S U B E D K Y T I
B M O N A S L A N I M I R C N
O P R T X D E D I C A T E D K
L O E T H L I M U J G O S A F
N L D I L A S F H A E Y E K U
F I R A U E M E N L N E A S A
I C B S X V B Q C Y I Y R O I
G E W O Y O A Y R R U R C E S
H S G I R A C T T Y S A H T G
T E Y A P T C A F I I R U E Q
E O R Q A E F I C D L B A U Y
R G Z B T A E T J T S I F O C
A O H O J U H U O B I L T F R
U I R N O D R O G A C O E U H
Q P I X E O S P R E V E N T U

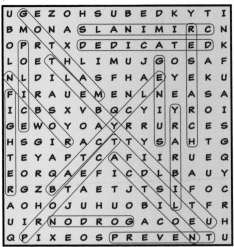